The Two Headed Coin

Founded in 1807, John Wiley & Sons is the oldest independent publishing company in the United States. With offices in North America, Europe, Australia, and Asia, Wiley is globally committed to developing and marketing print and electronic products and services for our customers' professional and personal knowledge and understanding.

The Wiley Finance series contains books written specifically for finance and investment professionals as well as sophisticated individual investors and their financial advisors. Book topics range from portfolio management to e-commerce, risk management, financial engineering, valuation, and financial instrument analysis, as well as much more.

For a list of available titles, visit our website at www.WileyFinance.com.

The Two Headed Coin

Unifying Strategy and Risk in Pursuit of Performance

JAMES L. DARROCH AND
DAVID WM. FINNIE

WILEY

Published by John Wiley & Sons, Inc., Hoboken, New Jersey.
Published simultaneously in Canada.

For general information on our other products and services or for technical support, please contact our Customer Care Department within the United States at (800) 762-2974, outside the United States at (317) 572-3993, or fax (317) 572-4002.

Wiley publishes in a variety of print and electronic formats and by print-on-demand. Some material included with standard print versions of this book may not be included in e-books or in print-on-demand. If this book refers to media such as a CD or DVD that is not included in the version you purchased, you may download this material at http://booksupport.wiley.com. For more information about Wiley products, visit www.wiley.com.

Library of Congress Cataloging-in-Publication Data:

Names: Darroch, James L. (James Lionel), 1951- author. | Finnie, David W., author.
Title: The two headed coin : unifying strategy and risk in pursuit of performance / James L. Darroch and David Wm. Finnie.
Description: Hoboken, New Jersey : Wiley, [2021] | Series: Wiley finance series | Includes index.
Identifiers: LCCN 2021000093 (print) | LCCN 2021000094 (ebook) | ISBN 9781119794202 (hardback) | ISBN 9781119794226 (adobe pdf) | ISBN 9781119794219 (epub)
Subjects: LCSH: Risk management.
Classification: LCC HD61 .D35 2021 (print) | LCC HD61 (ebook) | DDC 332.1068/1—dc23
LC record available at https://lccn.loc.gov/2021000093
LC ebook record available at https://lccn.loc.gov/2021000094

Cover Design: Wiley
Cover Images: © tokenphoto/Getty Images,
© iStock/Getty Images

SKY10025919_033121

To my wife, Brenda Blackstock, and our son, Daniel.

—James

To my wife, Marilyn Finnie, and our growing family—Geoffrey Finnie and Sidita Zhabjaku; Gillian Finnie, Ilia Baranov, and their daughter, Alice; and Colin Finnie.

—David

Contents

Preface

Risk Is Good and Uncertainty Is the Reality!

We have been working together now for well over a decade. Our journey started with designing a comprehensive risk management education program for the Risk Management Group at the Bank of Montreal (BMO). Following that we developed several strategy and risk programs for the Schulich Executive Education Centre (SEEC) and worked on a risk program for bank directors at the Global Risk Institute in Financial Services. We have learned much along the way from our professional colleagues and the participants. Although our backgrounds are in strategy and risk management for financial institutions, we have worked with people from many different industries, including not-for-profits.

We thought it was time to share what we have learned from financial institutions (FIs), which are among the leaders in integrating strategy and risk. This should be no surprise because that is their business. We believe that it is worthwhile to see what is at the leading edge of the integration so that other public and even private companies can reflect on the appropriateness of their integration. We also think our ideas will be useful for people starting their careers in risk at FIs. To that end, we try to balance the needs of a broad audience with the challenge of being relevant to risk professionals.

Here are the highlights we cover in this book:

- The elements of both strategy and risk management are common sense.
- Both strategy and risk management are broad in scope and inclusive.
- Achieving fit of the elements is complex.
- Bringing risk awareness into the conversation is the necessary complement needed to achieve fit in a dynamic world.
- Consequently, although the journey starts with strategy, recognizing risk and uncertainty is the flip side of the coin and the needed complement to ensure completeness and integration.

STRATEGY IS THE STARTING POINT!

This of course raises the question, "What is strategy?"[1] There are many approaches to this but let us lay out a fairly classic position largely associated with Michael Porter and many of his Harvard colleagues.[2] Strategy is an intentional activity: it is goal oriented. Porter provides a succinct summary of this position:

> *A company can outperform rivals only if it can establish a difference that it can preserve. It must deliver greater value to customers or create comparable value at a lower cost or do both. The arithmetic of superior profitability then follows: delivering greater value allows a company to charge higher unit prices; greater efficiency results in lower average unit costs.*[3]

There are several key points to the above. First, "creating a difference" or positioning is the key. Porter elaborates: "The essence of strategy is choosing to perform activities differently than rivals do."[4] Strategy is about being unique, and this requires a unique set of activities and, as we shall discuss later, a unique set of risks. The second fundamental point to notice is the focus is on profitability. Please note the focus on *costs* not *prices*. The point is that if you are creating comparable value and have the lower cost structure, you will be more profitable, as you will be if you can create more value. The third fundamental point is the need to preserve the position. Generally, in our discussion when we employ the term *sustainability,* it refers to maintaining a more profitable position, not corporate responsibility.

This positioning approach focuses on the desired outcome for perception of the product/service, which leads to the desired economic results. But achieving this result demands a process.[5] The process outlines the sequence of actions, including consultation, that will produce a simple and comprehensive mission statement that addresses the following:

- Mission—why we exist
- Values—what we believe in and how we will behave
- Vision—what we want to be
- Strategy—what our competitive game plan will be
  - Objectives = ends
  - Scope = domain (customer or offering, geographic location, and vertical integration)
  - Advantage = means
- Balanced scorecard—how we will monitor and implement the plan[6]

To elaborate, the process must include specific goals or ends that guide decision-making. The mission is to solve a customer's problem, but to do this, it is essential that we create the appropriate perception of our brand. In today's world, the brand is affected not only by its ability to solve the problem but also by other corporate actions, such as social values the company promotes.[7] Being clear on the scope is critical because strategy is as much about what not to do as it is what to do. It should also be clear that our values and the reputation that we desire place restrictions on the means that we can employ to accomplish our objectives. The "Statement on the Purpose of a Corporation" by the Business Roundtable in September 2019 makes it clear that it is inappropriate to employ means that don't consider a broad range of stakeholders.[8] Finally, the nature of our competitive advantage must be linked to an understanding of the risks it generates—both upside and downside—and how those risks are managed to protect value and build resiliency. Throughout this book we emphasize that strategy and risk, in an integrated approach, both focus on creating a sustainable business.[9]

And it is a classic mistake to divorce content from process. The two are interdependent and link strategy formulation (content) to execution (process). In short, involvement in the formulation or development process improves the content in terms of its ability to be executed but more significantly improves the quality of the content by involving more expertise. It also has the benefit of enhancing engagement or commitment over compliance. But this means engaging a broader set of stakeholders if the process is to be best in class.[10] The process presents a number of steps or actions to gather diverse insights and unify them to pursue corporate goals. It is the fit of all the elements that drives competitive advantage and sustainability of the advantage because the processes that achieve fit are difficult to duplicate.[11] You know you have achieved fit when the elements of your strategy are mutually reinforcing, rather than being at odds with, or independent of, one another.

One of us learned this the hard way in an executive seminar designed to embed strategic processes into the thinking of the second level of management, that is, the management level below the C-Suite. The C-Suite executives had determined what the strategic process should be without consulting their reports. The focus on the content of the strategic process actually violated the assumptions of the strategic planning process that they were trying to embed.[12] The failure to consult was evidence of a culture that did not value transparency and openness. When the question was raised as to why the C-Suite executives were not at the session, the hopes of embedding the new process came crashing down. Leadership needed to set the agenda but also invite active participation to include what they were not aware of.

Failure to do so doomed the change management hopes of the C-Suite. To put it more simply, the strategy journey is not linear—it has twists and turns.

We view goals beyond profits as a needed complement to Porter's definition of strategy. But without superior profits it is challenging for established companies to attract the resources needed to win and grow.[13] The recognition that these resources go beyond capital creates linkage to the growing social demands being placed on companies by employees and even investors.[14] An organization's values as established by the board are essential for creating a healthy culture and giving meaning to the work of its employees. By meaning, we mean participating in value creation, not simply being the guardians against value destruction, or being the department of NO! Fundamental to our understanding of giving meaning to employees are those in risk oversight who are essential players to be involved in the strategy process from the start.

Your strategic goals and position create the risks that you need to manage. This comes from not only a strategy professor but also a risk professional. As a strategist, working with risk professionals such as David taught James that strategy was creating risks that were being managed ex post when risk thinking or risk considerations needed to be brought into the strategy process ex ante.[15] This has since been recognized by Kevin Buehler, Andrew Freeman, and Ron Hulme[16] at McKinsey and more recently by Daniela Gius, Jean-Christophe Mieszala, Ernesto Panayiotou, and Thomas Poppensieker, also at McKinsey.[17] Buehler et al. also noted that the type of rigorous analytics and use of statistical tools common to risk management in financial institutions was becoming increasingly common in other business areas.[18]

We realized early on in our collaboration that the strategy, specifically the goals and positioning theme made concrete in the organization's value proposition, determined the risks that must be managed. This is because in creating value for customers/clients the organization must deal with both risk and uncertainty.[19] The positioning theme explores the ceiling on what customers will pay.[20] The financial executives and especially the risk manager help determine what is the minimum price that must be charged for the business to be economically sustainable.[21] The science of risk management employs statistical tools to determine the probability of losses—for the organization to survive, it must consider the impact of losses on pricing and capital reserves. This concept is fundamental to the capital structure of the firm. Holding reserves against capital loss establishes a boundary between risk management and uncertainty. Beyond the limit set for unexpected losses,[22] which is partly determined by market forces of investor demands for returns and creditor demands for safety, lies the world of uncertainty. Failure to recognize how this highlights the element of art in risk management leads to myopic strategies, poor risk management, and organizational failure.

Our business and teaching experiences have further taught us how these concepts can be applied to any organization and improve their strategic processes and business success.[23]

WHAT IS RISK? WHAT IS UNCERTAINTY?

Our ongoing engagement with diverse organizations has also helped us to understand the challenges created by the term *risk*. For many, risk is something to be avoided or eliminated; to us, risk is good because if there is no risk, there is no profit. But in the modern world, virtually all risk can be transferred to others, as Nobel Laureate Robert Merton has noted.[24] Oddly enough, the implications of this was recognized by Frank Knight in his classic work on *Risk, Uncertainty and Profit.*[25] Despite Knight's status among risk scholars, he held that uncertainty, not risk, was the source of profit. The question for the strategic risk manager then becomes, to what level of uncertainty or unexpected loss do I want protection from and how much will markets allow? The science and art of strategy and risk management meet in this decision.[26] In our everyday lives we make a similar decision when we decide on insurance deductibles in either health or property and casualty (P&C) insurance. When making that decision, we confront our willingness to accept the possibility of negative outcomes up to a certain limit but transfer the risk beyond that point to someone else.

This means we must learn to manage risk, and to do that, we need to identify, assess, or quantify and monitor our risks. There is both a content and process side to doing this. Superior risk management can lead to competitive advantage, as we will show in later chapters. The process side is fundamentally important because here we embrace the people managing the risk process. The risk process is entirely geared toward enabling and informing the organizational strategy and day-to-day business decisions made by the lines of business with risk-rich information and insights. This requires that risk awareness be embedded in the entire organizational culture so that risk management takes place at the first line of defense.[27]

We also need to embrace a definition of risk that at the minimum has both an upside and downside.[28] But it would be better to embrace one in which the upside exceeds the downside, because these are the risks worth taking.[29] For the general reader, understand that *strategic risk* has both an upside and a downside. The future can exceed our wildest dreams or make real your worst nightmare. For people from the FI world, think market risk, not credit risk.[30] Recognizing the upside helps people working in risk functions make the work more meaningful because although saying "no" to projects is important to the business, avoiding problems is generally not as

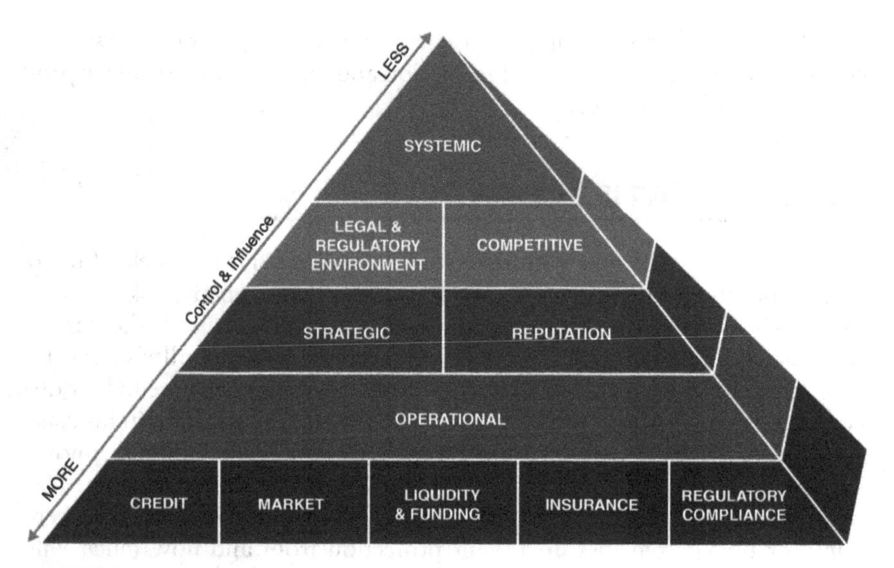

FIGURE P.1 Royal Bank of Canada's Risk Pyramid 2014[31]
Source: Royal Bank of Canada Annual Report 2014, The Royal Bank of Canada's Risk Governance Framework (2014), 49–50. © 2014, Royal Bank of Canada.

well recognized as contributing to success.[32] There are advantages to participating in profit centers that are not as readily available to cost centers. So, it is important that the risk function be recognized as contributing to the overall profitability of the business by helping the lines of business take the right risks in the right way for the right return.

Royal Bank of Canada is among the 30 global banks deemed too big to fail by the Financial Stability Board in Basel. It is also worth noting that it escaped the 2007–2008 financial crisis as did the other Canadian banks relatively unscathed, suggesting a robust approach to risk management. The bank developed a very appealing graphic that provides not only a typology of different risks but also presents them in a hierarchical fashion based on the organization's ability to control the risks (see Figure P.1).[33]

We take risks in the expectation of gains; the question is which risks we should take and how should they be managed and priced.[34] Royal Bank of Canada's pyramid sets out several different risks that need to be identified and managed. Implicit in the hierarchy is that the lower levels of the pyramid need to be managed to make the higher levels manageable. This is made clear by the way that operational risk can affect all the financial risks. For the moment we also want to make clear a distinction between operational risk and financial risks.[35] Generally, financial risks are susceptible to scientific measurement, which is often an approximation via statistical tools based on historical experience within a certain confidence level. Parts of operational risk may be susceptible to scientific measurement, too. But, one does not take operational risk for regulatory purposes. Operational risks are taken as necessary to fulfill the organizational strategy and objectives. Operational risks, and compliance efforts, are a cost of doing business. There is another dimension to operational risk.[36] Many operational risks provide the opportunity for learning.[37] Although operational risk is hard to profit from, it directly affects the cost structure of the firm. If the risk is controlled to the right level, using effective cost-benefit analysis, the firm is able to build risk understanding into its cost structure and, thereby, create competitive advantage in its costs. This makes clear the need for risk management to be dynamic and holistic: it must be complete in scope and integrated.

When we started working together, we discussed elements of *reputation risk*, but the term was not really in vogue. It is now, and it has important implications for how we view management.[38] Financial risk management in FIs has always had a strong commitment to financial stakeholders, but once reputation is recognized as an asset, it becomes imperative to move beyond a shareholder model to a stakeholder model.[39] Royal Bank of Canada points to the lower degree of control over reputation, and we believe this is because although reputation is generally the outcome of delivering on your value promise, external elements can affect your reputation. So, it is not just the actuality of your performance, it is the perception of what you do. With the outbreak of trade tensions in 2020, the country of origin can have a significant impact on a company's reputation unrelated to past performance. This broadening of the scope of risk management takes us deeper into the realm of uncertainty and risk management as art, not just science. And it makes risk management strategic.

Our process framework identifies the elements and relationships in managing the strategy-risk-governance process (see Figure P.2). It assumes an intentional view of strategy by starting with the strategy to be achieved, moving through risk to ensure only the strategy-supportive risks are maintained to support a strategic- and risk-based competitive advantage. That competitive advantage leads to strong performance and the desired reputation. Above all the execution activities exists the governance processes supporting ethical approaches, appropriate behaviors, and a strong organizational culture. Beneath the execution actions are the enablers—including risk appetite, data capabilities, and strong and appropriate infrastructure and systems including all organizational capabilities. Because these goals are to be accomplished in the future, the strategist must deal with both risk and uncertainty that lies beyond the confidence level.[40] The framework shown in Figure P.2 provides a graphic representation of how to integrate strategy and risk.

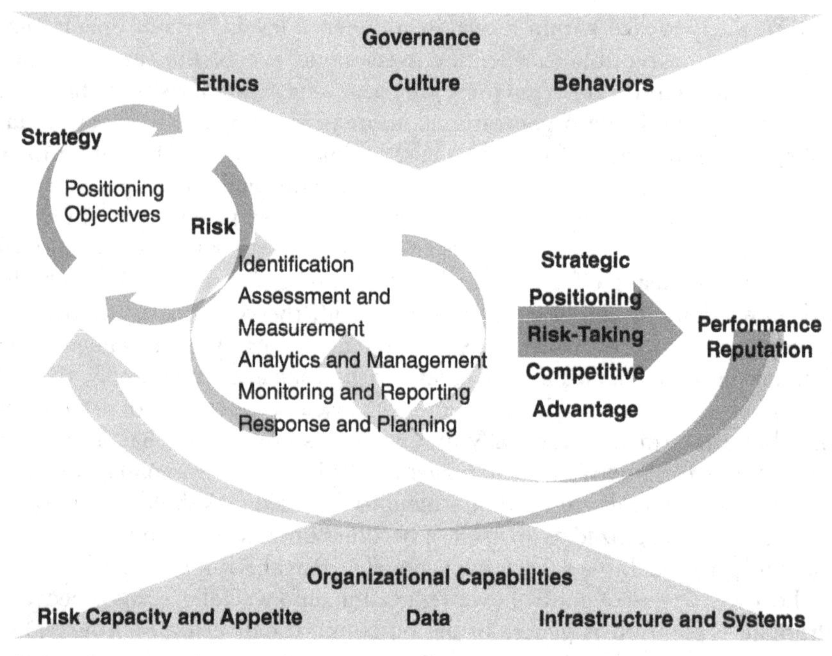

FIGURE P.2 The Strategy-Risk-Governance Process

It needs to be understood that strategists and risk managers may have different approaches to the same issue. For example, if the problem is earnings volatility rather than hedging exposures, a change in the balance of product lines may be the answer. For a FI this might mean increasing the percentage of retail operations; for a consumer goods company it might mean adding a lower-priced brand to the product line to protect against changes in the business cycle.

However, for our purpose we need to emphasize creating customer value and stakeholder management[41] as central to the business objectives. Setting risk appetite and tolerances is essential to the strategic process if risk is to be managed and is too often ignored by the last line, or fourth line, of defense: the board.[42]

There are multiple facets to the relationship between strategy and risk. The book seeks to consider more deeply these aspects in the following chapters:

- Chapter 1: Strategy and Risk: Two Sides of the Same Coin
- Chapter 2: Executing on the Plan and Discovering New Risks

- Chapter 3: Which Risks to Keep
- Chapter 4: How Do We Achieve Independent Risk Governance and Improve Performance?
- Chapter 5: Who Has the Specific Knowledge to Design the Risk Architecture: Why You Need an Independent Risk Function
- Chapter 6: Enterprise Risk Management and Competitive Advantage
- Chapter 7: What Reputation Do We Want? With Whom?
- Chapter 8: Uncertainty, Scenario Planning, and Real Options
- Chapter 9: Risk Culture and Ethics: Can You Have Excellence and Consistency at the Same Time?
- Chapter 10: The Top of the Pyramid: The CEO as Integrator of Strategy and Risk and the Board as the Fourth Line of Defense
- Epilogue: Decision-Making at the Restaurant: Creating and Executing a Risk-Aware Strategy

The journey starts by exploring two partners making strategic choices that create the risks that must be managed in a risk-return framework. Chapters 1 and 2 explore the dialectic between strategy and risk in developing the plan and the dialectic between executing to turn the dream into reality. These two chapters provide a touchstone for the rest of the book. The third chapter addresses the fundamental strategy-risk decision: how to determine which risks are fundamental to the strategic positioning and goals and must be retained and managed. Each firm will have a different solution set and we can only guide them in discovering which risks are fundamental to them. This leads to a consideration of the scope of enterprise risk management (ERM): it must be all inclusive and integrated to capture the interdependencies that unite risk and strategy. Chapter 4 argues that you need a focal point for risk management to standardize processes to ensure consistent outcomes. This requires a dedicated senior risk professional reporting to the chief executive officer (CEO) and possibly the board. In FIs, this typically is the chief risk officer (CRO).[43] The role of the independent risk function and this executive is developed in Chapter 5. Closely tied to Chapter 2 is the notion of competitive advantage, and this is the focus of Chapter 6. Changes in consumer perceptions make reputation an important asset to be managed and Chapter 7 explores the relevant issues. Although uncertainty is bounded by certain considerations of risk management, it doesn't go away. Scenario planning and real options provide a framework for managing uncertainty. Moreover, scenario planning provides an opportunity to counter CEO optimism by providing the "outside view" to debias the forecast and incorporate insights from behavioral economics.[44] Finally, strategy and risk management are both about creating a commitment to the goals of the organization, and this means a focus on culture and ethics.

Many large losses are the result of adverse behaviors, not purposeful risk choices. In the concluding chapter the issue of conflict and alignment are discussed in the context of governance. The role of the CEO is examined as the ultimate locus of the reconciliation of strategic risk decisions within the context of board governance as the fourth line of defense. The Epilogue revisits the partners and reveals the decisions that they made in light of their strategic positioning and the awareness of the risks that it created.

NOTES

1. This of course is the title of a famous article by Michael E. Porter, "What Is Strategy?" *Harvard Business Review* (November–December 1996).
2. For a discussion of differing positions please see Henry Mintzberg, Joseph Lampel, and Bruce Ahlstrand, *Strategy Safari: A Guided Tour through the Wilds of Strategic Management* (New York: The Free Press, 1998).
3. Porter, "What Is Strategy?," 62.
4. Porter, "What Is Strategy?," 64.
5. David J. Collis and Michael G. Rukstad, "Can You Say What Your Strategy Is?" *Harvard Business Review* (April 2008).
6. Collis and Rukstad, "Can You Say What Your Strategy Is?"
7. This is explored more fully in Chapter 7.
8. Business Roundtable, "Statement on the Purpose of a Corporation," August 10, 2019, https://opportunity.businessroundtable.org/ourcommitment/.
9. We consider resiliency, or sustainability, to be critical and we have included an exploration of this in Appendix II.
10. It is only appropriate to pay homage to the founder of this approach: Ed Freeman. See R. Edward Freeman, *Strategic Management: A Stakeholder Approach* (Boston: Pitman, 1984).
11. Porter, "What Is Strategy?," 70.
12. For the curious, the CEO was trying to embed Hoshin Planning, a popular approach at the time.
13. For start-ups, the promise of growth may be sufficient as we have seen with many unicorns. For other organizations, the promise of promoting artistic accomplishment, public purpose, or some other worthy goal may be enough to attract resources from investors who share those goals.
14. Larry Fink, "Larry Fink's Annual Letter to CEOs: A Sense of Purpose," accessed July 18, 2018, https://www.blackrock.com/corporate/investor-relations/larry-fink-ceo-letter. See also Julie Battilania, Anne-Claire Pache, Metin Sengul, and Marissa Kimsey, "The Dual-Purpose Playbook," *Harvard Business Review* (March–April 2019); Adi Ignatius, "Profit and Purpose," *Harvard Business Review* (March 2019); and James Mackintosh, "A Davos Debate: What Is Finance For?" *The Wall Street Journal* (January 24, 2019).
15. This is very well discussed in Gary Klein, Tim Koller, and Dan Lovallo, "Premortems: Being Smart at the Start," *McKinsey Quarterly* (March 2019).

16. James should have paid more attention to the work of Kevin Buehler, Andrew Freeman, and Ron Hulme when he read it. See Kevin Buehler, Andrew Freeman, and Ron Hulme, "The New Arsenal of Risk Management," *Harvard Business Review* (September 2008) and "Owning the Right Risks," *Harvard Business Review* (September 2008). Part III, "Linking ERM to Strategy and Strategic Risk Management" in John R. S. Fraser, Betty J. Simkins, and Kristina Narvaez, eds., *Implementing Enterprise Risk Management: Case Studies and Best Practices* (Hoboken, NJ: Wiley, 2015) is well worth a look, as are many other chapters and cases in this book.
17. Daniela Gius, Jean-Christophe Mieszala, Ernesto Panayiotou, and Thomas Poppensieker, "Value and Resilience through Better Risk Management, *McKinsey & Company Risk Practice,* (October 2018, https://www.mckinsey.com/business-functions/risk/our-insights/value-and-resilience-through-better-risk-management). This approach is also apparent in Fraser, Simkins, and Narvaez, *Implementing Enterprise Risk Management.*
18. The selection of many cases from outside the financial services industry in Fraser, Simkins, and Narvaez, *Implementing Enterprise Risk Management,* clearly demonstrates this.
19. See the discussion of Frank Knight's work in Chapter 3.
20. Differentiation raises the ceiling, but if the ceiling is set, then achieving the lowest cost structure is the way to superior profitability.
21. Of course, you can charge less with the idea of future customer profitability, lower costs due to achieving scale, or learning curve effects, but if you do this you must prepare for the contingencies of these not occurring.
22. Expected loss is the average loss predicted to occur using historical loss analysis in normal business conditions over a specified period of time. Unexpected loss is the potential for loss above expectations due to extreme events and is often expressed as the average total loss above the expected loss using a defined confidence level.
23. See Joseba Eceiza, Piotr Kaminski, and Thomas Poppensieker "Nonfinancial Risk Today: Getting Risk and the Business Aligned," *McKinsey & Company* (January 2017).
24. Robert C. Merton, "You Have More Capital Than You Think," *Harvard Business Review* (November 2005).
25. Frank H. Knight, *Risk, Uncertainty and Profit,* 2nd ed. (New York: Reprints of Economic Classics, 1964), https://mises.org/library/risk-uncertainty-and-profit. See, in particular, the Preface to the 1933 reissue and page 19.
26. David R. Koenig, *Governance Reimagined: Organizational Design, Risk, and Value Creation* (Northfield, MN: B Right Governance Publications, 2018), 218. Pages 89–90 make the following observation in a section entitled, Quantification as a Coping Mechanism: "Since risk and uncertainty make us uneasy—we naturally prefer to move further down on the Risk of the Unknown factor chart—we may attempt to turn subjective risk assessments into objective measures, or quantifications. In effect, we attempt to convert uncertainty, which is not measurable, into risk, which is believed to be measurable."

27. Later we will discuss the three lines of defense model and the implications for the balance of centralization and decentralization. Koenig, *Governance Reimagined,* 161, makes the same point as does James Lam in Chapter 6 in James Lam, *Implementing Enterprise Risk Management: From Methods to Applications* (Hoboken, NJ: Wiley, 2017).
28. James Lam makes the same point in his recent edition. Lam, *Implementing Enterprise Risk Management.*
29. We thank David R. Koenig for pointing this out.
30. Later we will discuss the upside to credit risk, but in general the downside exceeds the upside. It is also the reason we do not discuss cyber risk—although it could be the source of competitive advantage at the moment, we doubt many firms are so confident as to claim this as a source of competitive advantage. See Oliver Bevan, Jim Boehm, Merlina Manocaran, and Rolf Riemenschnitter, "Cybersecurity and the Risk Function," *McKinsey & Company Risk Practice,* November 2018, https://www.mckinsey.com/business-functions/risk/our-insights/cybersecurity-and-the-risk-function; Jim Boehm, Peter Merrath, Thomas Poppensieker, Rolf Riemenschnitter, and Tobias Stahle, "Cyber Risk Measurement and the Holistic Cybersecurity Approach," *McKinsey Quarterly,* November 2018, https://www.mckinsey.com/business-functions/risk/our-insights/cyber-risk-measurement-and-the-holistic-cybersecurity-approach?cid=other-eml-alt-mip-mck-oth-1811&hlkid=c0daad3b6cdf461f9a5fbd5beaf94692&hctky=1961840&hdpid=2d71440f-329f-4038-8100-e353a5c2d01
31. Royal Bank of Canada, "Annual Report," 52.
32. See Dan Cable and Freek Vermeulen, "Making Work Meaningful: A Leader's Guide," *McKinsey Quarterly* (October 2018) and Alexis Krivkovich and Cindy Levy, "Managing the People Side of Risk," *Corporate Finance Practice, McKinsey Company,* May 2013, https://www.mckinsey.com/business-functions/risk/our-insights/managing-the-people-side-of-risk.
33. The positioning of operational risk is important for us. Royal Bank of Canada, however, has continued to refine the pyramid for their risk management and governance purposes. See Royal Bank of Canada, "Annual Report" (2014): 52, https://www.rbc.com/investor-relations/_assets-custom/pdf/ar_2014_e.pdf.
34. Some of the risks, such as regulatory, can be viewed as calculating the cost-benefit as to the degree of compliance, rather than being taken for the sake of "gains" per se.
35. For a very interesting discussion on learnable risks and competitive advantage, see David Apgar, *Risk Intelligence: Learning to Manage What We Don't Know* (Boston: Harvard Business Review Press, 2006). We do recognize that superior use of statistical tools can also lead to competitive advantage as Capital One demonstrated in the sub-prime credit card market and Goldman Sachs in the 2007 financial crisis.
36. Compliance is becoming a more significant issue. See Bevan, Kaminski, Kristensen, Poppensieker, and Pravdic, "The Compliance Function at an Inflection Point."
37. On the importance of risks governed by nonrandom processes, see Apgar, *Risk Intelligence.*

38. For a recent discussion, see Owen Parker, Ryan Krause, and Cynthia E. Devers "How Firm Reputation Shapes Managerial Discretion," *Academy of Management Review* 44, no. 2 (2019): 254–78.
39. It is only appropriate to pay homage to the founder of this approach, Ed Freeman. See R. Edward Freeman, *Strategic Management: A Stakeholder Approach* (Boston: Pitman, 1984). This is still an evolving field; see Jay B. Barney, Measuring Firm Performance in a Way That Is Consistent With Strategic Management Theory. *Academy of Management Discoveries* 6:1 (2020): 5–7.
40. See the discussion of the relationship between risk and uncertainty in our discussion of Frank Knight's work in Chapter 3.
41. Essential to our understanding of positioning is a focus on the customer and creating value for the customer. We concur with the insights presented in Roger Martin, "The Age of Customer Capitalism," *Harvard Business Review* (January 2010).
42. See Gius, Mieszala, Panayiotou, and Poppensieker, "Value and Resilience through Better Risk Management," which asserts the following: "Boards spend only 9 percent of their time on risk—slightly less than they did in 2015. Other questions in the survey results in this McKinsey paper revealed that only 6 percent of respondents believe that they are effective in managing risk (again, less than in 2015)." The survey interviewed a large number of listed companies in the UK in 2016.
43. This may be the chief financial officer in many organizations. See McKinsey & Company, "The New CFO Mandate: Prioritize, Transform, Repeat," December 3, 2018, https://www.mckinsey.com/business-functions/strategy-and-corporate-finance/our-insights/the-new-cfo-mandate-prioritize-transform-repeat.
44. See Dan Lovallo and Daniel Kahneman, "Delusions of Success: How Optimism Undermines Executives' Decisions," *Harvard Business Review* (July 2003); Bill Javetski and Tim Koller, "Debiasing the Corporation: An Interview with Nobel Laureate Richard Thaler," *McKinsey Corporate Finance Practice,* May 2017, https://assets.mckinsey.com/~/media/70B0411CF4524543B396B4AE2B44A827.ashx; Tobias Baer, Sven Heiligtag, and Hamid Samandari, "The Business Logic in Debiasing," McKinsey & Co, May 2017, https://www.mckinsey.com/business-functions/risk/our-insights/the-business-logic-in-debiasing; and Tim Koller and Dan Lovallo, "Taking the 'Outside View,'" *Bias Busters,* McKinsey & Co., 2018.

Acknowledgments

JAMES L. DARROCH

When I started this project, I knew I needed a coauthor whose experiences and knowledge complemented mine. I was incredibly fortunate to be joined by my friend, David Finnie. David has been an inspirational collaborator and mentor over the years.

I owe debts to numerous people who have assisted me in the journey that led to this book. It started with my PhD committee chaired by Al Litvak, who remained an inspiration, coauthor, and friend for many years. Dezso Horvath challenged my strategic thinking and Dawson Brewer and Sy Friedland, who remained lifelong friends, challenged my financial thinking. This gave me a solid foundation for what followed.

I was fortunate to have Paul Cantor as a mentor in implementation, leadership, and governance when I worked with Paul at the Toronto Leadership Centre. It was a transformative experience to work with him and financial sector supervisors from around the world: Brian Quinn, Bob Clarke, Michael Mackenzie, Jorge Patino, David Scott, Richard Farrant, and Bill Ryback to name a few. This was my introduction to risk management.

I was then fortunate to meet David Finnie and develop the risk curriculum for the Bank of Montreal (BMO) with Fred Gorbet. This was my PhD in risk under the tutelage of Michel Maila, Mike Frow, David, Phillippe Sarfati, Tony Preccia, Milo Rado, Fred Shen, and many others. Developing the material with these mentors was an unbelievable experience and then to bring it to the classroom for BMO professionals sharpened my learnings and brought the realities of the challenges of risk management home. Working with Cory Jack at BMO also helped me learn about leadership and the challenges of implementing enterprise risk management.

Interestingly, David, Michel, Paul, Corey, and I were all reunited at the Global Risk Institute for Financial Services. We worked on creating a risk program for directors of financial institutions. After that Corey and I continued to work together in the Financial Services Leadership Program at Canadian Imperial Bank of Commerce (CIBC), where we had the privilege of working with emerging leaders at CIBC. This was the most recent stage of my journey in executive education and consulting.

Although I have worked with many executives, two people stand out for their role in this book. David Koenig was kind enough to read an early draft.

His comments significantly improved the work. Francois Desjardin, while he was CEO of Laurentian Bank, not only made detailed comments on an early draft but took considerable time to discuss with us the importance of branding and the relationship of the CEO to the board. I hope we captured the insights of David and Francois, because they opened my eyes.

I would be remiss if I didn't express my gratitude to my many coauthors. Some especially stand out: Pat Meredith, who brought me into her project, which resulted in the Donner Award–winning *Stumbling Giants*. My contribution and understanding of Canadian public policy owe a great deal to my Schulich colleagues: Al Litvak, Charley McMillan, Fred Gorbet, Jim Gillies, and Tom Wilson. Although I was unaware of the connection while writing, I see the continuation of the work I did with David Weitzner.

The scope of the book owes much to my colleagues in the Financial Services Program at Schulich. I was fortunate to be brought back to the program and want to thank Lois Tullo, Lee Watchorn, Bernard Hyams, Desmond Alvares, Christine Tekker, and Andrew Lin.

This book is as much a result of teaching as research, so I want to thank the many Schulich students who took my courses and contributed their thoughts and insights on strategy, risk, and governance. Their challenging questions have forced me to rethink many issues addressed in this book. And key to the success of these courses were my executive assistants, JoAnne Stein, Filomena Ticzon, and Jennifer Fernandez.

The team at Wiley have provided superb support through the process of publication, so I want to express my gratitude to Kevin Harreld, Susan Cerra, Samantha Enders, and Susan Geraghty. You really made a difference. And, finally, thanks to some friends whose support in discussing many of the issues addressed in this book has been invaluable: Eileen Fischer, Moren Levesque, Dirk Matten, and Christine Oliver. Their support kept me going through some tough times.

DAVID WM. FINNIE

I want to thank James Darroch for inviting me to join him on this project. James and I have worked together many times over the years, and I have always learned from him and enjoyed our time together. I find his knowledge and understanding to be complementary to mine and, as a result, with his involvement, I am able to go beyond what I can accomplish on my own.

Over the years I have worked with tremendous thought leaders in business and risk. I owe a deep debt of gratitude to these individuals.

I entered the realm of risk management during my time at Bank of Montreal (BMO) and worked with many people in the trading business and new risk functions. I learned a tremendous amount from my first two bosses, Phil Wilson and Michel Maila. Both were thought leaders, although in very different ways. I learned about people, behaviors, and leadership from Phil and risk concepts, approaches, and philosophies from Michel. I also worked with several wonderful business and risk contributors. Jean Desgagné, Mike Frow, Geoff Hydon, Paul Marchand, and Tony Peccia taught me about the key concepts in their risk and operational specialties. During this time, I was fortunate enough to have some tremendous people agree to work for and with me. I want to thank Greg Frank, Sandy Howlett, James Ireland, Sarah Knapp, Robin Li, Graham Pugh, Phillipe Sarfati, and Fred Shen. I learned far more working with them than I believe they were able to learn from me.

I was able to make the transition into risk management due to great support from Ellen Costello and David Hyma. I worked with them and Shelley Weiss and their trading floor teams to create business-supportive risk solutions. It was with them and in this environment that I began my risk and, ultimately, risk and strategic management, journey.

It was while I was at BMO that I was able to lead the development of the risk curriculum, and it was in this effort that I first met James Darroch. This project enabled me to work very closely with James and the other people he mentions. While James learned about risk, I learned about curriculum design and development and working with educators in a high-performance setting.

I was able to take what I had learned at BMO to a number of other organizations where I met and worked with some valuable individuals. From American Express Company, I thank Kai Talarek and Bud Herrmann for their support. At Teachers Pension Fund, I want to thank a tremendous leader and risk thinker, Barb Zvan. At Global Risk Institute in Financial Services I was able to work with many of the people already mentioned along with Paul Cantor. Paul was a noteworthy chair of the board from whom I learned many governance lessons. At Central 1 Credit Union I had an excellent team from whom I learned about the credit union movement and with whom I implemented a strong, business-supportive, risk-disciplined capability. I want to thank Chris Galloway, Phil Hemming, James Ireland, Phil Kennedy, Martin Kyle, and Dan O'Connor. I also want to thank their staff with whom we as a team were able to accomplish so much.

Part of working in any financial institution is the interaction with the regulators. Over the years I worked with and learned from individuals in the Office of the Superintendent of Financial Services (OSFI), the Chicago Federal Reserve Board, the New York State Banking Authority, and the UK Financial Services Authority. More recently, I worked with individuals from British Columbia's and Ontario's financial regulators and would like to thank Mehrdad Rastan and Guy Hubert for sharing their ideas and thoughts freely and supporting my team's efforts to create a strong risk foundation at Central 1. I particularly want to thank Mehrdad for his patience as we moved to overcome the many obstacles to implementing an appropriate risk function.

I want to thank my wife, Marilyn Finnie. Marilyn has spent untold hours challenging and educating me in the numerous fields in which she has become an expert, many of which have a direct bearing on financial institution business, technology, and risk management.

Finally, I want to thank David Koenig and Francois Desjardins. They were able to take an early draft of James's and my work, provide very valuable insights and suggestions, help us develop some of our ideas further, and lead us to greater clarity in our writing. And, of course, I join James in thanking the wonderful team at Wiley. They made this publishing journey seem effortless.

About the Authors

James Darroch is the CIT Chair in Financial Services at the Schulich School of Business, York University.

He teaches strategy and risk management with an emphasis on financial institutions. His book coauthored with Pat Meredith, *Stumbling Giants: Transforming Canada's Banks for the Information Age* (Toronto: Rotman University of Toronto Press, 2017), was the winner of the 2018 Donner Prize.

He holds an MBA and PhD from the Schulich School, where he has taught for over 30 years. He also has extensive executive education and consulting experience.

James is married and has a son, Daniel.

***

David Wm. Finnie is an accomplished senior executive combining strong strategic leadership with 20+ years in executive leadership across many disciplines. His impressive track record includes creating or contributing to the strategic visions and risk management capabilities of Bank of Montreal, American Express Company, Global Risk Institute in Financial Institutions (GRI), and Central 1 Credit Union (C1).

David has been able to attract, retain, develop, coach, and mentor outstanding individuals and he has won staff-nominated equality and leadership awards. He is most proud of the high-performance teams he has been able to create and lead.

David is an avid cyclist and Nordic skier. He is married to Marilyn Finnie and has three children, Geoffrey, Gillian, and Colin, and one granddaughter, Alice.

CHAPTER 1

Strategy and Risk

Two Sides of the Same Coin

Strategy and risk are two sides of the same coin. Both aspire to create profits in an uncertain future.[1] The classic strategy question is: What business is the organization in? This starting point determines the organization's purpose, that is, what problem it is solving for its targeted market, and should make clear what inherent risks it will face. For example, if you are a detergent maker in 2020, it is important that your product not only cleans safely but also is environmentally friendly and childproof. Because a major goal of the firm is to create economic value, not just accounting profits, risk management with the calculation of economic capital is fundamental to the strategy process. Both strategy and risk management confront important cash flow, income statement, and balance sheet issues. *Strategy and risk meet in pricing and capital because these are the two tools to deal with expected losses (ELs) and unexpected losses (ULs) arising from the risks that an organization takes in creating and claiming value.*[2] Because we will say more about economic capital later, for now, let us provide a simple definition. Economic capital is the capital required to support the economics of the business including the necessary infrastructure (critical assets for operations) and risks. This means if the unexpected happens, you have a reserve that enables you to survive for a length of time calculated by probability and market conditions. The higher the relative economic capital, the longer you are likely to stay in business. But the more challenging it is to achieve return on equity (ROE) or return on asset (ROA) goals, the higher the capital reserve you'll likely need.

However, it is important to realize that the firm's strategy, specifically the goals and the position created by the value proposition, is the starting point: it initiates the dialogue that leads to strategy formulation and implementation.

In practical terms this means that the strategic processes determine what risks/uncertainty the firm must accept and manage. By manage we simply mean that the firm first identifies, then accepts, certain risks, mitigates others, and transfers others. In the strategy-risk-governance process shown in Figure 1.1, it is important to recognize the feedback loops linking strategy and risk. Strategy informs risk and, in turn, risk informs strategy.

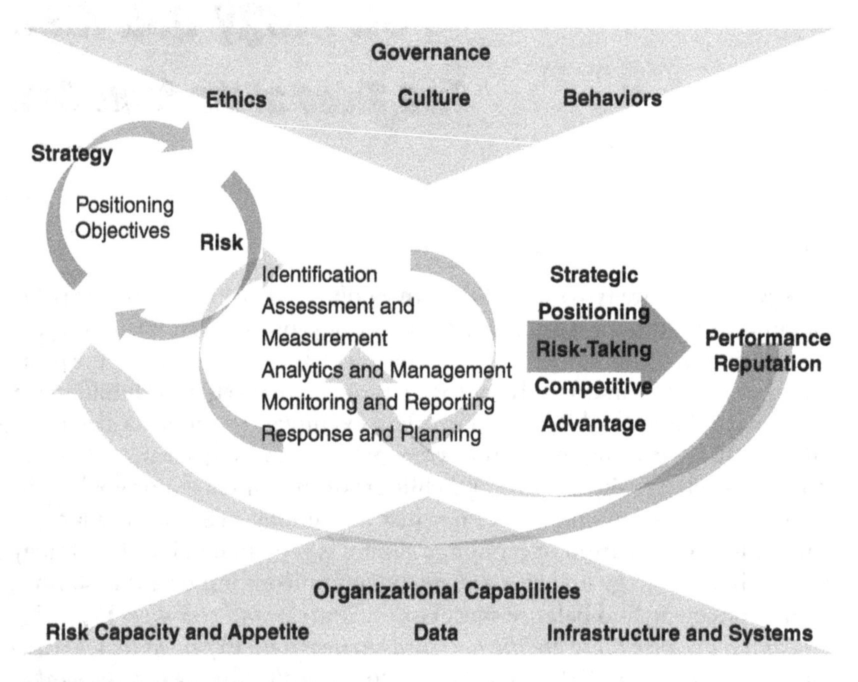

FIGURE 1.1 The Strategy-Risk-Governance Process

Table 1.1 illustrates the similarities and complementarities among strategy, risk, and brand management. We decided to include brand management and culture because it helps to illustrate that management of risk involves the entire organization, as does brand management, and it is affected by the organization's culture. This is not to downplay the role of the C-Suite specialists, but rather to highlight that the specialists coordinate the activities of the entire organization to achieve the desired outcomes. This will be amplified in our later discussion of the three lines of defense model.[3]

If risk-taking is fundamental to business and profits, then it must be understood ex ante in order to deal with identifiable risks through pricing and contingency reserves (capital), and this requires that it be an essential

TABLE 1.1 Strategy, Risk Management, Brand, and Culture

Scope and Role	Strategy	Risk Management	Brand	Culture
Enterprise Wide	Yes	Yes	Yes	Yes, but with pockets of different cultures
Integrating	Yes	Yes	Yes	Yes in a functional organization; no in a dysfunctional one
Goal articulation	Mission statement	Risk appetite	Presenting the organization as it wants to be seen by the target segment(s)	Having the desired culture integrate the subcultures
	Formulation, for example, profitability, market share, etc.	Risk tolerances	Brand equity Edelman Trust Barometer	
Organization requirements[4]	Capability to execute the strategy including MIS and performance and risk analytics	Capability to execute the risk process and complete performance and risk analytics	Integration at C-Suite to ensure coordination at all levels	Attention to nurturing the appropriate behaviors and actions
Embedding in the organization	Dialogue on concerns Implementation Organizational structure	Risk-based decisioning Risk processes	Brand awareness	Leadership displaying the desired behavior and use of symbols
Pricing impact	Differentiation/low cost	Expected loss	To portray value relative to competitors	Impact on perception of differentiation by customers
Contingency planning	Generation of options, alternatives	Resiliency, business continuity, and proactive response planning	Issues and crisis management	Employee engagement and organizational health plans and activities
Uncertainty	Scenario planning Contingency planning	Economic capital: capital at risk, stressed capital at risk, fat tails	Monitoring of social media	Surveys to measure what the culture is

part of the strategy formulation and execution process.[5] Once one starts to probe the relationship between pricing and positioning in the classic Porter[6] sense, as well as the role of capital in sustainable competitive advantage, it becomes obvious that risk identification and management is built into the DNA of strategy; the only question is whether it is explicit or implicit. Fundamental to our approach is to portray how the process of resource allocation basic to strategy, suggests the development of risk capacity as part of the implementation process. In order to avoid execution pitfalls, including mispricing, the creation of risk capacity must also predate strategic moves. We do accept that this capacity may take place in a dynamic context so that it may need further development as strategic plans unfold, but the essential components must be in place prior to the strategic move if the dialectic of strategy and risk is to be realized.

It similarly follows that the risk capacity of the organization should be greater than its risk appetite, which should be greater than its risk tolerances and limits.[7] A specific statement of risk appetite is the essential complement to the articulation of strategic goals. The risk appetite statement provides the authority to take risk and, importantly, helps to tell the organization *what not to do*—which is also fundamental to strategic positioning to avoid mission creep. This is important because mission creep can lead to a misalignment of the organization's aspirations and its ability to manage the associated risks. However, the mere statement of a risk appetite without having developed the organizational capability to understand, assess/measure, monitor, and report on the risks is meaningless. These resources include management time to determine whether the risk capacity is matched to the risk appetite aspirations. Similarly, performance must be evaluated against both the strategy and the risk limits.

The board delegates authority to the CEO to execute the board-approved strategy. Similarly, creating a clear risk appetite statement is critical for corporate governance because this is a key board-approved statement of authority for the CEO and organizational leadership. It needs to clearly articulate the risks the management is authorized to take. There have been many papers and texts on risk appetite frameworks since 2012 when the Committee of Sponsoring Organizations of the Treadway Commission (COSO) released the discussion paper, "Enterprise Risk Management—Understanding and Communicating Risk Appetite."[8] COSO made it clear that this was an important topic for all organizations. Financial institutions (FIs) implemented approaches based on the principles provided by the Financial Stability Board (FSB) released in 2013.[9] This results in a great deal of commonality in the frameworks and advice. Key elements of risk appetite frameworks invariably include these elements:

- The concepts of risk capacity and appetite
- Governance requirements in terms of policies, authorities, principles, and ongoing monitoring and reporting
- Metrics, limits, and triggers linked to income and capital for approved risk-taking
- Management plans for risk incident responses
- Communication requirements to ensure all risk-takers are aware of the appetite and requirements

The FSB explicitly notes that "for the purpose of these Principles, the risk appetite framework does not include the processes to establish the strategy, develop the business plan, and the models and systems to measure and aggregate risks."[10] However, increasingly, good risk appetite statements are capturing the integration with strategy and the business plan and begin with a statement such as "[The organization] will take risks only in support of executing its business strategy."

Implicit in this admittedly vague statement is the connection between risk and performance. But most risk appetite frameworks do not adequately address this link.[11] Performance oversight, including the development of objectives, metrics and triggers, monitoring and reporting requirements, and resource budgeting, are the responsibility of the organization's finance team. This is appropriate, just as the oversight of similar risk activities is the responsibility of the risk team. A performance and risk appetite approach can be the mechanism to bring the two oversight roles together to provide the businesses with clear performance and risk objectives and governance approaches.

James Lam notes that fundamental questions to be addressed in a risk appetite framework include "What are the strategies for the overall organization and individual business units? What are the key assumptions underlying those strategies?"[12] Cubillas Ding of Celent notes that "in many instances, firms have fully operationalized and embedded risk appetite within their organizations yet not seen the influence of those changes on key decision-making processes."[13] In light of these two quotations, it is clear that risk appetite statements are still developing, with much work yet to be done. This oversight is also an important governance concern because a meta-analysis of leading academic research by Deloitte concludes that good governance has a positive impact on performance.[14]

Without going into detail on how to construct a risk appetite statement, we suggest two amplifications to the described COSO and FSB elements:

- When reading the finished risk appetite statement, the reader must be able to clearly discern the organization's purpose, strategy, and business model; and,
- Every risk appetite statement or limit must provide the performance outcome to be driven by the risk-taking activities.[15]

If done correctly, the integration of risk into strategy will be complete and the organization will focus on taking risks to drive competitive advantage and profitability. It is, of course, the CEO's responsibility to execute the board-approved strategy within the risk appetite statements.[16]

There is an extensive literature on the process of setting strategic goals and the importance of this is well-known to most executives. But has your organization infused an understanding of a risk appetite and tolerances into the strategic process?[17] Establishing the tolerances makes the risk appetite statement more concrete and actionable. Accomplishing goals demands risk-taking, so it is essential your strategic processes focus not just on returns but also on risk and return. The inclusion of a risk dimension is imperative because an understanding of risk sets an essential parameter for determining the pricing structure for a sustainable business model by ascertaining the *minimum* price that can be charged and have economic profits in a dynamic market.[18] If firms do not create economic value then they are simply transferring value from the owners to the customers and/or suppliers. Although this may be a desirable outcome for the customers and suppliers it is not sustainable and certainly precludes raising capital for growth.

STRATEGIC POSITIONING AND RISK

We should start with an exploration of the relationships concerning positioning and risk. Weitzner and Darroch (2010) explored just such a relationship and we will elaborate on their thinking. At the heart of positioning is the value offering an organization presents to customers[19] and the capability of the offering to deliver value to the stakeholders of the organization.[20] Although we start with the broad concept of stakeholders, it must be recognized that for a for-profit organization to have a sustainable strategy, the value proposition to customers must have the potential to create economic profit for the providers of capital needed to finance the venture.[21] We have chosen the term *potential* in order to capture the future orientation of both risk and strategy as well as to prepare the way for considering the role of expectations in creating shareholder value and issues for reputation risk management. Financial types may see this as another way of expressing risk and expected return. Organizations promise to deliver value to customers and stakeholders in the near and not so near future. An essential element to the evaluation of the potential of this promise to deliver at the quoted price involves a risk assessment by customers and investors.[22] In this assessment, both will consider the chances of positive and negative surprises.

STRATEGY AND RISK IN A START-UP

To further our exploration of the links among strategy, positioning, and risk, we could provide examples from any number of industries. Each would provide the links in slightly different ways, and some would draw immediate attention to certain inherent risks, but any would bring out the basic points we wish to raise. For ease of explanation and understanding, let us examine the key points based on a new restaurant operation. Consider a well-known chef and very capable and experienced restaurant manager/sommelier who decide to open their own restaurant. They wish to benefit from their respective reputations for exceptional food preparation and presentation and high-quality and responsive service. At the start, the pair assume that they do not need external financing beyond supplier credit.

We accept that the restaurant business has its own inherent risks although these vary across the many types of restaurant operations. Further, we recognize that strategic positioning is a multidimensional concept, but would like to start our exploration with pricing. To some degree the two partners will be price takers as a start-up. Customers will evaluate the offering of the new restaurant based on previous experiences with the two and decide to try based on the pricing relative to existing offerings. Although we could and will complicate this scenario, let us stay with this for a moment. The two partners will make a strategic decision on how to position their new restaurant. They can either price well below existing players, at about the same level, or significantly higher. This is a common problem for new entrants. Whatever positioning theme they choose will determine a specific set of risks that need to be identified and managed. Although we are aware that the executive team may achieve superior performance via superior implementation of a strategy including risk management, for purposes of discussion we take the extreme position that a strategy must be unique if it is to create above-average profitability for its owners. Then at least some of the risks relevant to that positioning must be unique also.[23]

If we use market tests to determine pricing options, then it follows that we must focus on cost drivers to ascertain whether there is an opportunity to create economic profits for the two partners.[24] Can the two partners source inputs, including labor, at a price that will enable them to drive a wedge between their direct and other costs and the price that they can charge? Although the input prices may be relatively easy to calculate, waste and quality of labor are important elements in the overall cost structure. Can the sources of waste be identified and controlled so that their losses do not destroy the economic profit created by the wedge between price and costs?[25] And how would the restaurant avoid the temptation to source lower-quality inputs to lessen cost pressures because this would damage the high-quality positioning theme and complicate operations?[26] Managing for ELs to meet your statistical goals is a challenge, not a given. The statistical tools used to calculate ELs essentially set a target.

Clearly another important cost driver will be volume or capacity use. The two partners will analyze the competitive landscape and estimate how many customers they can expect.[27] In going through this exercise, it is essential that the partners consider the distribution of customer demand, not a weekly average, because unused capacity from Monday's dinner does not create extra capacity for Friday's dinner. The same holds that unused capacity from Saturday's brunch does not create extra capacity for Saturday's dinner. The fixed capacity constraint forces the partners to consider the pattern and level of capacity use. There is also the strategic consideration of using pricing strategies for different days or menus to level capacity and invite trial. These choices will also interact with location and operating hours decisions. Here we see another major driver in volatility of earnings. It is important to understand that to manage performance we need to consider the drivers of the risks. For example, if freshness is important to quality of food, we need to assess location in terms of access to appropriate produce. Although sauces and so on can mitigate the impact of less-than-fresh goods, we chose to expose our partners to these risks and now need to manage the impact on performance.

We also need to consider the number of turns, that is, the number of times all the tables in the restaurant are in use, in relation to capacity use. At one extreme the manager can manage the bookings to accommodate a reasonable flow in the kitchen. You remove stress from the chef but place constraints on customers. Alternatively the decision could be made to go with an early and a late service. Although this would place more stress on the kitchen it could be mitigated by offering a more limited or even prix fixe menu that would allow for significant ahead-of-time preparation. Both would be consistent with a high-end position, but each has its own upside and downside in terms of returns. The question is how to align capacity and production.

Some readers may be thinking that although all that has been described is true, there are additional ways to expand capacity, such as longer hours or expanding to breakfast or lunch service. Let us consider two viable options and their implications. First, we can expand capacity by having a patio during the appropriate seasons.[28] This is an interesting option that affects other strategic decisions, primarily the location decision. An open patio close to a busy road may be suitable for a sports bar, but not a fine dining establishment. Not only does this limit the possible locations but also probably drives up the costs associated with real estate. Introducing or amplifying the seasonality issue may have an important impact on estimating cash flows. How does seasonality affect menu choices and then regular customers and hence cash flow at risk (CFaR)?[29] Do we price in the off-season months to break even and hope for good weather in the patio season, or do we budget for a healthy profit during every season? Whatever the choice, the uncertainty of the impact of weather will add new volatility to our earnings, and we must take measures to protect ourselves. This is the realm of ULs.

A second option evolves from having a take-out service, especially appealing in the age of independent food delivery services such as Uber Eats and other services. Now recall that the excellence of food and service is fundamental to our positioning. We are giving up on differentiating via service because this is now eliminated through pick-up and delivery, and the quality of the food is not likely to be improved with either option. This may or not be an issue. Regular customers will understand and adjust their expectations, but suppose they are using the restaurant as a catering service for a dinner party for noncustomers. This will be the first encounter they have with the restaurant's offering and they are likely to be somewhat disappointed. Although the partners have expanded the market, it comes at the price of new downside risk arising from the loss of control over key dimensions of their positioning and exposing them to negative word of mouth.

We accept there are options to manage capacity but note that it does not alter the fundamental problem but rather changes the parameters and in general adds complexity. Efforts to solve these constraints by operational changes impact other areas of risk such as the strategic risk of positioning and will generally create new operational risks arising from the complexities of dealing with multiple service offerings, thereby requiring new operations and processes as well as expanded human resource management to mitigate risks arising from human decisions.

A focus on positioning, however, provides the clearest way of assessing how the interaction of different risk types condition possible mitigants. Because the partners had determined to position their establishment as a fine dining establishment, it is unlikely that opening for breakfast is an option. We can think of no such positioning—except for some hotels. It should be noted that we are not trying to put limitations on innovation but rather suggest that an increased level of innovation generally leads to a perception of increased risk—in this case by customers and investors. One clear example of this issue is the vacant niche. If there is a vacant strategic position, before leaping into filling it, consider why no one else has. The assumption that competitors are dumb is often a recipe for disaster—if no one else is doing it, ask yourself why? Strategic positioning is as clear in telling you what not to do as it is in what to do.

Let us explore some other elements of positioning in terms of the breadth versus the specificity of the product offering. In general, trying to be all things to all people is a recipe for disaster. But think of the challenge facing our partners. First, they have established reputations for providing a certain type of value. Do they build on this asset or do they seek to provide something new? What if the heart of their previous value proposition was being innovative not classic? If they build on their existing strengths, how does that affect strategic rivalry? Can they open in their existing locale or will competition be too intense? If they seek a new locale, how well will their reputations travel? The strategic positioning process must constantly be factoring in elements from the risk dimension. This is clearly an important issue facing all businesses as they seek to leverage their brands or other assets.

Consider the effect of the reputation of the manager on a specific strategic decision: the wine list. Should the restaurant seek to be known as the place to go for oenophiles or should it position itself in a slightly different manner as friendly to wine aficionados? If it seeks to be a destination for oenophiles it is committed to building a significant wine cellar and earning recognition in publications such as *Wine Spectator*. Are the skills of the manager/sommelier up to the task—does the risk capacity match the challenge? If so, then this decision allows for additional differentiation because the restaurant will become known for enhancing the dining experience through the pairing of wine and food. The margins to be earned from allocating resources are significant, but so too are the risks. The first risk affects cash flows. To make this a profitable activity the owners will be purchasing wines that they may have to hold for several years and cash will be locked in. Although buying early reduces initial price, it also leads to inventory issues when a vintage fails to deliver on its initial promise. To some degree there are portfolio effects here because some wines may outperform their initial promise and garner superior earnings.[30] There are also operational risks arising from the storage of the wine. The investment in the wine cellar also can create significant entry barriers for new entrants by raising the capital costs of entry and thus contribute to the sustainability of the strategy. This risk, driven by social trends and perhaps magnified by social media, is a risk faced by all industries. Think of the current discussions concerning selling guns or high-sugar or fatty foods.[31] Assuming the status quo is akin to the proverbial ostrich sticking its head in the sand.

There is another risk that is ignored by many risk managers—changes in consumer taste that lead to lower demand and hence lower valuations of certain wine types.[32] In this context, we should note that the value of renowned wines increases as they age and reach maturity. Sommeliers are not just buying wines for next month's consumption but investing with a long time horizon, and over that long time horizon consumer tastes can and do change. Consider the traditional way of valuing French Bordeaux wines by appellation designating their origin by locale or the movement away from heavily oaked chardonnays. There has been a long-held belief in the mythic importance of terroir, or the soil and other natural endowments that alone can produce great wine. In recent years, this has come under attack and the belief that the technology of wine making has a far greater impact has gained prominence. Many further believe that this view is supported by the influential wine critic Robert M. Parker Jr.[33] Although it has been argued that Parker's opinion affects only a small percentage of buyers, that is precisely the segment that is under discussion. Think of the impact on the trading portfolio of an FI if a new method of valuation suddenly achieved significant acceptance in the marketplace. If you do this, then you will understand the risk on the wine inventory of some restaurants.

Yet consider the wine-friendly positioning that would require far less in the way of investment in a wine cellar at the cost of losing one dimension of differentiation. Could we make a choice that would mitigate this loss? We can by allowing true aficionados to bring their own wine and charging a reasonable corkage fee. We are now differentiated by involving the customer in creating the dining experience. Note that the risk transfer is not complete because the partners are still responsible for the proper serving of the wine to what is likely to be a very demanding customer. This element of operational risk would be heightened depending on when the transfer of the wine bottle takes place.[34] The longer it is in the restaurant presumably the higher the corkage fee but so too the greater the operational risk of proper storage. To return to a previous point, there are different ways of creating customer value, and it is essential to identify the specific risks created by the management of value chain activities to execute the delivery of the promise.

We would like to draw some simple lessons from the described scenario. The first is the dialectic between strategy and risk. As an organization formulates its strategic position it must identify and prioritize the risks inherent in its positioning and put in place monitoring processes as well as controls and mitigants. Given the scarcity of resources then it becomes important to prioritize risks to make the allocation of resources to these tasks effective and efficient.[35] Complicating this task is the interaction of different risk types as the possible solutions to the capacity problem demonstrated. Your actions can change the shape of the risks confronting you, but they will not make risk go away. Identifying every risk type and assigning accountability for them creates silos, not solutions.[36] The effect of choice, as seen, often results in risk migrations, transformations, amplifications, and diversification. This is a key element in effective risk management and will be dealt with in Appendix I. This bad news is tempered by remembering that in a world of no risk, there are no economic profits, only accounting profits.

Organizations must create economic profits, not just accounting profits to create value for investors.

In Chapter 2 we will discover how executing on the plan leads to the discovery of new risks.

NOTES

1. We will return to the issue of risk and uncertainty in our discussion of Frank Knight's work in Chapter 3.
2. Essential to our understanding of positioning is a focus on the customer and creating value for the customer. We concur with the insights presented in Roger Martin, "The Age of Customer Capitalism," *Harvard Business Review,* January 2010.
3. See Chapter 4.
4. This highlights that performance analytics is the flip side of risk analytics.
5. We explore the process issues and discuss different approaches to capital in Chapter 3.
6. Michael E. Porter, *Competitive Strategy: Techniques for Analyzing Industries and Competitors* (New York: Free Press, 1980).
7. This topic is explored more fully in James Darroch and David Finnie, "Risk Appetite and Tolerance in Competitive Strategy," in John Fraser and Betty J. Simkins, eds., *Enterprise Risk Management: Today's Leading Research and Best Practices for Tomorrow's Executives,* 2nd ed. (Hoboken, NJ: Wiley, forthcoming).
8. Larry Rittenberg and Frank Martens, "Understanding and Communicating Risk Appetite," COSO, January 2012, https://www.coso.org/Documents/ERM-Understanding-and-Communicating-Risk-Appetite.pdf. COSO started its life as the National Commission on Fraudulent Financial Reporting in 1985 when it was sponsored by "five major professional associations headquartered in the United States: the American Accounting Association (AAA), the American Institute of Certified Public Accountants (AICPA), Financial Executives International (FEI), The Institute of Internal Auditors (IIA), and the National Association of Accountants (now the Institute of Management Accountants [IMA]). Wholly independent of each of the sponsoring organizations, the Commission included representatives from industry, public accounting, investment firms, and the New York Stock Exchange." COSO About Us, January 2, 2020, https://www.coso.org/Pages/aboutus.aspx.
9. Financial Stability Board, "Principles for an Effective Risk Appetite Framework," November 18, 2013, http://www.fsb.org/wp-content/uploads/r_131118.pdf.
10. Financial Stability Board, "Principles for An Effective Risk Appetite Framework," 3.

11. See Patricia Jackson, "Risk Appetite and Risk Responsibilities," Ernst & Young, February 15, 2019, https://www.ey.com/Publication/vwLUAssets/ey-risk-governance-2020-risk-appetite-and-risk-responsibilities/$FILE/ey-risk-governance-2020-risk-appetite-and-risk-responsibilities.pdf.
12. James Lam, "Implementing an Effective Risk Appetite," IMA, August 2015, https://www.imanet.org/-/media/8150b134bafd42aaaf5267bf49d6d2a3.ashx.
13. Cubillas Ding, "Next-Generation Risk Appetite Management: Getting Real about Achieving Impact in Uncertain Time," Celent, March 2016.
14. Deloitte, "Good Governance Driving Corporate Performance? A Meta-Analysis of Academic Research & Invitation to Engage in the Dialogue," December 2016, https://www2.deloitte.com/content/dam/Deloitte/nl/Documents/risk/deloitte-nl-risk-good-governance-driving-corporate-performance.pdf.
15. To some degree this is implicit in the COSO statement: "Risk appetite is the amount of risk, on a broad level, an organization is willing to accept in pursuit of value. Each organization pursues various objectives to add value and should broadly understand the risk it is willing to undertake in doing so." "Understanding and Communicating Risk Appetite," January 2, 2020, https://www.coso.org/Documents/ERM-Understanding-and-Communicating-Risk-Appetite.pdf.
16. And it is the board's responsibility to monitor this. See Chapter 10.
17. Note that this assumes that you have previously determined your risk appetite.
18. Stern Stewart, now Stern Value Management (SVM), created the metric *economic value added (EVA)* to analyze economic profits. SVM's homepage offers this definition of EVA:

    Economic Value Added (EVA®) measures the wealth a company creates (or destroys) each year. It is a company's after-tax profit from operations minus a charge for the cost of all capital employed to produce those profits – not just the cost of debt, but the cost of equity as well.

    EVA® can be drilled down to a business unit, geographical area, project, client, product or service. It allows us to measure value creation at the most basic level of a corporation's operations, greatly improving decision making. (https://sternvaluemanagement.com/economic-value-added-eva)

    David R. Koenig emphasizes this point in a different way:

    Chris Matten, the former group financial controller of Swiss Bank Corporation and former Managing Director (Corporate Stewardship) of Temasek Holdings, said that risk is the single biggest expense not found on any income statement. His insight is especially important for us as we consider motivation and incentives. If our incentive design, whether extrinsic or intrinsic, does not properly account for the risk it creates, then it will have a distorted impact. To take on risk, we need economic capital, which has a cost if we wish to acquire it in the marketplace. That cost should be recognized. (David R. Koenig, Governance

Reimagined: Organizational Design, Risk, and Value Creation [*Northfield, MN: B Right Governance Publications, 2018*], *156)*

Many FIs now show a capital charge in sections on the profitability of different lines of business.

19. We have chosen the neutral term *organization* because we believe that the same logic holds for all organizations whether they are for-profit or not-for-profit. The nature of the value creation and value claiming may differ, but the logic is the same. Consider the current philosophical divide in the US. Republicans and Democrats differ not only over the possible arenas for value creation by government but also over the value-claiming mechanism—taxes. Having chosen the neutral term *organization,* we must then employ the stakeholder concept. However, we will also argue later that the choice of the term *stakeholder* is not just for semantic reasons but also for strategic reasons. A narrow focus on "shareholders" or "owners" may unduly curtail the perspective needed to consider all the issues in managing risks to the organization's reputation.
20. For a recent discussion of the importance of stakeholders to strategy, see Richard L. Priem, Ryan Krause, Caterina Tantalo, and Ann McFadyen, "Promoting Long-Term Shareholder Value by 'Competing' for Essential Stakeholders: A New Multi-Sided Market Logic for Top Managers," *Academy of Management Perspectives* (April 17, 2019).
21. In this book we will always stress that the returns generated must create economic profits, not accounting profits, because this is essential to the link between strategy formulation and risk. Moreover, it is important to consider that the providers of debt capital will also be focused on economic, not accounting, profits. Later on this leads to a discussion of the relationship between positioning strategy and income statement and balance sheet positioning.
22. We will use the term *investors* to cover all providers of scarce resources including equity, debt, and human capital.
23. Michael E. Porter takes this position and examines the role of fit in sustainable competitive advantage. We are extending this concept to the world of risk. See "What Is Strategy," *Harvard Business Review* (November–December 1996). Porter also recognizes the difficulty of copying the fit that is an essential component of high-performing strategies.
24. We recognize that we are assuming that the partners are aligned on the profit goals and that this is not a lifestyle business that the partners want to be in for nonfinancial reasons. This is an important consideration because if the industry is populated by lifestyle rivals it becomes more difficult to earn economic profits. Competitor analysis is an important element of industry analysis and the entry decision. It is also one of the important ways to make your analysis future oriented and dynamic by considering the response of rivals as Michael Porter's famous five forces framework make clear. See Michael E Porter, "The Five Competitive Forces That Shape Strategy," *Harvard Business Review* (January 2008).
25. An interesting recent development in this area is the creation of the food sharing app Olio. This app allows consumers to buy surplus produce from restaurants,

cafes, and supermarkets. See Hazel Sheffield, "The Food Waste Warriors Harvesting Success," *Financial Times* (December 31, 2019).

26. An important insight from Porter's value chain logic is the need to maximize the entire chain. Maximizing one silo actually prevents maximizing the entire range of interconnected activities.
27. Some readers may recognize that the partners are implicitly building a model with all its inherent risks; we will return to this later.
28. Seasonality is, of course, a general issue for many businesses.
29. There is a saying in the entrepreneurial world, "Cash is king." Students are often surprised that you can be profitable but out of business when you run out of cash. Therefore, it is important to estimate your highest negative cash flow. In a sense this is comparable to liquidity management in a FI—in both cases, if you are out of cash, you are out of business. However, consultants at McKinsey have argued that just as VaR is the appropriate risk measure for FIs on the assumption that investments can be sold in a relatively short time frame, the appropriate measure for non-FIs is how much cash a company can lose over the appropriate time frame. Hence CFaR is the appropriate risk measure. Claude Genereux, Eric Lamarre, and Thomas-Olivier Leautier, "The Special Challenge of Measuring Industrial Company Risk," *McKinsey on Finance* 6 (Winter 2003), https://www.mckinsey.com/client_service/corporate_finance/latest_thinking/mckinsey_on_finance/~/media/C5BAB75D838B403582F1FB87B5E24A7F.ashx.
30. See Emiko Terazono, "Burgundy Cheered as Region's Wines Outperform Gold," *Financial Times* (January 21, 2019).
31. Changes in attitudes toward the treatment of animals could lead to a real backlash, for example, as has happened with foie gras or game. Even if your regular customers enjoy these foods, they may not want to run the gauntlet of protesters. A broad understanding of the potential impacts of social changes is essential to anticipate possible impacts on your products/services. See Sara Germano, "Acknowledge, Apologize, Investigate: How Big Brands Combat Online Outrage," *The Wall Street Journal* (February 19, 2019).
32. Olivier Gergaud and Victor Ginsburgh, "Natural Endowments, Production Technologies, Quality of Wines in Bordeaux. Is It Possible to Produce Wine on Paved Roads?" *American Association of Wine Economists* Working Paper No. 2 (2007).
33. See Robert M. Parker Jr., *Parker's Wine Buyers Guide,* 7th ed. (New York: Simon & Schuster, 2008) or "Making Sense of Terroir," *Wine Advocate* (January 7, 2019), https://shopcru.com/learn-about-wine/making-sense-of-terroir.
34. For the aficionado we are concerned about the phenomenon of "bottle shock"—the temporary impact on a wine's flavor from being shaken in transport.
35. This is a general issue; see Oliver Bevan, Matthew Freiman, Kanika Pasricha, Hamid Samandari, and Olivia White, "Transforming Risk Efficiency and Effectiveness," *McKinsey & Company Risk Practice* (April 25, 2019), https://www.mckinsey.com/business-functions/risk/our-insights/transforming-risk-efficiency-and-effectiveness.

36. The impact of silos on business performance is not sufficiently recognized. See the very interesting book by the *Financial Times* columnist, Gillian Tett, *The Silo Effect: The Peril of Expertise and the Promise of Breaking Down Barriers* (New York: Simon & Schuster, 2015) and Tiziana Casciaro, Tiziana, Amy C. Edmondson, and Sujin Jang, "Cross Silo Leadership," *Harvard Business Review* (May–June 2019).

CHAPTER 2

Executing on the Plan and Discovering New Risks

In Chapter 1 we developed the link between strategy and risk management in guiding the decision-making to formulate the business plan. Now, let us consider how to bring the plan to life, in other words, explore the relationship of positioning on value chain management. This is a fundamental choice facing all organizations. Think of how Apple, Nike, Walmart, and other high-performing organizations manage their value-adding activities to focus on their unique capabilities.

In our case, should the partners create (manufacture) their own deserts or should they outsource to a well-known local pastry chef? It is important to recognize that pastry baking is a different specialized skill set from cooking. In the early days of the venture there are advantages to outsourcing. First, the use of a well-known outsider may create halo effects that enhance the perceived quality of the new restaurant. It will probably be less expensive than hiring a pastry chef full-time and should reduce complexity in the kitchen. In addition to these benefits, it may make it possible to expand other offerings on the menu. We can view this decision as a risk transfer decision driven by the positioning theme. Most of the upside in terms of reputation goes to the outside supplier, who will get most of the credit for success, and any failures will likely accrue to the restaurant. Transferring operational risk here does not make the risk go away; it simply changes the shape. You now have inventory risk. There is also an element of vendor and financial risk depending on how the supplier contract is structured.[1] If the outside supplier is the more powerful player in this relationship, that person may impose contractual conditions on unsold goods that will create cash flow problems. Although the decision may appear to change the fixed cost of a captive chef into a variable cost, the structure of the contract could actually be creating fixed cash flow obligations similar to fixed costs. The manner in which operational leverage affects the capacity to take risk is an issue for all organizations, and this is where decisions concerning cash flows at risk (CFaR) become important.

Ultimately the decision is a strategic one linking positioning to value chain management. Which decision better accomplishes fulfilling the value proposition of the positioning theme? It should also be noted that the decision is a dynamic one that may change over time. For reputation reasons, the partners may start with a famous outside supplier but supplement those choices with internally prepared choices as the reputation of the restaurant gains greater recognition. We should also consider how learning affects risk management.[2] Over time the restaurant manager should learn more about the preferences of customers and be able both to enhance customer satisfaction by providing the desired offering while reducing waste. A clear win-win. The extent of the win, however, may be tempered by what competitors are learning from the restaurant's success and developing new tactics to limit the success.

In this scenario we have primarily focused on the inter-relationships among positioning, pricing, and risk. The positioning is the key risk management activity, and the pricing decisions drive risk/return. We have also tried to emphasize the relationship between organizational governance and market governance. The organization has a clear governance responsibility in identifying and managing the risks associated with its strategy and in a sustainable strategy it accomplishes this through pricing for expected losses (ELs). Yet, it must be recognized that there is a ceiling on the price that can be charged that is essentially a function of the market.[3] This relationship makes it incumbent on organizations to have explicit risk management strategies. However, let us return to our two partners. Let us assume for a moment that they chose a scenic riverside location and took out the appropriate insurance policies related to weather and so forth. Let us go even further and say that they anticipated business continuity issues arising from floods and insured that. What risks remain?

We need to return to the previous discussion of how to determine the level of risks transferred. If all the risks of the location are transferred, then presumably all the gains associated with taking this locational risk would also be transferred. Consequently, the more likely real-world scenario is that the partners decide to accept (retain) and manage a certain level of risk. Either implicitly or explicitly they have determined their risk appetite. To make economic profits an organization must take risk and to have a sustainable position, those risks must be managed, and that demands an understanding of risk capacity and the development of a risk appetite statement.

All of the previous decisions that we have discussed affect the risk capacity of the organization. The degree of capital reserves, operational leverage, understanding of the risk drivers, and transparency of the risk decisions and the appropriate culture all affect the ability to take any risks, not just new risks. For example, the decision to hold wine inventory reduces our capital buffer.[4] So, too, do the decisions on how we manage our value chain in the context of operational leverage. Fixed contracts and other devices increase our operating leverage by turning variable costs into fixed ones. However, they also have the advantage of securing strategic assets. Careful thought must always be given to the relationship between strategic assets and risk drivers.

Although before we were in the realm of ELs and flows, we are now in a different realm: the realm of the balance sheet, or stocks. Organizations must hold resources or access to resources to weather the unexpected. The questions are how much and what kind. To return to our previous discussion of the wine cellar, it is important to recognize this as a capital asset—albeit with market and liquidity risk. The wine or portions of the inventory can be sold; the issue is how easily and at what price as we see the interaction of liquidity and asset prices.[5] But this takes us back to the demands of investors versus the comfort of having surplus resources. The partners may believe that the restaurant business is cyclical and accept that each venture has a limited life span. If this is the thinking, then the strategic decision would be to go very light in holding resources for contingencies because this will limit current returns.[6] The point is that reducing idle resources limits organizational resilience. Take the opposite time horizon: the partners are building a business for their children to take over. Rather than managing to maximize return on investment (ROI) they would be more likely to focus on creating the needed cash flow to support family needs and doing the best to build up a cushion to get them through the "bad times."[7] It is also possible that in developing their positioning theme the two partners realize that they lack sufficient resources. Do they cut back on their dream—or at least develop a staged plan—or seek external investors? If they seek external investors, to what degree are they willing to accept the loss of control imposed by the demands of the investors?

It is not our purpose to say which is correct but rather to note that the process of resource allocation fundamental to strategy requires a specific understanding of the degree of control needed and a statement of risk appetite and tolerances if the manner of achieving strategic goals is to be understood. It is also worth considering risk migration and how risk changes shape. The consequence of this is that there must be a clear focus on the entire risk spectrum. If the specific risks are treated by individual specialists, the net effect may be to transfer the risk to another silo, not to effectively manage it.[8]

This discussion is somewhat static because it sees everything from the point of view of our two partners, but although they can influence how competitors respond, they can't control it. This forces our partners to consider how much of a buffer—cash in the bank, line of credit, and so on—they need before they can count on their venture to at least break even. In making this decision they need to consider not only how long it will take to build up their clientele but also how the response of other restaurants will affect the growth of their clientele and positioning. This aspect highlights the importance of the future for strategy and risk management. Later we will discuss how scenario planning is an important tool for dealing with this dynamic situation, but for the moment we simply want to highlight how the future orientation forces us to deal with uncertainty.

When you enter or alter your position in a competitive situation you have changed the dynamic, so to think that everything else will stay the same is fundamentally mistaken. Your actions, whether anticipated or not, will most likely change how others respond. So, it is imperative for your strategy that you anticipate what the likely reactions will be. But unlike the more "scientific" aspects of risk management, you need to be cognizant that the unexpected can happen. You will not have a historical database on rival responses. In some situations, if your positioning is quite distinct, your arrival may be welcomed as helping to bring new customers into the area. Or, you may be viewed as rivals for a fixed market—in which case, response may be swift and harsh if the rivals have the resources to do so. In this context, it is very similar to how you need to vet your assumptions about any frameworks or models you are using.[9]

Previously we noted that the partners were assessing cost drivers, capacity use, and the competitive landscape. They were implicitly building a model to help them make key business decisions. The model itself is a representation of reality using historical data and simplifying assumptions to predict future possible outcomes. In assessing the risks in this model, the partners need to be clear on the stability of the underlying inputs and assumptions—specifically, how often and to what extent do they vary over time? It is also imperative to understand the sensitivity of the decisions to be made to any given input or assumption. Clearly, the less stable an input or assumption and the more sensitive the model results are to any input or assumption, the more those must be tested through different model scenarios. Also, all assumptions should have a certainty factor—how much confidence can be placed on the assumption being correct?

These efforts to manage risks may create a new type of risk—in this case, model risk. Let us elaborate. The identification of risk and the assignment of accountability points to a planning process—perhaps an informal understanding or a more explicit business plan. The business plan can be seen as developing a model for the organization and, hence, the assumptions that are untested in the plan create something akin to model risk. We need a model to guide our actions and to simplify a complex reality, but confidence in the reality of the model may lead us to underestimate the complexities created in reality.[10] This can be extremely dangerous because our confidence in the reality of the model leads us to see events in a specific way. These preconceptions can guide us to have dangerously slow responses to what is happening.[11] The more complex the model, the greater the opportunity for failure. In making decisions using models, the partners must establish an understanding of where and when the model is most vulnerable and how they can fail. This enables them to establish feedback mechanisms to monitor how well the assumptions in the models meet conditions as time moves forward, into the uncertain future.

Our belief in the past as a guide to the future may blind us to significant changes—think inflection points and discontinuity. In the case of our restaurant partners the emergence of molecular cooking or plant-based foods may challenge some of their long-held beliefs and skills.[12] Watching niche or fad trends become mainstream is why attention to emerging risks is necessary.[13] Paying attention to changing consumer tastes is essential to creating customer value. To revisit a point we made with the wine inventory, it is not just the inventory that loses value, it is often the skills that created the inventory. The skill in cooking traditional meat may not be the same as preparing plant-based meals. Organizational slack may be necessary to prepare for the future—even if it reduces current returns.

THE ASSUMPTION OF GOAL CONGRUENCE AND THE IMPORTANCE OF CULTURE

If we go back to the notion of partnership, it was assumed that the partners would agree, but is that a good assumption? Maybe yes, maybe no. But it is worthwhile to explore how their different forms of expertise could lead to a clash. Given the positioning, the chef probably sees herself as an artist who will only use the finest materials to create what she wants. A celebrity chef a la Anne-Sophie Pic; Ferran Adria; Eric Ripert; Marco Pierre White; Clare Smyth; or the late Paul Bocuse, who trained under the first female chef to earn three Michelin stars, Eugenie Brazier[14]; and Joel Robichon will aspire to three Michelin stars.[15] Now if this will bring in the customers, all is well and good. But what if the dishes create a very limited market?[16] How will the manager with his planning and budgeting skills convince the chef of the need to adjust or go bankrupt? Although food may be an art, running a restaurant is also a business. One can see how problems lead to conflict that leads to broken partnerships.

Second, we haven't really focused explicitly on operational risk, which dramatically affects the positioning. The chef will have to find qualified suppliers and help. Although she is an artist, she is not the solo creator but rather an artist running an atelier that requires installing the appropriate procedures and supervision. It is not just about getting the right result—the chef can't reject too many dishes because this would frustrate waiting customers and create longer waits for everybody, as well as drive up the costs as the food is thrown out. The chef is not only key to the product part of the value proposition but also to the execution. This means managing the operational risks. And managing the operational risk means designing the appropriate processes and checks to produce the desired results. For the organization to succeed, masterpieces must be produced as close to every time as possible. The chef must accomplish the Herculean task of combining excellence with consistency. This is the challenge of managing operational risk to achieve an acceptable standard of masterpiece—as judged by the customer.

This is not just a challenge for the chef because the manager too must hire and train the appropriate waitstaff. Because this is a fine dining establishment, the waitstaff must not only be knowledgeable but their interactions with customers must be appropriate. This requires the waitstaff to be knowledgeable about the food, the wine,[17] *and* the customer. The waitstaff is critical in matching the expectations of the customer to the capabilities of the kitchen. If asked for an opinion, it is essential that the waitstaff provide an honest one.[18] If they don't, they become shills, not the trusted, knowledgeable advisors that good salespeople are. This role becomes especially important with repeat customers. Here, again, there is the source of a potential conflict between artistry and market demands. When the menu changes, a customer favorite may disappear. Now if this is an issue of seasonality, the customers will understand it is a quality issue, but if it is simply the chef being an "artist," it is unlikely the customer will understand. We are sure that many artists get tired of repeating their hits, but it is the price of maintaining steady customers.

Now it should be acknowledged that some may accept erratic quality but what will be the impact on pricing and market demand?[19] And some may accept a lower level of artistry for consistency, as the fast food industry demonstrates.[20] There are many possible positions, and of those some will succeed and some will fail. Our focus is not so much on evaluating the quality of the positioning as recognizing the impact of operational risk on all elements of delivery and on the promise of the value proposition.

Let us return to our example of the two restaurant owners to explore the relationship between goals and risk. Consider the decisions facing the two owners over short-term versus long-term profitability. Previously we noted that the partners would not seek external financing, but they came to realize that to maximize the value of their equity, they could use as much debt financing as possible. But this may expose the operation to near-term issues in generating the cash flow to cover the interest costs.[21] This decision increases liquidity, or cash flow, risk and consequently reduces capacity for other risks. Assuming that there are no covenants on the loans that restrict management decision-making and their cash burn rate of reserves, this puts a specific time horizon on when the operation must start generating positive cash flows. This is a decision involving uncertainty. Certainly, the owners can study the statistics concerning similar operations or have heuristics based on their experience, but there is no certainty that these numbers will apply to their specific situation.

The decision must be made as to how to prepare for this contingency. Assuming their resources are exhausted, they can follow one of the three following choices:

- Accept the risk
- Consider taking in another investor
- Change the menu/promotion/pricing to increase the likelihood of generating early customers

What merits consideration is that to manage the situation, the partners must explicitly consider ex ante the probability of success. Some will say, what will be will be and if things don't work out we will deal with it then. But that is very problematic because in that situation you are approaching potential providers of resources in a weaker position. *The weaker your position the more likely it is that investors or suppliers of credit will seek higher returns and the reduction of downside risk.* The reduction of downside may affect the positioning of the restaurant by imposing new controls on the discretion of the two partners. Proper risk management is about not only managing the downside risk, but also capturing as much of the upside as possible. The distinction is an important one. Accounting profits do not recognize fully the importance of risk return. Consequently a firm can be profitable in accounting terms but destroying value because the return is not compensating investors for the risks they are taking.

This scenario is not a simple situation. It is possible, for example, that the two partners have determined that if their concept is to be successful, it will be in a specific time horizon. Although in some instances the calculation of economic capital, which enables you to survive the unexpected, is as much an art as a science as applying generalizations, even statistical ones, to specific situations, it is itself uncertain. But, the partners may have a gut feel from their experience in the industry that if the restaurant doesn't pass the market test in six months, it never will.[22] If they are confident in this decision and have built it into their plan, then they will match resources to the opportunity and accept the judgment of the marketplace.

It is worthwhile to consider the links between the second and third options. The provider of external resources may say the menu is too exotic for this locale, that the restaurant needs to offer some more basic options. Depending on the chef's artistic inclinations, this may pose a problem and imperil the long-term positioning of the restaurant. After all, it is generally easier to move down market than up market.[23] The importance of managing ex ante is to maintain control of the vision. It is also worth considering how this situation could drive a wedge between the two partners. The chef may hold to the importance of the creative vision, while the manager may be more inclined to bend to business realities. At issue is the degree of goal congruence between the two owners. In larger organizations this can be seen as a governance issue: the degree of goal congruence between board and management and/or within the executive management ranks. In this situation, the agreement is under stress because the intensity that each holds to different goals of artistry versus survival may imperil the partnership.

There are other dimensions to the interaction of risk and artistry and that is in the acceptance of the menu by the patrons. Let us assume that the menu is posted online and in front of the restaurant for passersby. This leads to the following choice:

- The menu attracts diners with its novelty.
- Diners pass on the menu as being too exotic.

Consider why diners might pass first. Again, we want to simplify to make some fundamental points. Imagine a couple, in which one is a very traditional meat and potatoes person and the other is a vegan. Does the menu include options for both? For those who are thinking you can always add options, you need to remember the impact of options on positioning from the chef's point of view and the addition of complexity and increased likelihood of waste from the business point of view. You can't be everything to everybody for these reasons.

On a different tangent, the partners must decide on how family friendly to be. Encouraging younger people to develop taste is a worthwhile goal. Should there be the option of smaller servings for younger diners? If so, should those options be available for lighter eaters? Whatever the decision it will affect branding from the early customers and hence word of mouth and also the complexity of operations. Capacity to manage this complexity must be a preopening decision, or the restaurant risks losing the vision it started with.

In addition to positioning risk, we also need to consider how the goals interact with execution, or operational risk. Diners could be enchanted by the promise of the menu, which has created expectations of how the food will taste and even be presented. There are multiple dimensions to how this will play out. Let us explore the most important ones:

1. The diners love the meal and discuss it with friends leading to new customers.
2. The diners are disappointed because their preferred dish is sold out.
3. The server notices there is an issue and asks if the diners would like a change.
4. The diners send it back and request changes or a different meal.
5. The diners are disappointed but don't say anything to the server but vow never to come back and to warn their friends.
6. The meal is average and the diners' decision to return has more to do with convenience or some other factor not influenced by the superior quality of the food.

Obviously the first choice is the desired outcome. The second choice may or may not be problematic depending on what happens with the alternative dish. If it is available and exceeds expectation the result is not far behind the first in terms of desirability. If the second option doesn't meet expectations, then we are thrown into the world of the following four outcomes.

Although not optimal, possibility three demonstrates the importance of the staff beyond the owners. The server should act as the customer representative, even be the customer's advocate to ensure expectations are met. This may mean explaining what the chef was trying to achieve but accepting that the customer's needs must be met. In a sense, your frontline staff have the opportunity to turn a potential disaster into a win or to make the disaster much worse. The fourth possibility takes us into the realm of risk appetite and risk tolerances. The owners have decided what to offer and outcome four shows their offering is not meeting expectations. But the questions are, what is creating the gap between expectations and how large is the gap? Let's focus on the expectations first. Is the entree fully described on the menu? If it isn't, are the servers able to fully explain each dish in order to set the appropriate expectations? We have all had the experience of something looking fantastic on paper, only to change our minds when we learn more about the item under discussion. The role of the server is to narrow gaps between expectations and reality.

In terms of risk tolerances, there are two different metrics. The first is how often the item is ordered. If it is never ordered, what is the problem? Should it be offered as a special and have the server explain the dish in order to invite trial? If that doesn't work, it has failed the market test and needs to be taken off the menu because it is driving up waste. But there is a different way a menu item can fail and that is that it keeps being sent back. How many times can this happen before you change the dish to meet the complaints? You can persist in your vision and, given your business, you won't become a starving artist, but you will become a bankrupt artist. Yet, commitment to your vision demands that you establish parameters as to what is an acceptable return rate. To phrase it differently, what is an acceptable level of loss on each item? Can the losses on one item be offset by gains on other items, or does market pressure demand all items have a similar loss profile? And over what time frame? Managing a menu is the same as managing a portfolio of business lines or financial assets.

But we have ignored a very important dimension so far: organizational culture. Not only will our restaurant have its culture that includes awareness of all the risks we have discussed, it will be affected by the culture of the industry, which has shaped the attitudes of our staff—from kitchen workers to frontline. Later we will discuss issues relating to tipping and how incentives affect goal congruence and performance, but for the moment we want to focus on the culture of the industry, which is often problematic. We run the risk of providing a caricature, but we do it to make a point. As a customer, we love the chef as artist, but reading the biographies of many "artists," or even entrepreneurs such as Steve Jobs, these are difficult people for whom to work. Reflecting on the well-known food writer and TV personality Anthony Bourdain's[24] suicide an article in *The Wall Street Journal* makes the following comment:

> *When John Hinman, owner of Hinman's Bakery in Denver, became a pastry chef in the mid-1990s, he learned through a tradition of apprenticeship. Many restaurant kitchens are run in a strict hierarchy where rising within a pyramid structure confers the right to dominate those beneath. "It's brutal, the berating that goes on. You had to be tough. You had to be able to take it,"* Mr. Hinman says.
>
> *The food industry often draws non-conformist, Type-A perfectionists attracted to the unusual hours and the camaraderie of a kitchen crew he says. However, that spirit can lead to an unhealthy partying life stye. Mr. Hinman, a recovering alcoholic, in May co-founded a group called Culinary Hospitality Outreach & Wellness—CHOW, for short.*[25]

This is not a healthy culture in any era but may be especially destructive in the era of #MeToo—especially as sexism has been rampant in the industry.[26] Although a generally negative attitude toward an industry can lead to better organizations having a competitive advantage because they differentially attract the best people, the overall attitude to the industry will lessen the size of the overall pool. How can you expect your people to be advocates when they can't advocate for themselves? How can you attract the best people who always have options if you treat them badly? Although the answer is obvious, it isn't so obvious how you break out of the way in which you were socialized yourself. Changing tastes and preferences affect your ability to attract employees just as much as the value of your wine cellar. And excellent employees are the sine qua non of great customer experience.[27] Just as operational risk affects all other categories, so too does organizational culture and the recognition that what is acceptable can and will change—sometimes to your gain, sometimes to your detriment.

CONCLUSION

In a very real sense, you can see that managing a menu is similar to managing a portfolio of business lines. And how this portfolio is managed can force underlying tensions over what counts as success to surface. This conflict can exacerbate different views of what success means. Consider the extreme where the chef aspires to three Michelin stars and the manager is a recent MBA who is convinced of the role of big data and analysis in a successful operation.[28]

The key concepts that we have explored here are the challenges of creating a value proposition and delivering on it. This ties together strategy formulation and implementation as well as managing different risks that arise from the positioning. Management of the challenges will go a long way toward establishing the reputation of the organization. At the heart of establishing and maintaining a reputation is the decision of which risks to keep and which to transfer. Strategy and risk management are about making choices. That is the subject of Chapter 3.

NOTES

1. Vendor risk is a very hot topic right now. Vendor risk is most important with respect to contract and financial terms and information security and long-term viability (long-term contracts or dependence on a vendor require the vendor to be viable over the term of the contract—this is colored by substitutability and so on).

2. See David Apgar, *Risk Intelligence: Learning to Manage What We Don't Know* (Boston: Harvard Business Review Press, 2006).
3. It is possible in a way to escape the market discipline—be unique and count heavily on one-time purchasers. You can think of any very highly differentiated good here, but the price may be subject to heightened volatility because of the lack of a steady customer base. A restaurant in a unique tourist location may be such a case, but if tourism falls, so too does the business.
4. It might be more accurate to say the wine inventory introduces market risk into our capital buffer because the price and liquidity of wines are volatile.
5. It is important to note the interconnection of liquidity and solvency issues in a crisis. It is far easier to sell good assets in a time of crisis, but this drives down the prices of all assets.
6. One cannot help but think of the high returns generated by the "asset-light" strategy of Enron.
7. Any capital held above economic capital is idle. Economic capital is held to cover ULs and UL is the measure of the volatility of the EL with a certain confidence level. For example, to maintain a bond rating, the firm must be able to withstand the volatility of the EL at a level commiserate with the desired rating. This points to the fact that ELs are averages over time not steady loss levels.
8. See also Appendix I.
9. Consider the formal processes in FIs for vetting model risk that must be separate from the group creating the model. As we go forward this is increasingly the role of the board in the strategy process.
10. Later we will relate the issues here to risk homeostasis and scenario planning.
11. Later we will discuss how Goldman Sachs was unusual in identifying the emerging financial crisis, whereas others seem to have ignored tell-tale warning signs.
12. The surprisingly rapid success of the Beyond Meat Burger.
13. For example, see Emiko Terazono, "Big Business Acquires Taste for Plant-Based Meat," *Financial Times*, January 3, 2019, or Alan Smith, "Making Sense of Divisive Trends," *Financial Times* (December 31, 2018).
14. This tends to be a male-dominated field for reasons that may become apparent later in the chapter. However, recently Michelin paid tribute to nine three-star female chefs: Anne-Sophie Pic, Elena Arzak, Carme Ruscalleda, Annie Feolde, Nadia Santini, Luisa Marelli Valazza, Clare Smyth, Helene Darroze, and Dominique Crenn. The article was published online March 8, 2017, https://guide.michelin.com/hk/en/hong-kong-macau/features/世界頂尖女主廚/news. Wikipedia has a lengthier article on the topic of Michelin stars and female chefs: "List of Female Chefs with Michelin Stars," Wikipedia, November 19, 2018, https://en.wikipedia.org/wiki/List_of_female_chefs_with_Michelin_stars.
15. We excluded Gordon Ramsay because his shows reveal a man focused on both good food and business. This is probably also true for all long-term survivors in the business.
16. This is not just hypothetical. Sebastien Bras handed back his three stars and requested that his three-star restaurant Le Suquet be removed from the Michelin guide. See Mike Pomranz, "Chef Who Gave Back His Michelin Star 'Surprised'

to Find His Restaurant Back on the List," *Food & Wine*, January 22, 2019, https://www.foodandwine.com/news/michelin-stars-give-back-sebastien-bras-2019-list. For others, see Hillary Dixler Canavan, "Why Chefs 'Give Back' Their Michelin Stars," *Eater*, September 21, 2017, https://www.eater.com/2017/9/21/16345242/chefs-give-back-michelin-stars. This article has the telling quotation from chef Karen Keyngaert in Flanders after receiving her star: "in these economic times [it is] . . . more of a curse."

17. The wine knowledge may be limited because there is a sommelier, but some knowledge is important.
18. Creating an ethical organization is an important aspect of mitigating risks and lowering the costs of risk management. On the challenges of creating such an organization, see Nicholas Epley and Amit Kumar, "How to Design an Ethical Organization," *Harvard Business Review* (May–June 2019).
19. We will revisit this issue. The ability of an organization to survive hiccups can be called "*resiliency*" See David R. Koenig, *Governance Reimagined: Organizational Design, Risk, and Value Creation* (Northfield, MN: B Right Governance Publications, 2018), 136.
20. This was classically discussed by Theodore Levitt, "Production-Line Approach to Service," *Harvard Business Review* (September 1972) and "The Industrialization of Service," *Harvard Business Review* (September 1976).
21. We recognize that there may exist the possibility to enter a deferred interest agreement with a lender but prefer to keep the discussion as simple as possible.
22. The time frame of six months is arbitrary and chosen only to make the point concrete. Sometimes you can trust your gut. See Daniel Kahneman and Gary Klein, "Strategic Decisions: When Can You Trust Your Gut? *McKinsey Quarterly* (March 2010).
23. Although winning Michelin stars or rave reviews may mitigate this.
24. Bourdain was the executive chef at Brasserie Les Halles in Manhattan before writing the best-selling book, *Kitchen Confidential*. He later developed food shows for the Food Network, then the Travel Channel before moving to CNN. He died in 2018.
25. Katy McLaughlin and Natalia V. Osipova, "A Reckoning with the Dark Side of the Restaurant Industry," *The Wall Street Journal* (November 12, 2018).
26. See Jen Agg, *I Hear She's a Real Bitch* (New York: Doubleday Canada, 2017). Agg is a very well-known restaurant owner in Toronto, well loved by foodies and who appeared on Anthony Bourdain's show. There are several recent examples of celebratory chefs brought down by complaints.
27. Exactly what constitutes a good waitstaff depends on expectations of the customers. See Marie Le Conte, "Vive l'indifference: Why Rude French Waiters Should Be Celebrated," *The Guardian* (March 27, 2018), which examines the case of Guillaume Rey, the French waiter who was fired from a Vancouver restaurant for being rude. He defended himself by arguing that he was just French.
28. Julie Jargon, "How Restaurants Are Using Big Data as a Competitive Tool," *The Wall Street Journal* (October 2, 2018).

CHAPTER 3

Which Risks to Keep

More than a decade ago, the Nobel Prize–winning Robert C. Merton made the following observation:

> *Thanks to the inventiveness of the modern financial markets, managers can, in principle, engineer a company's capital structure so that virtually the only risks its shareholders, debt holders, trade creditors, pensioners, and other liability holders must bear are what I call value-adding risks. Those are the risks associated with positive-net-present-value activities in which the company has a comparative advantage. All other risks can be hedged or insured against through the financial markets.*[1]

Much of our understanding of the strategic value of risk management stems from this insight. But let's focus on the first key component: risk-based capital is expensive, far more expensive than debt, so it should be used strategically to support increasing shareholder value.[2] In practical terms, this means transferring risks to someone better able to manage them: take advantage of their competitive advantages so that you can take advantage of yours. Now Merton's observations were written prior to the 2007–2008 financial crisis, so some might be wondering if this still holds true. In the main, we would argue yes, but the crisis did call attention to one of the enduring principles of risk management: risk and uncertainty don't go away. The level of uncertainty that we can survive combined with what investors think about survival will determine the level of capital to be held. And defining this level of capital is complex—because the capital we need to remain viable must be readily accessible, or in finance speak, liquid. So, the risks we keep require us to build a wall of specific types of capital against uncertainty. But outside the wall, the unknown resides.

Risk transfer[3] alters the shape of risk, but you will retain some risk or may even take on new risks. There are two concepts here. The first is risk transfer or migration and the second is the common-sense element built into the risk process: that one should take risks only that are understood, able to be managed, and priced correctly. Huge losses occurred during the 2007–2008 financial crisis because banks and individuals chased returns, rather than understanding the classic principle of risk and return. Chasing returns led to taking risks that were either poorly understood or not understood at all.[4]

Risk migration happens through ongoing business and environmental changes and through conscious choice. The former can arise through the learning process discussed previously or through changes in market conditions. As competitors act and sociopolitical conditions shift, the risks faced and the exposures to those risks change.

For the latter, the risk manager makes a conscious decision. If one risk is better understood or better able to be managed, it makes sense to transact or manage to transform one risk into another. The specific example of market risk being transformed into counterparty risk happens when market risk is hedged, or managed. For example, you may reduce market risk by taking counterparty risk because the organization's risk capacity is better suited to manage counterparty risk. A simple example involves an individual or firm who is exposed to floating interest rates and who wishes to fix those rates to minimize the risk of interest costs escalating to a level beyond the ability to pay. The exchange of this risk to a third party can involve a payment and exposure to that third party, which is an exchange of market risk for counterparty risk. So, it is imperative that you retain or develop the capacity to manage the new sources of risk, just as we mentioned in the case of the sommelier and building a wine cellar.

But Merton's observations about focusing the use of scarce capital can be extended to the logic of supply chain management. What is the most capital-efficient way to obtain access to the resources that you need? To return to our restaurant example, recall the strategic decisions on wines, desserts, and so on. To maximize the use of scarce kitchen resources, it was essential to focus on what the restaurant owners could do better than others. Many of the more successful companies, such as Apple, Amazon, Nike, and Walmart, do exactly this: control what is strategically important and value adding. Walmart is widely admired for its control over the supply chain and their ability to derisk themselves. Amazon has also often been quoted as masters at this through their creation of the platform and the access to the information obtained through transaction processing. For Amazon, it controls the information, not storefronts or manufacturing.[5] Alibaba in China is a master of this with AliPay.[6]

But not all risks can be transferred, so it should be recognized what risks are retained. Take Apple: where does Apple focus its resources? First, it is important to note what Apple doesn't do, and that is manufacturing. Rather than manufacture, Apple is noted for its mastery of supply chain logistics. Gartner identified Apple as the leader in supply chain management, and its current CEO, Tim Cook, had been head of supply chain management.[7] Both clearly identify the importance of managing the supply chain for Apple, but the point of supply chain management is to free up resources so they can be concentrated on R&D, retailing, employee engagement, and compensation. Model companies such as Google with its games room understand that employee engagement is driven by more than compensation, but the ability to provide these extras, such as day care, requires having resources beyond the returns demanded by stakeholders.

But this strategy, which focuses resources and facilitates profitable growth, also creates new risks. The most obvious one is reputation risk. To some degree Apple is putting its reputation in the hands of its suppliers. If something goes wrong, you are not going to blame some nameless part manufacturer; you are going to blame Apple. And that is how it should be because you have trusted Apple to meet your needs or wants and this puts the obligation on it to select the right partners. This goes beyond outsourcing contract conditions and to partner selection, what many refer to as vendor risk. Various companies have been held accountable for their partners using child labor or having unfit conditions or being harmful to the environment. Just because consumers may benefit from lower prices, it does not mean that they have all abandoned the moral high ground.[8] As we will discuss later, taking social stands is becoming increasingly important to brands. Strategic choices create some risks unique to the organization's performance, which may in turn lead to the need for unique business and risk management capabilities, such as strong vendor management practices needed to be able to effectively outsource.

Producing economic profits means adjusting for risk through an understanding of economic capital. The Bank for International Settlements defines economic capital as follows:

> *Economic capital can be defined as the methods or practices that allow banks to consistently assess risk and attribute capital to cover the economic effects of risk-taking activities. Economic capital was originally developed by banks as a tool for capital allocation*

and performance assessment. For these purposes, economic capital measures mostly need to reliably and accurately measure risks in a relative sense, with less importance attached to the measurement of the overall level of risk or capital. Over time, the use of economic capital has been extended to applications that require accuracy in estimation of the level of capital (or risk), such as the quantification of the absolute level of internal capital needed by a bank. This evolution in the use of economic capital has been driven by both internal capital management needs of banks and regulatory initiatives, and has been facilitated by advances in risk quantification methodologies and the supporting technological infrastructure.[9]

Although this style of thinking is strongest in financial institutions (FIs), it should be reflected in the thinking of all firms because shareholders do set expectations for returns according to economic, not accountant, thinking. To deal with this, we would broaden the Bank for International Settlements definition. Economic capital is the capital required to support the economic performance and resiliency of the organization.[10] Economic capital includes risk-based capital as well as the capital needed to support key operational elements. These may include technology, plants and equipment, or other capital-intensive assets critical to the organization's strategy and operation.

In the case of our restaurant example, it is how much capital or lines of credit are set up when the restaurant opens to give the restaurant time to get established. If we think of potential investors, they will recognize the need for contingency funds, but the larger the funds the lower their returns, or the higher their share of the profits will be. And this is a zero-sum game, so our original partners' share is reduced.

Figure 3.1 illustrates another issue: the nature of uncertainty in our quantitative approach. Given the scale of the graphic it is important to note that both the left-hand and right-hand side of the distribution never touch the axis: they are asymptotic to the axis. This is important because the maximum possible loss is indeterminate—loss distributions have the possibility of extreme results. A common risk expression is the amount of loss possible with 99% confidence—the distribution does not tell you the possible magnitude of loss in the other 1%. In common parlance, risk never goes away. Many have employed the distinction made by Frank H. Knight in his 1921 classic *Risk, Uncertainty and Profit* between risk and uncertainty. Risk was measurable and uncertainty was not.[11] In this context it is important to remember what the purpose of Knight's book was: to understand the source of profits.

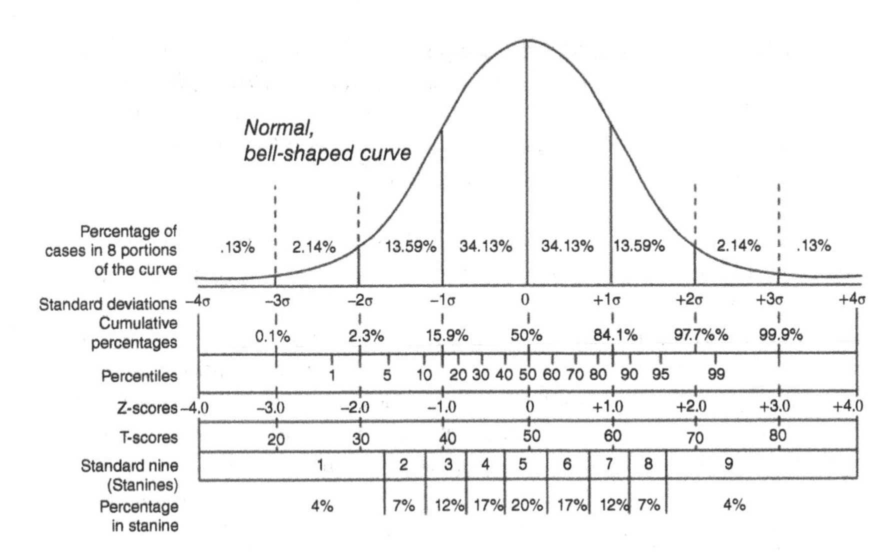

FIGURE 3.1 The Normal Distribution and Scales[12]
Source: Jeremy Kemp, The Normal Distribution and Scales, October 6, 2020. Licensed under public domain.

It will appear that a measurable uncertainty, or *proper risk,* as we shall use the term, is so far different from an unmeasurable one that it is not in effect an uncertainty at all. We shall accordingly restrict the term *uncertainty* to cases of the nonquantitative type. It is this "true" uncertainty, and not risk, as has been argued, that forms the basis of a valid theory of profit and accounts for the divergence between actual and theoretical competition.[13]

Think back to Merton's comments about what risks are retained. What he calls value-adding risks take us into the realm of uncertainty in Knight's world. Moreover, Knight was careful to limit the scope to which risk could be applied:

> *We should note, however, two other facts. First, the statistical treatment never gives closely accurate quantitative results. Even in such simple cases as mechanical games of chance it would never be final, short of an infinite number of instances, as already observed. Furthermore, the fact that a priori methods are inapplicable is connected with a much greater complication in the data, which again carries with it a difficulty, in fact impossibility, of securing the same degree of homogeneity in the instances classed together. This point will have to be gone into more fully. The second fact mentioned in regard to the two methods is that the hazards or*

> *probabilities met with in business do admit of a certain small degree of theoretical treatment, supplementing the application of experience data. Thus, in the case of fire risk on buildings, the fact that the cases are not really homogeneous may be offset in part by the use of judgment, if not calculation.*[14]

The limitations of probability calculations meant that uncertainty was the underlying source of profit. If risk never goes away, then risk managers must deal with uncertainty as a reality. Risk management is also an art.[15] And similar to all art, judgment and interpretation play a key role. Previously we discussed using models to simplify reality, understanding the assumptions in the model and their appropriateness to a changing reality reveals the importance of judgment. Many models have a key assumption that the future will be similar to the past.[16] This assumption is valid over short time frames and in very stable environments. But it needs to be understood that this assumption exists, and judgment is needed to continuously assess its applicability. This is a key source of uncertainty in risk modeling

Let's relate this to the assertion—"risk never goes away"—and Figure 3.1. If the curve is asymptotic then it is impossible to know either all alternative events or their specific probabilities. Rather, the use of the normal distribution in much of risk management enables us to determine the amount of economic capital we are willing to hold against unexpected events.[17] This establishes the limits on what we consider as unexpected. We hold that for practical purposes there is little difference between the unexpected and the uncertain.

Knight's thinking on the relationship between risk and uncertainty is tied to what is knowable. Langlois and Cosgel (1993) put it well: "Perhaps the most straightforward way to approach Knight's philosophy is to recall the distinction he constantly makes between the mechanical and the organic (biological) frameworks. Mechanistic thinking views human behavior and institutions as static, machine-like entities, whereas organistic thinking invokes notions such as change and process."[18] Because both strategy and risk management are about the future, it is imperative to consider the changes that make the future unknowable. Remember how our restaurant partners thought about how rivals would react. It is likely they even said to one another "Le Rendezvous down the street will probably change its menu to mimic our best sellers," but that is as much a guess as anything else. They can fool themselves by using subjective probabilities to look more scientific, but this is false precision, which generally leads to overconfidence and poor decisions. It is more useful to think of risk management as the science of approximation.

Before proceeding we need to reconcile quantitative risk management with Knight's assertions concerning how uncertainty, not risk, is the basis for a valid theory of profit or economic returns.[19] Knight provides the answer: "But the probability in which the student of business risk is interested is an estimate, though in a sense different from any of the propositions so far considered."[20] Quantitative risk management is extremely useful as long as the limitations are recognized. Knight's warning does not exclude modern risk techniques developed after publication of his work but rather warns us against putting too much trust in them. Queen's University psychologist, Gerald Wilde, first alerted us to the issue of risk homeostasis in 1982. Belief in our risk management framework can alter our perceptions of risk/uncertainty and lead to behavior that offsets the mitigation efforts.[21] In a later article, Wilde provides this salient example: "The introduction of childproof medicine vials has failed to limit the number of cases of accidental poisoning. These, in fact, became more frequent, apparently as the result of parents becoming less careful in the handling and storing of the 'safer' bottles." [22] A more modern example may be the hapless drivers who trust their GPS and drive into a lake[23] or the driver who was killed because he put too much trust into his car's autopilot and died after crashing into a concrete divider.[24]

An understanding of Knight's view on risk and uncertainty help us to guard against risk homeostasis by understanding how our perceptions can alter realty. When we consider some of the implications of behavioral economics and finance the significance of this link will become even more apparent.

The firm must decide how much risk it can be paid to take through effective pricing and how much capital it needs to take to hold against uncertainty. In both cases there is a market-imposed limitation. In terms of pricing, customers will not pay for a firm's above-average defects or far-below market-quality standards of service. We will discuss this in connection to the importance of operational risk. And investors expect a certain return, which limits the amount of capital a firm can hold against the unexpected. Risk appetite and establishing and monitoring risk tolerances are strategic decisions, as is getting paid properly for the risks taken. Communication of these goals or objectives is an important element of embedding the firm's strategy into operations.

This takes us back to a fundamental question: how do firms make money? The best firms develop a unique and sustainable strategic position that creates value for their customers by taking and, more importantly, managing risk.[25] A business model is then developed to deliver on their strategic proposition or promise and at the same time identify and manage the risks inherent to the strategy. This is because the way the business is undertaken establishes key risk exposures unique to the strategy. Certain risks are inherent in the business undertaken—examples such as credit risk for lending institutions, fiduciary risk for deposit or investing operations, plant operation risks for manufacturing firms, liquidity risk, strategic risk, and reputation risk for all firms. And how the business is governed, including the risk management capabilities established, provides the firm's risk identification, monitoring, reporting, and response capabilities. This also contributes to the cost structure of the business.

The implication of these choices is that the firm should primarily retain risks that are critical to its positioning and that the firm has, or can develop, the capabilities to manage such risks. Consider the cases of Apple and RIM in the smartphone market. Apple in many ways cannibalized its iPod to create a new mobile device for consumers. RIM, with its Blackberry network, created a secure email communication device primarily for business and government users. Apple initially targeted retail consumers and Blackberry initially thrived in the wholesale or industrial marketplace and with IT managers of large organizations. The strategic opportunities and risk in the two segments were initially distinct and required quite different resource allocations and organizational risk capabilities to create value for customers. For example, essential to RIM's strategy is a reliable network while Apple transferred network management to its telecom partners. This was a fundamental strategic decision that needed not only to be risk informed but also monitored to ensure the assumptions that led to the decision were holding. Because uncertainty is ever with us, we need to monitor to know when our risk capital walls are in danger of being breeched. We make decisions in a world of bounded uncertainty.

STRATEGIC POSITIONING AND RISK GOVERNANCE

Just as the term *risk* highlights issues arising from ambiguities created by the coexistence of everyday and technical language in the same organization, so too does *integrated risk management* highlight one of the central problems in management: decentralization versus centralization. A maxim of strategy was that we centralize for efficiency and decentralize for effectiveness. Many of the current spate of restaurant shows, including Gordon Ramsay's, point to the need for aggregation and integration. Assume the restaurant manager notes a decline in diners and decides to use his knowledge of the customers to deal with the problem. He changes the restaurant decor and ambience to enhance the dining experience, but although he gets new tries, he fails to get repeat visits. Encountering an old, but no longer current, customer on the street, the question is posed: "Why don't you come back?" The answer is the food is terrible. Similarly, good food in a dangerous location may fail to bring back loyal lunch customers in the evenings. Only an overall inclusive view can resolve the problem.

Integrated risk management also provides salient examples of why organizations need to centralize and decentralize. The waitstaff is clearly in the best position to identify when customers are having problems with the food.[26] Although the chef may note returning dishes, most chefs would be unlikely to place the blame on their art or their management of the processes basic to good execution. Unless the chef or the restaurant manager makes the waitstaff accountable for identifying issues with customers the chef will not change her food preparation. And unless the manager and chef listen to the customer service representatives and act on it, the restaurant is doomed. The example makes clear the need for independent risk oversight. The waitstaff can provide unbiased oversight of the quality of the dishes from the customer's perspective and the restaurant manager must provide independent oversight of the waitstaff to ensure the validity of their insights. The importance of independent risk oversight cannot be overemphasized.

The 2007–2008 financial crisis combined with the earlier collapse of companies such as Enron and Arthur Andersen drew attention to the importance of risk management for organizations, especially enterprise risk management (ERM). But all too often, the ERM challenge is seen as a process to be developed post-strategy formulation rather than as an integral part of the strategy formulation and implementation process that addresses the centralization/decentralization issues. The limitations of the sequential approach become obvious once the relationship between strategy and risk is made more transparent.

We will also need to put this into a governance framework because the board of directors are responsible for oversight of both strategy and risk management. Although from a prescriptive or best practices perspective strategy and risk management need to be intertwined at all levels of an organization, we can be assured that they at least formally meet at the CEO's office and at the board. Because of this we need to address what we mean by "corporate governance" even though this is a book essentially about interdependency of strategy and risk. To execute many of the ideas presented here good corporate governance is a prerequisite.

We further understand that for much of the 21st-century corporate governance has received increasing attention and that good corporate governance is often portrayed as the universal panacea to what ails the Western world.[27] For that reason, we wish to offer a working definition of corporate governance and then discuss the implications of this definition taken from the *Financial Times Lexicon:*

> *How a company is managed, in terms of the institutional systems and protocols meant* ***to ensure accountability and sound ethics.*** *The concept encompasses a variety of issues, including disclosure of information to shareholders and board members, remuneration of senior executives, potential conflicts of interest among managers and directors, supervisory structures, etc.*[28]

We would also add the importance of ensuring proper systems and protocols for how decisions are made and to ensure IT security, which is especially relevant in these times. We further wish to emphasize the following aspects of this definition. First, the emphasis on accountability. Translating this means processes must be in place that provide information flows to make accountability possible. It further suggests the need for clear goals—that is, for what individuals are being held accountable. This points to the centrality of the goal-setting process in strategy. The second point worth calling attention to is the ethical element. Ethics are important in part because of uncertainty. Although we can establish policies and codes for normal times, there will be exceptions when the correct response depends on an employee's discretion. This demands not only the appropriate training and education but also having the right values. Warren Buffet emphasizes this point in his hiring credo: "Somebody once said that in looking for people to hire, you look for three qualities: integrity, intelligence, and energy. And if you don't have the first, the other two will kill you. You think about it; it's true. If you hire somebody without [integrity], you really want them to be dumb and lazy."[29]

In addition, good governance takes place in a broader social context, not simply one of maximizing shareholder value. The modern organization needs to be conscious of maintaining the legitimacy of its purpose, not only in generating returns for shareholders but also contributing, or at least not detracting from, the social fabric in which it operates.[30] This can greatly complicate the task of reputation risk management, as we shall see in Chapter 7.

HOW DOES RISK MANAGEMENT HELP CLOSE THE GAP BETWEEN STRATEGY FORMULATION AND EXECUTION?

We should make clear the advantages for strategy execution that come from an explicit involvement of risk processes in creating a virtuous circle of strategy formulation and implementation. A focus on risk crystallizes several fundamental issues in strategic management. First, the very term *risk* has multiple meanings. At one point on the continuum is the classic definition developed by Frank Knight in *Risk, Uncertainty and Profit* (1921) and employed by professional risk managers: *risk* refers to situations in which the decision-maker can assign mathematical probabilities to the faced randomness. If strategy posits expected outcomes, then strategic risk resides in unexpected outcomes. Although the reader may say that the major difference between the two definitions is simply the difference that mathematics brings to unexpected outcomes, we will argue that the difference is much more profound. Central to the widely practiced prescriptive approach to strategy is the ability of organizations to shape their environment to achieve superior profits. The notion of control inherent in certain classic economic definitions of strategy is somewhat at odds with the more mathematical notions of randomness and distributions.

Yet the point to be developed here is not which definition is correct; that is a fool's game. The underlying issue—critically tied to strategy execution that we are exploring—is how different managerial or cultural attitudes are expressed in natural language. The goal is not to find one correct definition but rather to find or create a common language or perhaps help organizations become multilingual so that they understand the way key terms are employed. The multiple ways in which *risk* is used cannot be solved by prescribing the correct definition but only by creating a rich dictionary that puts the term into its correct context and facilitates an understanding of the mindsets that use the term in different ways. Embedding risk processes into strategy formulation and execution can be a major gateway into forging a communication process that embraces diversity of mindsets into the pursuit of a common goal. If your strategic language separates formulators and executers by a common language—as it is often asserted of the British and Americans—the strategy will not be understood and hence not executed.

Just as the term *risk* highlights issues arising from ambiguities created by the coexistence of everyday and technical language in the same organization, so too does ERM highlight one of the central problems in management mentioned previously: decentralization versus centralization. A maxim of strategy was that we centralize for efficiency and decentralize for effectiveness. ERM provides a salient example of why organizations need to centralize and decentralize. Consider an organization that is completely decentralized for effectiveness—individual lines of business manage their foreign exchange risks. The total cost of such a hedging strategy may be very high because the organization should be hedging its net, not its gross exposures. A similar issue may arise with insurance if it is not done in a centralized manner.[31] One can make a similar case for centralization in order to have a critical mass of technical skills and a corresponding need to set direction and standards. So, the need for leadership from the center is clear. Yet the importance of centralization does not diminish the need for decentralization.

Moreover, there is a very important tie between risk identification and strategy. Although in the short term the economic exposure to transactions can be hedged using financial instruments, what if there is a fundamental shift in the structure of the economic relationships? Consider sourcing. Canadian auto suppliers can hedge their transactional exposure but the sustainability of their firms and strategies may require a complete change in their sourcing strategies, as the Canadian dollar has fundamentally changed its position vis-à-vis the US dollar. Or to take another example, British companies can do their best to hedge their foreign exchange positions during the confusion caused by Brexit.[32] But once it all settles, what will be the long-term effects on the British pound? Confusing economic risk for transactional risk puts the entire organization at risk.

CONCLUSION: EMBRACING AND MANAGING RISK

In this chapter we have sought to introduce some key concepts that facilitate the dialogue between strategic and risk perspectives. An understanding of risk brings the economic roots of strategic thinking into sharp focus and addresses issues of economic sustainability by focusing on the minimum price. Concepts such as expected loss and unexpected loss are not just applicable to the sophisticated world of credit and investment banking but rather have an everyday import in linking value creation and value claiming. We have also tried to illustrate that risk management is not a sterile quantitative exercise but also an art that aims at anticipating how risk changes in response to strategic initiatives and affects the long-term sustainability of those initiatives.

We have also sought to bring attention to the importance of integrated risk management over simply enterprise-wide risk management (see Appendix II). Although the scope is important if risk management is to contribute to competitive advantage, it must be integrated into a strategic perspective, and this perspective must be embedded in the foundations and frontline employees of the organization if it is to have an impact. Controls are important for monitoring progress and aligning goals, but the controls must be put in the context of what goals the controls are supporting. An organization that seeks to control all risks, or, even worse, get rid of all risk, cannot create economic value. It may create accounting profits and be an extremely well-oiled machine, but it will not have the strategic vitality of an organization that embraces risk to create value for customers and through its management of those risks is able to claim value for itself.

In Chapter 4 we explore why ERM is needed to accomplish this value.

NOTES

1. Robert C. Merton, "You Have More Capital Than You Think," *Harvard Business Review* (November 2005). Kevin Buehler, Andrew Freeman, and Ron Hulme, "The New Arsenal of Risk Management," *Harvard Business Review* (September 2008) argues that an organization should only keep risk if it is the "natural owner" of the risk.
2. See the discussion of capital in Appendix II in which risk capital is defined as a forward-looking estimate of the maximum unexpected loss in market value that an asset, portfolio, or line of business could incur over a specified time interval with a defined confidence level due to any and all types of quantifiable risks (credit, market, and operational risks).
3. This is elaborated in the Appendix I.
4. Although Canadian banks were largely spared the pain of the 2007–2008 crisis, Canadian capital markets had a crisis in the commercial paper sector in 2009.
5. Admittedly Amazon does have larger warehouses. See Michael A. Cusumano, Annabelle Gawer, and David B. Yoffie. *The Business of Platforms: Strategy in the Age of Digital Competition, Innovation, and Power* (New York: HarperBusiness, 2019) and Geoffrey G. Parker, Marshall W. Van Alstyne, and Sangeet Paul Choudary, *Platform Revolution: How Networked Markets Are Transforming the Economy and How to Make Them Work for You* (New York: W. W. Norton, 2016).
6. On platform companies and control of assets see Cusumano, Gawer, and Yoffie, *The Business of Platforms*.
7. "Gartner Announces Rankings of the 2018 Supply Chain Top 25," May 17, 2018, https://www.gartner.com/newsroom/id/3875563.
8. See Chapter 6.
9. Bank for International Settlements, "Range of Practices and Issues in Economic Capital Frameworks," March 2009, https://www.bis.org/publ/bcbs152.pdf,1.
10. Resiliency and capital are elaborated in Appendix II.
11. See Richard N. Langlois and Metin M. Cosgel, "Frank Knight on Risk, Uncertainty, and the Firm," *Economic Inquiry* XXXI (July 1993): 457.

> *For instance, Knight's distinction between risk and uncertainty has been taken to differentiate between the measurability/unmeasurability or objectivity/ subjectivity of probability, or between the insurability/uninsurability of probabilistic outcomes . . .*
>
> *Moreover, as the latter had effectively routed the former (at least in principle) within the realm of theoretical economics, this framing of the distinction made it possible to ignore situations of uncertainty entirely: for if probability consists in a decision-maker's subjective assessment, then there is no state of the world whose probability cannot be articulated. By definition, all probabilistic calculations are matters of risk.*
>
> *Although this interpretation has passed into the consciousness of economists it remains dominant today.*

12. The author, Jeremy Kemp, kindly released this into the public domain, accessed October 6, 2020, https://commons.wikimedia.org/wiki/File:Normal_distribution_and_scales.gif.
13. Frank H. Knight, *Risk, Uncertainty and Profit,* 2nd ed. (New York: Reprints of Economic Classics, 1964), https://mises.org/sites/default/files/Risk,%20Uncertainty,%20and%20Profit_4.pdf.
14. Knight, *Risk, Uncertainty and Profit.* See also Langlois and Cosgel, "Frank Knight on Risk, Uncertainty, and the Firm," 456–65; Jochen Runde, "Clarifying Frank Knight's Discussion of the Meaning of Risk and Uncertainty," *Cambridge Journal of Economics* 22 (1998): 539–46; Yasuhiro Sakai, "J. M. Keynes on Probability versus F. H. Knight on Uncertainty: Reflections on the Miracle Year of 1921," *Evolutionary and Institutional Economics Review* 13 (2016): 1–21; Hans-Hermann Hoppe, "The Limits of Numerical Probability: Frank H. Knight and Ludwig von Mises and the Frequency Interpretation," *The Quarterly Journal of Austrian Economics* X, no. 1 (Spring 2007): 1–20.
15. David Weitzner and James Darroch, "The Limits of Strategic Rationality: Ethics, Enterprise Risk Management, and Governance," *Journal of Business Ethics* 31, no. 3 (March 2010): 361–72.
16. See the discussion of the normalcy bias in Chapter 5.
17. See Nassim Nicholas Taleb, *Fooled by Randomness: The Hidden Role of Chance in Life and in the Markets,* 2nd ed. (New York: Random House, 2005); *The Black Swan: The Impact of the Highly Improbable,* 2nd ed. (New York: Random House, 2010).
18. Langlois and Cosgel, "Frank Knight on Risk, Uncertainty, and the Firm," 458.
19. Knight, *Risk,* 20.
20. Knight, *Risk,* 139. Also see p. 134.
21. Gerald J. S. Wilde, "The Theory of Risk Homeostasis: Implications for Safety and Health," *Risk Analysis* 2, no. 4 (December 1982): 209–225. Also see Rick Nason, "Is Your Risk System Too Good," *The RMA Journal* (October 2009).
22. Gerald J. S. Wilde, 1998. "Risk Homeostasis Theory: An Overview," *Injury Prevention* (July 1998): 90.
23. Sarah Wolfe, "Driving into the Ocean and 8 Other Spectacular Fails as GPS Turns 25," *PRI,* February 17, 2014, https://www.pri.org/stories/2014-02-17/driving-ocean-and-8-other-spectacular-fails-gps-turns-25.
24. Guardian Staff and Agencies "Tesla Car That Crashed and Killed Driver Was Running on Autopilot, Firm Says," *The Guardian,* 2018, https://www.theguardian.com/technology/2018/mar/31/tesla-car-crash-autopilot-mountain-view.
25. This position follows the classic Michael Porter view that a "company can outperform its rivals only if it can establish a difference it can preserve." "What Is Strategy?" *Harvard Business Review* (November–December 1996): 62. Porter then makes clear that strategy rests on unique activities; see p. 64.
26. This is akin to why the first line of defense owns the risk—it is closest to the customer, as we shall see later.
27. Dominic Barton, "Capitalism for the Long Term," *Harvard Business Review* (March 2011) has argued that much of the ills of capitalism that affect business

legitimacy stemmed from poor corporate governance and leadership. He sees it as imperative that business leaders take a longer-term view. Another interesting perspective comes from Stephen Davis, Jon Lukomnik, and David Pitt-Watson, *The New Capitalists: How Citizen Investors Are Reshaping the Corporate Agenda* (Boston: Harvard Business School Press, 2006). Part of their argument is that corporations will be held to higher standards because the real owners of corporations are the general populace via pension funds. Whatever gains these owners capture through exploitation of externalities—for example, pollution—costs them a comparable amount through taxes. Although the practical impact of this insight is unclear, it does make sense to expand risk management to include a broader perspective to address legitimacy concerns.

28. Emphasis added. *Financial Times Lexicon,* September 19, 2019, http://markets.ft.com/research/Lexicon/Term?term=corporate-governance.
29. Marcel Schwantes, "Warren Buffet Says Integrity Is the Most Important Trait to Hire For. Ask These 12 Questions to Find It," *Inc.*, February 13, 2018, https://www.inc.com/marcel-schwantes/first-90-days-warren-buffetts-advice-for-hiring-based-on-3-traits.htm.
30. See Dominic Barton, Dezso Horvath, and Matthias Kipping, eds., *Re-Imagining Capitalism* (New York: Oxford University Press, 2016).
31. See Lisa Meulbroek, "A Better Way to Manage Risk," *Harvard Business Review* (February 2001).
32. As we are writing this in September 2019, the United Kingdom is in the process of negotiating its departure from the European Union. It has been a highly contentious and complex set of negotiations that is ongoing as we write.

CHAPTER 4

How Do We Achieve Independent Risk Governance and Improve Performance?

Although many books discuss what enterprise risk management (ERM) is and how to implement it, our discussion reverses the usual order because we wish to focus on the independence of risk oversight and that takes us immediately to governance. Royal Bank of Canada's[1] risk-governance framework provides an interesting overall view of a structure to ensure independent oversight to improve profitability by limiting the downside while promoting the upside. Figure 4.1 presents the structure. We recognize that this may be overkill for less complex or smaller organizations. So, we would like to call attention to the following key features. The first is the need for independent oversight. The agent cannot be the overseer. Second, there is a need to ensure the quality of the data provided to the oversight function. In all organizations there are a number of oversight functions and these can be combined in various ways depending on the needs of the organization and the nature of its operations. In smaller organizations risk and finance oversight could be combined within the finance function while data assurance could be delegated to the accounting function or other function responsible for management information and reporting. The nature of the reporting will also vary among organizations with large, sophisticated firms requiring extensive data analytics and ongoing reporting. Smaller firms will still need to monitor and report critical performance and risk metrics, but these may need to be carefully assessed to ensure critical metrics are included and costs are kept low.

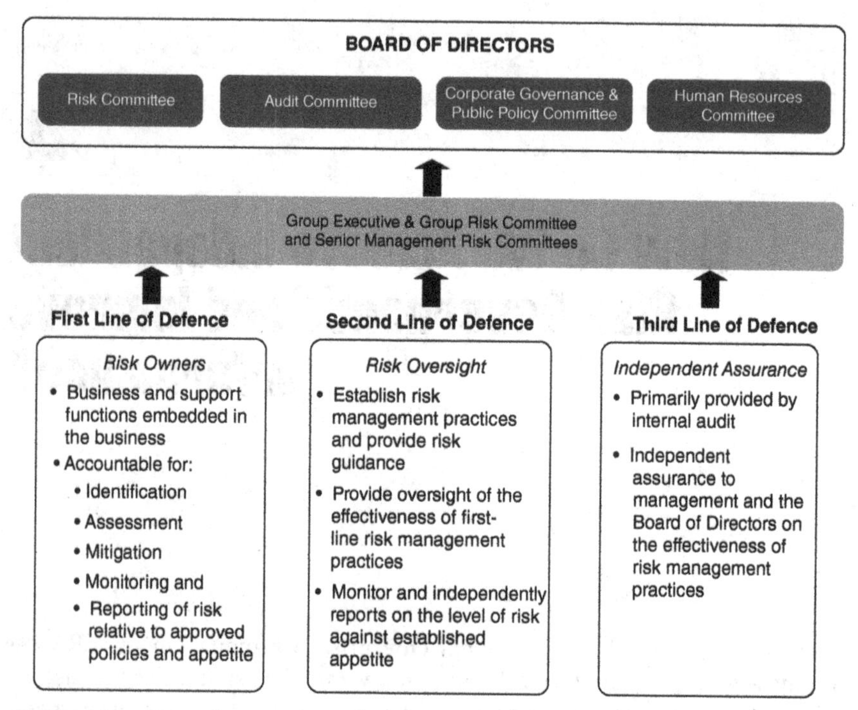

FIGURE 4.1 Royal Bank of Canada's Risk-Governance Framework[2]
Source: Royal Bank of Canada Annual Report 2014, The Royal Bank of Canada's Risk Governance Framework(2014), 49-50. © 2014, Royal Bank of Canada.

The framework uses "the Three Lines of Defence Model to ensure that risk in achieving our strategic objectives are appropriately and adequately managed."[3] The section then explains the roles of the different lines of defence:

The First Line of Defence is provided by the employees across the businesses as well as support functions embedded in the businesses that are responsible for providing products and services, and for the execution of activities. The First Line of Defence has ownership and accountability for:

- *Risk identification, assessment, mitigation, monitoring and reporting in accordance with established enterprise risk policies and Risk Appetite;*
- *Ensuring appropriate and adequate capabilities to manage risks relevant to the businesses; and*

- *Alignment of business and operational strategies with our strong Risk Conduct and Risk Appetite.*

The Second Line of Defence is provided by areas with independent oversight accountabilities residing in functions such as GRM [Group Risk Management]. Global Compliance, and other areas within our Control and Group Functions (such as Corporate Treasury, Law, Human Resources, Finance, Technology and Operations, Corporate Taxation and Enterprise Strategy Group). The Second Line of Defence:

- *Establishes the enterprise level risk management frameworks and policies, and provides risk guidance;*
- *Provides oversight of the effectiveness of first line risk management practices; and*
- *Monitors and independently reports on the level of risk relative to established appetite.*

GRM, under the direction of the CRO [Chief Risk Officer], is responsible for the oversight of a number of significant risks we face. GRM also provides oversight of Strategic Risk through the CRO and the Group Executive, who have responsibility for ensuring business Risk Appetite and strategies align with Enterprise Risk Appetite. Global Compliance is responsible for our policies and processes designed to mitigate and manage regulatory compliance risk. In addition to GRM and Global Compliance, other Control and Group Functions have designated roles supporting our enterprise-wide risk management program.

The Third Line of Defence is primarily provided by internal audit, and provides independent assurance to senior management and the Board of Directors on the effectiveness of risk management policies, processes and practices in all areas of our organization.

This describes Royal Bank of Canada's approach to ERM, which is integrated and comprehensive, or all-inclusive in the pyramid structure and scope definitions given in the line of defense descriptions. Recently, many financial institutions (FIs) have added the concept of "constructive challenge" to the second line of defense and "control processes and practices" to the third line. Later, we will explore the meaning of ERM and the processes that are embedded in the framework necessary to make it work, but there is a prior issue. In Royal Bank of Canada's description, you will frequently see the use of the word *independent,* but what we need is a clear conceptual understanding of who gets to decide on what: the issue of "decision rights." From the start, the board has the final say, but how does the board decide to allocate the rights?[4]

This is an area of thought that received considerable attention from Michael C. Jensen and William H. Meckling. To understand the allocation of decision rights in a manner that is efficient and appropriate to maximize organizational performance, the decision-maker must possess the appropriate knowledge. In the terms of Jensen and Meckling, this means "specific knowledge," which is costly to transfer.[5] So the issue for us, and for those implementing independent risk processes, is who has this specific knowledge to make the decision?

Let us start with the first line of defense, which broadly speaking is the line of business. What specific knowledge does the first line of defense have? They do, or should, understand the products, clients, and specific business environments better than anyone else because they are closest to the them. That is their business and expertise. So, what else is there to know? Well, for starters, they are just one line of business in a portfolio of businesses.[6] The second line of defense has broader knowledge of the entire context, that is, where does this line of business fit with the other lines of business in an organization with multiple lines of business? But to know this, the second line of defense must have the specific knowledge of how to measure the risks in such a way that they can be integrated and aggregated with all the other risks to know how to put the specific risks identified by the first line into context. We don't want to get into specifics at this time but consider the problem of risk concentration. The line of business in retail mortgages may know in advance its limits, but if it seeks an exception to those limits, will they know how retail mortgages are correlated to other lines of business? Probably not, but it is these correlations that lead to an element of the concentration problem.

You may notice the second line of defense in risk governance is far broader than just the risk function (group risk management for Royal Bank of Canada), because there are other areas of specific knowledge that affect the first line of defense; however, our focus is on the role of the risk function in risk oversight. The risk function, and specifically the person in charge of that function, in FIs, the CRO and in other organizations typically someone in treasury or a finance function, needs to design the processes to guide the first line to carry out their assessments in a manner that enables integration and aggregation with the other areas. This is one area of their specific knowledge and we will discuss details of this later.

To be clear, the business practices and the risks arising from them are then identified by the first line; constructively challenged and independently measured, monitored, and reported on by the second line; and tested by the third line. Internal audit is looking for effective processes, including documentation, the existence of critical controls, and the operation and effectiveness of those controls. Internal audit does not have the skill to provide assurance on risk management practices—they provide assurance that the line follows the risk function's requirements effectively (among other things such as making sure fire safety codes are met, etc.).

Finally, the third line of defense must ensure the integrity of the processes designed by the second line. The designer of a process is not in the position to determine the integrity of the process nor to assure it is being properly carried out. The board needs the assurance primarily provided by internal audit that the processes are designed to identify and to measure all the risks being taken by the first line and that the processes are being carried out with integrity. The third line has specific knowledge in compliance, or quality assurance.

The three areas of specific knowledge are different but complementary to provide risk oversight of the entire organization in a way that enables the information to be reported in an integrated manner to the board. The allocation of decision rights to the various lines of defense essentially centralizes process design and decentralizes the specific application of these processes to those closest to the client/product. Jensen and Meckling elegantly demonstrate the trade-off between centralization and decentralization on total organizational costs. They balance the costs arising from inconsistent objectives and costs owing to poor information to show that allocating decision rights to balance centralization and decentralization leads to the lowest total organizational cost.[7]

At the risk of oversimplification, the second and third lines have specific knowledge to put in place or validate processes to facilitate the first line systematically gathering risk information in a process monitored for quality assurance. To put it more generally, we have centralized a specific risk management process in the second line of defense in Royal Bank of Canada's framework.[8] The organization structure necessary to ensure performance needs to employ centralization and decentralization to ensure the proper synchronizing of the specific knowledge of different skills. The implication of this decentralization to achieve risk oversight is that risk awareness must be defused throughout the entire organization in a process designed by the risk function.

WHAT DO WE MEAN BY ERM?

Before turning to the role of the coordinator of risk management in the second line, generally the CRO in FIs or the chief financial officer (CFO)[9] in nonfinancial corporations, we need to define what we mean by ERM.

There are several definitions of ERM. James Lam's definition seems to capture the key ingredients, especially of financial risk:

> *ERM is an integrated and continuous process for managing enterprise-wide risks—including strategic, financial, operational, compliance, and reputational risks—in order to minimize unexpected performance variance and maximize intrinsic firm value. This process empowers the board and management to make more informed risk/return decisions by addressing fundamental requirements with respect to governance and policy (including risk appetite), risk analytics, risk management, and monitoring and reporting.*[10]

An important moment in the history of risk management was the release of The Committee of Sponsoring Organizations of the Treadway Commission (COSO)[11] in 2004, which held that ERM encompasses these actions:

- Aligning risk appetite and strategy
- Enhancing risk response decisions
- Reducing organizational surprises and losses
- Identifying and managing multiple and cross-enterprise risks
- Seizing opportunities
- Improving deployment of capital

Although the Lam definition has the merit of specifically calling attention to the need for integration, the COSO definition explicitly raises a few things implied by Lam.

Our definition for ERM is as follows:

> *A comprehensive and well-understood framework for recognizing and managing all risks throughout the business operation within the context of the current and future business model, financial characteristics, organizational capabilities, and strategic objectives.*

Now, this definition implies some things and suffers in the same way that Lam's does in that regard. We will deal with those implied elements as we go through the things that have been added.

First, we have added the term *well understood*. It is critical that the risk framework be understood and acted on throughout the organization. Risk is managed in every functional area and by managers with differing expertise and areas of specialization. The risk framework must be understood by all. This leads us to one of our pet peeves—many risk managers talk the language of risk. They use modeling and stochastic calculus terms, they speak to show expertise rather than to provide clarity, and they like to think of themselves as "rocket scientists." Risk managers must speak the language of business and use the appropriate processes to embed risk awareness into the organization.

The second term we have added is *recognize,* as in the need to recognize risks. Later, we will also add the concept of current and future time. The point is that risk management is not static, and it must adapt to changes within the organization and across business conditions. As things change, so do the risks that are faced and that need to be managed.

The definition we have provided simply states *all risks*. This is to reflect the fact that the lists of risks and their definitions have never been static in our career as risk managers. Once we only had credit and market risk. Operational risk soon showed up as everything but credit and market risk. Now we have these risks:

- Strategic risk, sometimes called business risk
- Reputation risk
- Operational risk including subcategories called operations risk and model risk
- Credit, counterparty, and issuer risk
- Traded credit risk
- Market risk
- Liquidity risk (and sometimes *liquidity and funding risk*)

The point is that as events unfold, general categories become more specific promoting quicker and easier identification and hence improved awareness and management. This aspect is captured by the term *emerging risk*.

The final piece that we have added is the context of the business and the environment in which it operates. We have provided four contextual elements:

- Business model (how we make money or how we execute the strategy)[12]
- Financial characteristics
- Organizational capabilities
- Strategic objectives

These four contextual elements speak to the need to understand the organization and to place the level and type of appropriate risk and the extent of risk management within that context.

With respect to the business model, it is important to consider which risks are inherent in the business, which can be managed, and which need to be mitigated or offset in some manner.[13] The business model also determines the nature and extent of the risk function within the organization.[14] The tremendous amount of financial innovation that preceded the 2007–2008 financial crisis demanded new risk management tools. A quick look at the survivors and the failures clearly demonstrates that each model demanded different risk and organizational capabilities.[15] A more pedestrian example would be a lowest cost commercial enterprise. Clearly this company can weather more price volatility than a higher cost enterprise. This may determine the level of hedging each undertakes.[16] It is always important to consider the business model and the level of operational leverage in determining the amount of risk a firm can afford.

Financial characteristics follows this same logic. A firm with a heavy debt load involves higher risk than a firm with less leverage and, therefore, is less able to carry other, additional risks. All aspects of the financial characteristics need to be considered. The leverage element, or the capital strength of the firm, only considers one side. The income stream is the first financial defense against loss, and it needs to be able to cover all expected losses. The capital is the second defense against loss, and it needs to be sufficient to cover unexpected losses up to a consciously agreed-on level.[17]

As we have noted elsewhere in this book, capital needs to be considered as an economic construct, not simply an accounting one. Economic capital considers all the economic aspects of the capital base including size, quality, risk coverage, and critical functional needs. With this in mind, it is imperative to consider the quality and accessibility of the capital. Regulatory regimes following the Basel approaches recognize capital quality through the tiering of capital and the introduction of nonviable contingent capital (NVCC).[18] Although NVCC is described as a measure to limit moral hazard, it also provides capital at the time it is most needed.

However, the amount of capital is a result of simple accounting math—the value of assets less the value of liabilities. The simple math becomes complicated very quickly because both assets and liabilities have a diverse range of characteristics affecting liquidity or the ability of the firm to use this capital to absorb losses. Long-term assets such as machinery, IT investments, land, and buildings are highly illiquid, may be very specialized, and often suffer large haircuts in value if sold quickly or in distressed circumstances. If this is the primary source of capital, that capital is not readily available for loss absorption. These assets may also be critical to the viability of the firm and may not be available for sale except on resolution. Even many liquid short-term assets lose value in times of distress and their capital value can be far less than current market value.

All of this results in key building blocks for effective enterprise risk management:

- Clearly articulated corporate objectives, values, and principles
- An understanding of corporate capabilities
- A comprehensive understanding of risk, organizational behaviors, and corporate culture
- Effective organizational design
- Appropriate data, risk models, and processes
- Timely and action-orientated risk monitoring and reporting

These building blocks come in a variety of sizes and complexities. For any business, there will be a minimum requirement for these blocks, what is described in gaming circles as the table stakes. If the organization does not have the table stakes necessary for that business, it shouldn't be in the game. Risk management capacity must be in place prior to risk-taking if disaster is to be avoided.

We mentioned that the financial innovation of the early 2000s led to a business model that required a different level of organizational capability than did the previous era. It is imperative that the capabilities of the firm guide the risk-taking activities—this means that the risk management capabilities must be in place prior to engaging in the activities that create the risk.[19] Organizational capabilities include management expertise, systems capabilities, models, operational processes, and board and executive understanding and awareness. An example of related diversification that went awry was American Express's venture into credit cards. Although credit cards would seem to be very similar to American Express's classic travel and entertainment card, there are differences, and these were exacerbated by the problems of 2007 that made American Express's expansion into the market a source of problems.[20]

And, of course, risk management is meaningless if it does not reflect and support the strategic objectives—as we want to emphasize. Lam implies this with his "maximize firm value" statement, and COSO states this explicitly in its "aligning risk appetite and strategy" comment.[21] The only context added to this requirement is the time element previously mentioned.

Perhaps central to the praise that has come the way of Canadian banks post-2008 is due in no small measure to the recognition of the hierarchical nature of risk and where strategy fits (see Figure P.1). Royal Bank of Canada's pyramid structure also makes clear the importance of an integrated approach, which provides one solution to breaking down risk silos.

Let us look at the logic of our revised risk pyramid shown in Figure 4.2 before going on to explain why we are putting strategy closer to the top of the pyramid. Royal Bank of Canada's pyramid is defined by the degree of control that Royal Bank of Canada can exert over the risk category, and from the risk manager's point of view this makes perfect sense because the CRO is concerned both ex ante and ex post with the risks created by the firm's strategy because ex post is a positive feedback loop for learning.

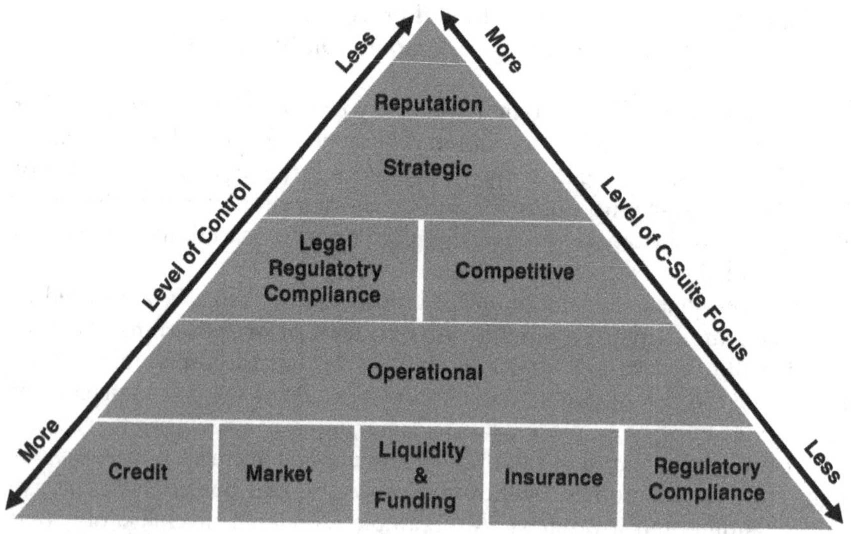

FIGURE 4.2 A Modified Risk Strategy Pyramid Emphasizing the Challenge of Strategy and Reputation Risk
Source: Royal Bank of Canada Annual Report 2014, 52 © 2014, Royal Bank of Canada.

We are more concerned with strategy formulation ex ante and how the formulation of strategy in a dialectic with risk leads to superior execution. Having said that, we would also like to differ on one point with Royal Bank of Canada's risk pyramid. We would argue that reputation risk is less controllable than strategic risk—especially in an era of social networking and broader stakeholder engagement.[22] The desired reputation that is consistent with the firm's value offering or proposition is highly controllable, but how it is perceived and communicated through social media is considerably less so. Take the case of P&G. For years the company fought the rumor that its logo of the man in the moon surrounded by a constellation of stars represented Satanism.[23] Despite numerous efforts including obtaining support from people such as Billy Graham, a renowned evangelist, the rumor persisted. Eventually P&G decided to move to a new logo—to the disappointment of some long-standing employees. Ultimately, we suppose that P&G did have control over the issue, although the demise of the well-known logo may suggest the degree of control was not all that was desired. And did the change in logo actually end the perception of ties with Satanism? In the age of social networking it seems reasonable to posit that control over external perceptions of your reputation are becoming increasingly challenging.

Perhaps an even more challenging task for managing reputation arises from actions taken by parties that are closely connected to the organization. Take the case of Danish companies and the Danish newspaper, Jyllands-Posten, which published what they believed to be humorous or satirical cartoons of the Prophet Mohammed on September 30, 2005. This outraged many in the Islamic world.[24] The reputations of many Danish companies were severely damaged by this unforeseen and uncontrollable event. There is an important lesson for global companies concerning clash of values. This incident can be seen as a clash between differing cultural values of free speech and religious observance. There is no correct answer as to who is right because each side is correct inside their value systems, which determine how the event is perceived.[25] As with many other forces, globalization promotes common values but can heighten conflict between differing fundamental values. And the issue is complex because accepting "foreign" values can lead to issues in the "domestic" market.

Because of the very strong links between strategic value propositions and reputation it is important to understand from the start what they have in common and where they differ. The company must have a very clear understanding of what the desired or intended relationship between its value proposition and its reputation is. If reputation risk is to be managed, then the organization must be very clear on what reputation it wants and how it can be measured. Although not all aspects of reputation may be manageable, organizations must ensure the ones that can be managed are and be aware of potential impact from those that cannot be managed.[26] In this context, the interconnectedness of risks can be managed only from an integrated point of view.

Before we move on, we want to emphasize that it is important to understand why the relationship between strategy and risk is hierarchical and well captured in a pyramid structure. It is the strategy that either creates the risk or chooses to be exposed to the different risk types in specific ways. For that reason, even if the risks are less controllable it does not follow that they merit less consideration. If this point is recognized, then it becomes imperative that all information concerning all risk types are considered in developing the strategic positioning theme. The need for this integrative view of risk is further expanded on in Appendix I where we note that in order for management to decide which risks to take and keep—those risks that create the opportunity for profit—an integrative approach is needed.

To return to our restaurant example and noting that as a service industry there is an inverted pyramid[27] to ensure achieving the desired outcome at the customer interrace, we view the server as the first line of defense. Servers are positioned to advise customers on the meal and to notice if their recommendations have gone awry. If the servers fail to notice, then the restaurant manager functions as the second line of defense because the manager is also at the front of the house and positioned to notice and resolve any problematic issues. Finally, one can identify the chef at the pass, approving any dishes that go out, as the third line of defense. The chef's role is to ensure that all appropriate procedures have been followed in preparing the meal. It is this oversight of all kitchen operations that ensures product quality.

The careful reader might take issue with this hierarchy and see the chef as the first line of defense, as the creator of the product. We have chosen to view risk management from the view of the entire organization. But it is interesting to note that, in choosing the appropriate risk management structures, smaller organizations or organizations with different power structures might need to modify Royal Bank of Canada's approach as we have to fit with our restaurant example. The crux of the issue is to identify the risks and have oversight over how they are identified and managed.

NOTES

1. There is a short description of Royal Bank of Canada in the Preface.
2. Royal Bank of Canada, "Annual Report" (2014): 49–50, https://www.rbc.com/investor-relations/_assets-custom/pdf/ar_2014_e.pdf.
3. Royal Bank of Canada, "Annual Report," 49–50.
4. See Michael C. Jensen and William H. Meckling, "Specific and General Knowledge, and Organizational Structure," in Lars Werin and Hans Wijkander, eds., *Contract Economics* (Oxford, UK: Blackwell, 1990), 16. Also available at https://papers.ssrn.com/sol3/papers.cfm?abstract_id=6658. James Lam is also interesting on this point. See James Lam, *Implementing Enterprise Risk Management: From Methods to Applications* (Hoboken, NJ: Wiley, 2017), Chapter 8.
5. Jensen and Meckling, "Specific and General Knowledge, and Organizational Structure."
6. To return to our restaurant example, generally CSRs have a knowledge of the wine list, but it does not match that of the sommelier who the CSR will call over for customers seeking guidance.
7. Jensen and Meckling, "Specific and General Knowledge, and Organizational Structure," Figure 1, p. 18.

8. This is our area of focus, but Figure 3.1 reveals other dimensions of risk are involved.
9. See McKinsey Strategy and Corporate Finance Practice "The New CFO Mandate: Prioritize, Transform, Repeat," November 2018, https://www.mckinsey.com/business-functions/strategy-and-corporate-finance/our-insights/the-new-cfo-mandate-prioritize-transform-repeat.
10. Lam, *Implementing Enterprise Risk Management,* Chapter 1.
11. COSO, *Enterprise Risk Management Integrated Framework* (September 2004).
12. For a good discussion of business models, see Marc de Jong and Menno van Dijk, "Disrupting Beliefs: A New Approach to Business Model Innovation," *McKinsey Quarterly* (July 2015). They provide this important insight into what is meant by a business model:

> *Every industry is built around long-standing, often implicit, beliefs about how to make money. In retail, for example, it's believed that purchasing power and format determine the bottom line. In telecommunications, customer retention and average revenue per user are seen as fundamental. Success in pharmaceuticals is believed to depend on the time needed to obtain approval from the US Food and Drug Administration. Assets and regulations define returns in oil and gas. In the media industry, hits drive profitability. And so on.*

13. Adrian Slywotzky has published some very interesting articles on this topic. See Adrian Slywotzky, "What Are the Risks You Should Be Taking?" *Harvard Business Review* (October 2004); Adrian J. Slywotzky and John Drizik "Countering the Biggest Risk of All," *Harvard Business Review* (September 2005); and Adrian Slywotzky and Anne Field, "Turning Strategic Risk into Growth Opportunities," *Harvard Business Review* (September 2008).
14. A Canadian example is in the late 1990s: ScotiaBank had a utilitarian approach to its client base. It offered first-generation derivatives to its clients based on client need and allowed very little in the way of open positions. However, CIBC opened a New York trading desk and offered highly sophisticated derivatives as it tried to expand its trading business and as it built proprietary positions. Scotia's business model depended on throughput and low cost and CIBC's business model relied on innovation and sophistication.
15. And governance to which we will return later.
16. Hedging is an important topic because investors may want to purchase the risk that managers want to hedge away. There are important agency issues to consider.
17. See the discussion in the Foreword.
18. Introduced by BIS in early 2011 for implementation by January 1, 2013, accessed September 19, 2019, https://www.bis.org/bcbs/basel3/b3_bank_sup_reforms.pdf.
19. There is an exception to this as discussed in David Apgar, *Risk Intelligence: Learning to Manage What We Don't Know* (Boston: Harvard Business Review Press, 2006), Chapter 2.

20. Robin Sidel, "Bruised AmEx Returns To Roots," *The Wall Street Journal* (March 2, 2009).
21. Lam notes that the 2004 COSO did not fully address the relationship between risk and reward that is fundamental to our more strategic view of risk. He also notes efforts to improve the framework. Lam, *Implementing Enterprise Risk Management*, Chapter 7.
22. It would seem that Royal Bank of Canada's thinking may be moving in this direction because the 2019 annual report has strategic and reputation risk on the same level.
23. Kathleen Fearn-Banks, *Crisis Communications: A Casebook Approach* (Mahwah, NJ: Lawrence Erlbaum, 2002), 66; Ronald J. Alsop, *The 18 Immutable Laws of Corporate Reputation: Creating, Protecting and Repairing Your Most Valuable Asset* (New York: Free Press. 2004), 46–47.
24. http://news.bbc.co.uk/2/hi/4677976.stm.
25. David Weitzner and James Darroch "The Limits of Strategic Rationality: Ethics, Enterprise Risk Management, and Governance," *Journal of Business Ethics* 31, no. 3 (March 2010): 361–72.
26. The desired reputation has significant impact on strategic decision-making. See Owen Parker, Ryan Krause, and Cynthia E. Devers, "How Firm Reputation Shapes Managerial Discretion," *Academy of Management Review* 44, no. 2 (2019): 254–78.
27. We will expand on the notion of the inverted pyramid in Chapter 9.

CHAPTER 5

Who Has the Specific Knowledge to Design the Risk Architecture?

Why You Need an Independent Risk Function

Previously we discussed the three lines of defense approach to enterprise risk management (ERM). Now it is time to consider the challenges in implementing such an approach. If all the risks of an organization are to be aggregated, then there must be a common risk approach to make this possible. Such an approach must create a common language, sometimes referred to as the risk taxonomy, so that all participants have an understanding of key concepts, especially risk, and have processes that promote a unifying approach. The architect of the process is the Chief Risk Officer (CRO) in discussion with the C-Suite executives and the board. So, you need a focal point and architect, typically a CRO or in smaller organizations a financial officer, or other oversight function executive, familiar with risk management.

THE STRATEGY-RISK-GOVERNANCE PROCESS

For many people, process and process requirements send a shudder down the spine. Process is often seen as onerous, constraining, and time consuming. Others see good, well-designed process as critical to providing steady, repeatable operations and to freeing up time to deal with areas requiring more attention. We see good process as an enabler of organization performance. Figure 5.1 illustrates a strong strategy-risk-governance process and was shown in the Preface as Figure P.2.[1] As previously noted, this approach begins with strategy formulation and integrates risk knowledge, understanding, and capabilities to develop a unique competitive advantage that drives strong performance and the desired reputation. The oversight function and requirement for strong ethics and culture are illustrated as the top elements feeding into the process and the organizational capabilities are illustrated as the bottom elements supporting and feeding into the process. The series of arrows throughout the process illustrate the need for links and feedback loops. Not shown, but integral to the approach, is the realm of uncertainty surrounding the activities and decisions.

FIGURE 5.1 The Strategy-Risk-Governance Process

A good process is usually defined as a series of actions, steps, or tasks to accomplish an objective (or objectives). From this definition, a couple of elements necessary for a process to be good are evident.

- The objective(s) must reflect these characteristics:
  - Valuable to the organization
  - Inclusive
  - Well-defined and clear to ensure it is (they are) fully understood
  - Measurable where possible to ensure they are met
  - Founded on important qualitative dimensions

- The tasks must also have these characteristics:
  - Well defined and clearly specified
  - Appropriately sequenced
  - Contributory to ensure benefits can be recognized and resolve is maintained

Further, a good process must also be aligned with the values of the organization and be achievable with the resources available. The objective(s) of the process must fit with the business strategy. Rob Davis provides a list of criteria for evaluating appropriate processes and more detailed descriptions of each: effective, efficient, relevant, valid, usable, used, reused, managed, and measured.[2]

The objectives of the risk process will depend on the level of risk awareness and understanding, risk capability, and risk preparedness in the organization. These are dimensions of organizational risk maturity. In a risk-mature organization, the key objective for the risk process is to ensure business strategies and actions are risk-informed and risk-appropriate.[3] Although this sounds simple, the span of business decisions affected is very broad. A complete list is not provided here because each organization in each industry will have its own business interests, activities, and strategies. A short list would include these elements:

- Effective pricing—ensure expected losses (ELs)[4] are included in product and services pricing
- Appropriate capitalization—ensure the organization has adequate capital of sufficient quality to weather unexpected losses (ULs)
- Resource deployment and prioritization—ensure businesses are provided appropriate resources (capital, risk appetite,[5] expense) for profitability, growth, and development

The selection of strategic goals directly affects the inherent risks and may introduce new risks or risk sensitivities. The strategy concepts of positioning and objective setting in Figure 5.1 were introduced and discussed already.

The risk elements of the process[6] include five individual process steps, and each of these has a specific objective in support of the primary objective:

1. *Risk identification:* Identify all the risks affecting business performance.
2. *Assessment and measurement:* Understand the magnitude, sources, direction, and key drivers of the risk exposures.
3. *Analytics and management:* Develop deeper understanding of possible performance outcomes and likelihoods.

4. *Monitoring and reporting:* Know the current risk exposure position and clearly communicate with key stakeholders.
5. *Response and planning:* Be prepared for the unexpected.

The risk portion of the process steps are ordered to reflect these situations:

- Only risks that are identified can be assessed and measured.
- Only risks that can be assessed and measured can be understood, explored in greater detail, and effectively managed.
- Only risks that are understood can be properly monitored and communicated.
- Only for risks that are understood and actively tracked can proactive plans be created.

Although the steps are in order, the cycle never completes. As the business environment changes and new strategic opportunities are developed, the risks must be reviewed, new risks identified, and the process continues. The progression and iterative processes are captured by the arrows built into the diagram.

Risk identification involves the detection and description of risks that could compromise the ability of the organization to achieve its business objectives.

The identification process begins with a clear statement of the business purpose—this is the link to strategy. The purpose should provide information on the inherent risks in the business. For example, at a minimum, a lending business includes the risk of borrower defaults (credit risk), the asset/liability risk involved in funding the lending assets (market and liquidity risk), and the operational risks including handling the ongoing interest and principal payments for both assets and liabilities, monitoring adherence to any covenants and perfecting any security.

The business model employed may introduce new risks or amplify or mute existing risks. In the lending business, a new risk may be created using hedge instruments (reduces the market risk but introduces counterparty risk) and the size of the asset and liability maturity gaps changes the market and liquidity risks. The key in identification is not to just note risk categories such as market or credit risk but rather identify specific drivers of performance outcomes. For example, investment portfolios and trading books are often subject to interest rate movements. The key risk drivers may be the market and investment structure (e.g., term, liquidity), broad macroeconomic factors (e.g., quantitative easing, business cycles), specific market volatility expectations, and specific events (e.g., flight to quality).[7]

The preceding material on risk identification is relevant for known or familiar risks. These are risks that the organization has knowledge of, experience with, and the organizational capability to recognize, assess, and manage. Emerging risks are those that are either known risks that are changing in unfamiliar ways or new risks that have never been seen before. An example of the former is the mid-2000s U.S. home mortgage market and, of the latter, the introduction of complex derivatives in the late-1980s and early 1990s.

Current examples of emerging risks that are often identified[8] include unsustainable national deficit levels, levels of inequality, climate change, escalating cross-species contaminations, and the wide variety of cyber risks. In recent conversations, several people have identified the emergence of blockchain and smart contracts, viral outbreaks, commodity pricing, and China's intentions as emerging risks worth considering. Of course, an emerging risk identified for one organization is not necessarily important for another organization.[9]

Identification of emerging risks relies on the following:

- Deep, broad, and multidisciplinary learning and experience[10]
- Combined analytical and intuitive thinking
- Multiple perspectives—in-out, macro-micro, past-present-future
- Knowledge of diverse human behaviors at a practical level
- Thinking about entanglements and connections rather than isolates
- Willingness to consider contrarian views

Information can come from standard sources that watch for changing emphasis or perspective but can also include rumor sheets, internet blogs, and the views of contrarians, alarmists, and flakes. One way of thinking about emerging risk is to consider how changes are making things that were once loosely correlated more highly correlated. While reviewing information and views it is important to be wary of the following biases:

- The ambiguity effect—when people choose the option with a known probability over the one with an unknown probability
- The bandwagon effect—the tendency of people to want to belong to the majority
- The normalcy bias—the tendency to underestimate the probability and consequences of a disaster because the world will continue as it always has

If we are to look beyond the recent, immediate, and obvious, we need to be aware of these deep-seated cognitive biases.

Risk assessment and measurement is about building an understanding of the magnitude, sources, direction, and key drivers of the risk exposures and their impact on strategy. There are risks that can be measured and those that can only be assessed. Assessment is largely a qualitative exercise relying on analytical and intuitive thinking. There may be the possibility of using some existing risk measurement approaches although the lack of data and clear insight into the performance and risk drivers imply that this must be done with caution.

Assessment relies on the same skills, perspectives, and approaches outlined in the previous discussion on the identification of emerging risks. Assessment often must deal with the lack of recognizable patterns, uncertain significance of observable data, and ambiguous consequences and implications. And, as with all aspects of economic systems, interactions and interconnectedness can be complex. The objective of assessment is sense-making to inform business strategic choices and actions.

The approaches need to use multiple approaches—no single evaluative tool is adequate because all have biases and shortcomings. There is a need to use quantitative and qualitative approaches creatively to build context-specific insight. The assessment should look for patterns and drivers of behaviors, and ideas, goals, and ways and means matter. It is important to constantly imagine and reconsider as possibilities are revealed.

There are many risk measurement approaches and they defy listing in this chapter. However, there are several commonalities. Measurement approaches provide the ability to convert the barrage of data into insightful and actionable information. This provides the ability to better understand the forces driving the risks faced and opportunities available. If used properly, measurement approaches enable complex performance and risk information to be communicated in a common language, a business language.

To use measurement approaches effectively, you should do the following:

- Transform data into information.
- Explore the information and its meaning.
- Apply experience and judgment to what the information and models seem to tell you.
- Ensure that any model used for decision-making is independently vetted and that all model risks are understood and managed.

Data, as implied, are central to most risk measurement approaches. Data are also often the greatest challenges to effective measurement.

Measurement approaches transform historical data to develop models of future possible events. Data quality and reliability must be high, and the data limitations must be fully understood. Any measurement approach is a filtered and simplified view of reality. Risk models use very sophisticated tools to generate future potential states and statistical tools to describe the resulting distribution of these potential states. It is necessary to use knowledge of the applied approaches and combine them with business understanding and experience to interpret the resulting information.

Effective risk management is a journey of discovery. As further discussed in Appendix I, risks transform and migrate; they emerge and dissipate. Business needs change and risk exposures and management actions change with them. Markets also change and experience different conditions that may not be adequately reflected in risk measures based on past conditions. It is necessary to undertake ongoing analysis to fully understand the possible factors driving business performance through time. The objective of this process step is to develop risk insights and a deeper understanding of possible performance outcomes to inform business management.

One of our favorite lines is from Tolkien's description of Aragorn: "All that is gold does not glitter."[11] It is necessary in risk management to look beyond the immediate and obvious and to explore business conditions, behaviors, and ongoing outcomes to discover evolving factors affecting performance and risk drivers, including changing interconnections, dependencies, and relationships. Common techniques are to undertake scenario analysis and stress testing. It is important to consider probable, possible, and catastrophic scenarios to understand future possible states. Ask the what-if questions.[12]

Business loss event analysis is another technique. It is based on reviews of reported losses from within the industry to assess the organization's exposure to similar events or risk drivers. Of course, all material losses experienced by the organization should be reviewed to ensure that the risk drivers are identified, and any driver of ULs are built into future risk approaches. A final technique previously identified as an aid to risk identification is income statement decomposition. As noted, this approach helps identify drivers of outcomes and vulnerabilities. The outcome of this analysis is a better understanding of performance and risk drivers and the effectiveness of the business and risk management approaches.

Monitoring and reporting are linked from the perspective of needing to report past and current risk positions. Reporting also requires a forward-looking view so it is also related to risk analytics. Combined, the objective is to capture risk exposures and clearly communicate with key stakeholders, including risk-takers, business leaders, regulators, and the board. Under risk identification, it was noted that all risks should be identified. In risk monitoring and reporting, there is the need to include only material risks and risks that are changing (they may become material). The monitoring and reporting need to reflect the volatility of the underlying risk drivers, business positioning, and sensitivities. They must also consider the liquidity holding periods and the time required for management to act.

Reporting must provide information on past and current exposures, the changes in the exposures, and reasons for the changes. The reasons for the changes must reflect the changes in the underlying risk drivers. It must also be forward looking. It is important to provide insights into how the exposures may change in the future given expected business activities and market conditions. The forward-looking perspective also allows for an action orientation. If limits are being approached or other issues are arising, necessary management actions can be identified, implemented and tracked.

The keys to creating effective business plans and/or contingency plans to address risks are a clear understanding of exposures and the underlying risk drivers and the critical business vulnerabilities. The identification, assessment, and analytic process steps provide this capability. The monitoring process step allows for the identification of risk driver changes and an assessment of the level of risk in the environment. A crisis may not be able to be predicted but increasing risk can be. The plans must consider the volatility of underlying risk drivers. How quickly the environment can change affects the nature of the required plans.

Another key element is management's ability and willingness to act. The plans, of course, must establish how decisions are made and who has the authority to act. However, committees and the need to work across functions or even organizational structures can significantly affect management's ability to act. Inexperience and certain locked-in perspectives or biases can affect management's willingness to act. Slow decision-making in normal conditions may be a warning sign that decisions will not be made or will be made too slowly in times of crisis.[13]

Market and market participant behaviors also affect an organization's plans, particularly in systemic crises. Each organization's competitive environment is different, so it is important to identify what the large competitors are most likely to do and how to respond. In regulated industries such as financial services, the actions of the regulatory authorities and legislative bodies also play a significant role. In times of crisis, an organization needs to fully understand the resolution frameworks, both formal and informal, created by these areas. As seen in the 2007–2008 financial crisis, the market turmoil increased as the US government initially walked away from the informal process of supporting large financial institutions and allowed

Lehman Brothers Holdings Inc. to fail. But it is important to understand that "bailouts" have been a mainstay of US public policy—at least dating from the 1979 bailout of Chrysler due to these reasons:

- National security implications
- Saving jobs
- Saving suppliers
- Improving American automobiles[14]

The warning here is to be careful if you think your business and or industry is essential to the national economy. In 2019, US farmers received help during the trade wars while many retail firms and strip malls were going bankrupt. Risk management is about avoiding the need for bailouts.

MEETING THE OBJECTIVE AND THE CATEGORIZATION OF RISKS

The objective of the risk process, as noted, is to ensure business strategies and actions are risk-informed and risk-appropriate. The risk process is described here as a series of process steps to accomplish this objective. Implicit in this is that the risk process is a part of the larger strategic process. Any change in strategy involves a change in risk profile, and this implies that the risk process is never ended. As strategies and business decisions are considered, the effect of the expected outcomes need to be assessed through the risk process. The effects need to be investigated prior to the decision to ensure the risks associated with the outcomes are appropriate for the organization and that they can be effectively managed.

As we mentioned, this is challenging. In their insightful *Harvard Business Review* article, Kaplan and Mikes offer one way to achieve such a common understanding by providing a categorization of risks:

- Preventable risks
- Strategic risks
- External risks[15]

It is pointed out that each risk category requires a different approach. Preventable risks are clearly known and are addressed by the control framework. Strategic risk requires a discussion concerning the likelihood and impact of such risks, akin to our discussion of ELs and ULs. External risks require preparation for unexpected future events via stress testing and other scenario planning tools.[16] For each of these three risk categories the CRO or the risk function has an essential role in coordinating and facilitating the discussion of the risks. The crux of making a centralized-decentralized structure work is knowing what to centralize—the framework—and how to decentralize operations to where the specific knowledge is. Kaplan and Mikes provide just such an approach.

But we are just describing the tip of the iceberg, as Mikes recognizes in the following comment: "Models are not decision makers; people are. So, the real issue is the culture that you have around modeling."[17] The Institute of Risk Management defines risk culture as follows: "risk culture is a term describing the values, beliefs, knowledge, attitudes and understanding about risk shared by a group of people with a common purpose. This applies to all organisations—including private companies, public bodies, governments and not-for-profits."[18] This means embedding risk appreciation into the strategy and the overall organization culture—especially if the first line of defense is the line of business that may not have risk at the forefront of their thinking. For this to happen the overall organization culture must embrace certain values:

- Transparency and openness
- Demanding clear roles and responsibilities
- Embracing constructive challenge to pursue the best results

These values create the conditions for dialogues, of which we will say more in Chapter 8, but some key points need to be made here. A common purpose focused on results is what enables a genuine exchange from different perspectives while establishing criteria for resolution. In language made popular in the history of science, for the discussion to have meaning, it must take place inside a common paradigm. The strategy/risk culture is that paradigm. The clear roles and responsibilities are also key to a productive dialogue because it establishes the initial boundaries and legitimacy of the views; whereas all may have opinions, not all opinions are equally valid, so it is important to have a framework that makes clear what makes participation in the discussion legitimate. However, the very basis for legitimacy may also be the basis for bias. So, transparency and openness establish the right to participate, but formal roles do not confer final decision rights. Only the perspective that led to better performance within the risk/return parameters of the organization do that.

Buehler, Freeman, and Hulme provide a realistic depiction of risk culture at most companies as fragmented. Often, the board lacks the expertise, the CRO has limited influence on decision-making, and the CFO has a siloed view of risk. Although the treasurer may have a sophisticated view of risk, the business units lack the capability of understanding or measuring risks. This fragmentation limits the CEO's capacity to dialogue about risk leaving her to decide by her "gut."[19] The fragmentation is in part the result of the lack of risk awareness in the organizational culture. The business unit and even the customer service representative, or the waitstaff in our restaurant, are in the ideal position to identify risks arising from the customer interface, more formally, because they are the first line of defense.[20] A healthy organizational culture has a healthy risk awareness component.

THE RISK ARCHITECTURE

Our modified risk pyramid shown in Figure 5.2 illustrates some key points about risk architecture. First, the scope of analysis for risk is company-wide. Second, the narrowing of the pyramid suggests that at the highest level of the corporation risks must be aggregated and integrated. This includes not only risks that can be measured quantitatively but also those that require qualitative assessment. Another take on how risk discussions can be integrated comes from Kaplan and Mikes: "Managers can develop a companywide risk perspective by anchoring their discussions in strategic planning, the one integrative process that most well-run companies already have."[21] Consequently, risk must be embedded in the overall organizational culture.

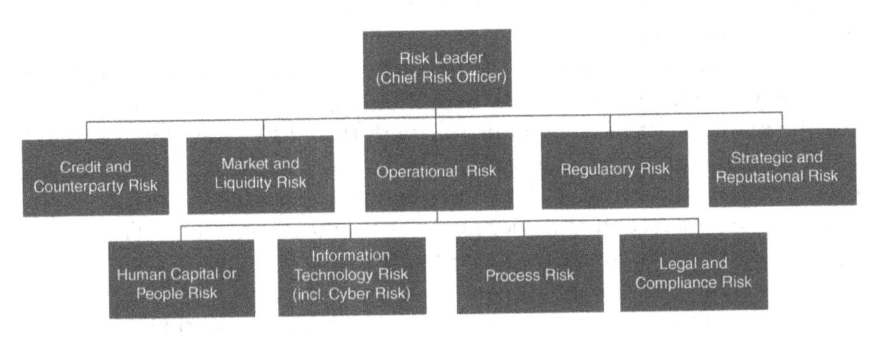

FIGURE 5.2 Generic Risk Function Chart

But as we previously mentioned, the risk perspective frequently comes from a perspective or culture that is very different from the growth culture that frequently characterizes strategic planning perspectives. As Kaplan and Mikes note: "Risk management is nonintuitive; it runs counter to many individual and organizational biases."[22] The flip side of the coin must be acknowledged too. Many risk managers, especially those from a credit background, may find the upside of strategic planning difficult to embrace. And some risk managers we have worked with want to negate risk without understanding that to do so will also limit or even negate profits. Depending on the firm's risk culture, a focal point for both risk and strategy may be needed to spur the debate.

In trying to popularize the need for risk thinking in an organization, it is essential to demonstrate the advantages of the enterprise wide and integrative nature of the ERM. One forceful way to accomplish this is to demonstrate the cost savings that comes from the approach. An early recognition of this can be seen in Lisa K. Meulbroek's work on Honeywell and Insurance.[23] She convincingly demonstrates that a silo-based approach to managing insurable risks was not cost-effective because the possibility of some events precluded the possibility of others. So, insuring all was a waste of money. The point can be made even more simply by considering foreign exchange transactions (FX). In order to avoid exposure to FX risks, you might decide to hedge the exposure. But the cost-effective way to do this is not to hedge every single transaction but the net exposure. Hence, the value comes from a firm-wide integrative approach.

Although the benefits of an enterprise-wide integrative approach have been clear for a considerable time, the difficulties of achieving it have been just as well known. The challenge is the same as embedding strategy in the organization: how do you balance centralization and decentralization? Going back to the three lines of defense, the front line owns the risk, but it is the second line of defense, risk oversight, that establishes the guidelines. For the moment, let us equate this role with the CRO. How does the CRO fulfill this role on an ex ante basis? The CRO must be a leader in establishing process for setting and quantifying where possible the risk capacity, appetite, tolerances, and resiliency planning for the organization. This means managing risk to maximize the value of the firm.

Just as the leader in any organization must do the CRO is responsible for establishing the framework for risk identification, reporting, and monitoring. The process must ensure that the frontline understands the risk, as well as the board. This demands the creation of an appropriate risk culture that is supported with quantitative tools and qualitative assessment frameworks. Because the process must not negate risk-taking, but support risk management, it must take place in a culture that has achieved the right balance between risk and reward. Neither excessive conservatism nor excessive risk-taking is good risk management. The reporting system must establish clear roles and responsibilities so that individuals can be held accountable. Once this structure is put in place, then it becomes time to staff.

CREATION OF A RISK FUNCTION

As noted in the Preface, our careers and involvement in risk management have spanned the past three decades. As a result, we have designed and built or witnessed the creation of risk functionality across several organizations. We have seen efforts that have struggled and those that have worked to build truly high-performance teams. This experience has taught us a lot about organizational behavior, leadership, and effective teamwork. Those are all worthy topics we will leave for another day, although much of what we provide on the creation of effective risk functionality will brush up against those topics.

It is important to begin with the understanding that risk management is not about risk elimination as we have noted elsewhere. It is about understanding risk exposures and working to capture those risks that provide a distinct advantage.

With the growth of market risk understanding and the complexities of many capital markets instruments, risk became associated with quantitative models and analysis. Given these complexities and the extent to which models are used in risk, there is a role for quants. *But the math without the business and risk understanding will not result in an effective ability to take and manage risk to create competitive advantage.*

It is also important to be clear that building a risk function, as described here, is not about creating a risk management function—the businesses and operational areas must manage the risks they take in driving profits and running their areas. The risk function, or second line of defense, is about creating the guidelines within which risks can be taken, providing independent tracking of risk-taking activities, behaviors, and outcomes, and providing risk insights to support effective strategic and business decisions. The "Dr. No" credit officer or BPU (business prevention unit) of decades past is not relevant in today's understanding of a risk function unless you are unfortunate enough to have an individual or function operating in that way in your organization.

If a risk function is responsible for creating the guidelines, providing independent tracking, and providing risk insights, what are the actual activities that take place? There are usually four activities within risk functions that provide these outcomes:

- Creating the independent risk framework—this includes tracking legislative and regulatory requirements and changes; creating policy documents including board/corporate risk policies, the risk appetite statement, and management risk standards; and creating and documenting the processes to be followed for risk assessments, approvals, and follow-up

- Onboarding new participants in the organization's ecosystem—this includes adjudication, including constructive challenge, of line of business client reviews (lending is the commonly recognized activity), strategic partnerships, and vendor engagement
- Running the ongoing monitoring and reporting of risk exposures against approved authorities, including risk limits—this involves monitoring positions on appropriate frequencies; reporting risk positions to management, executives, and the board; and escalating any issues for action and resolution
- Performing risk and performance analytics—this involves tracking corporate vulnerabilities and risk exposures and developing forward-looking assessments; reviewing and monitoring signals for emerging risks and adverse business trends; undertaking scenario analysis to understand the probable, possible, and catastrophic outcomes; and providing the key analytical support for the organization's resiliency plans, including risk incident resolutions and recovery planning

Another important factor to contemplate is the fact that risks change through time. Risk transformations require a level of vigilance and exploration beyond the risk exposure monitoring and reporting mentioned previously. This falls into the fourth bullet—performance and risk analytics.

These activities can be organized in different ways to reflect an organization's specific risk activities, operating model, and level of centralization. A common organizational approach used by financial institutions is to have all or most of the activities associated with credit risk in a credit risk department. That department may develop and update the credit policies and standards, provide input on credit limits, and review and concur (or not) with lending officers' recommendations[24] to advance a loan product to a borrower. A common financial institution risk organization structure would be based on risk types. A generic representation of this is provided in Figure 5.2.

These risk structures, whether in financial institutions or commercial entities, are beginning to be transformed into "agile" structures more closely aligned with business processes. The four activities just listed are structured closer to the agile approach then the traditional design in the organization chart in Figure 5.2.

Also, seeing the risk function as a collection of activities and purposes rather than a simple organizational structure as in the figure enables us to understand the breadth and nature of the capabilities required by the staff of a risk function. We are not going to go into technical capabilities, such as understanding of capital markets or cyber security, because those capabilities are dependent on the nature of the organization's business activities. We are going to focus on the complementary capabilities to these technical skills.

In our opinion, the three key attributes required beyond the technical, analytical capabilities include these:

- An understanding of how the business makes money
- Diversification of backgrounds, thought process, and perspectives
- A driving curiosity of why things happen the way they do

The first attribute includes a clear understanding of strategy, business objectives, and business interactions with stakeholders—what drives sustainable, long-term profitability. It is impossible to understand risk dynamics if the underlying business is not understood. As mentioned elsewhere, the organization's strategy and business model—how the organization makes money—directly affects the types of risks the organization takes and the ones that best align with creating and maintaining competitive advantage.

A common risk technique for testing risk identification is income statement decomposition. In this approach, the analyst decomposes the income statement into specific performance and risk drivers—those factors that affect the outcomes experienced through the income statement. This approach requires some accounting knowledge but relies on an understanding of the business dynamics. In some cases, unexplained income or expense volatility can result in identification of otherwise unknown risks.

The most engaged and empowered market and liquidity risk team either of us has been involved with included training on how the bank within which they operated made money. Each risk professional was provided the opportunity to spend time with the treasury function to understand funding, transfer pricing, liquidity management, and asset/liability management.

The second attribute reflects the fact that risk is an art and the context within which the business operates is always changing, resulting in changes in risk profile, risk transformations, and emerging risks. Performance and risk analytics rely on differing perspectives to enable the creation of scenarios to test resiliency and recovery and the ability to identify and assess emerging risks.[25]

Effective risk functions include staff with deep, broad, and multidisciplinary learning and experience. In describing risk activities, it is possible to reflect on macroeconomic factors, business results as reflected in the financial statements, management accounting allocation processes, analytical and quantitative modeling, and business analysis, including all strategic elements. A very broad set of capabilities requires a very diverse staff. In one risk function we both experienced, the team consisted of PhDs in mathematics, statistics, and economics; MSCs in mathematics, engineering, and computer science; MAs in philosophy and English literature; MBAs in finance, financial accounting, organizational behavior, and strategy; CMAs; and a number of BAs in different disciplines. It was a diverse team that introduced many innovative and thoughtful risk approaches that were recognized by industry peers, regulators, and outside consultants as improvements over the preexisting approaches many relied on.

The diversity of these backgrounds leads to the recognition that intuitive approaches to risk are as important as the quantitative. This captures the art in the risk function. It also provides against common biases in business decision-making, such as dealing with the previously mentioned ambiguity and bandwagon effects and normalcy bias. The differing perspectives force the team to look beyond the recent, immediately obvious, and easily understood.

The outcome of the diversity in the risk staff leads to the third attribute—curiosity about why things happen the way they do. In considering the organization's future and assessing and measuring risk possibilities, it is important to recognize that the business world is complex, adaptive, and ambiguous. Behavioral patterns shift and the significance of performance and risk drivers change over time. And, of course, there are the famous, unknown unknowns. It is important to look beyond the obvious and dig out the factors most important to the organization's execution of its strategy and most relevant to creating risk-based competitive advantage. It is an ongoing process of discovery. What was true yesterday may not be true today and can be very different as the world evolves.

A fourth element not listed is the ability to provide constructive challenge. This is a communication, emotional intelligence, and relationship management skill that is required by all risk professionals.

The foregoing has focused on the risk function within the organization at a staff level. Effective board risk committees also require certain capabilities and ways of thinking about and approaching performance and risk dynamics for the organization. The board risk committee is an element of the independent risk oversight function and must be considered as an important element within the organization's risk function. Key attributes for a member of a risk committee include risk acumen, certain personal attributes such as the ability to provide constructive challenge, and strong business acumen in order to evaluate the risk issues within the strategic and business opportunity context. These are captured in DCRO's "Qualified Risk Director Guidelines."[26]

CONCLUSION

As discussed previously in the context of insurance and FX management, individual risk must be put into context. And this makes a focal point: the CRO imperative—the function is what matters even if the title differs in different organizations. Centralization through a senior risk professional is what enables the consciousness of risk to permeate the organization. And this is what makes it possible to decentralize risk management to the lines of business yet to have the capacity to aggregate and integrate.

NOTES

1. This is the same as Figure P.2.
2. Rob Davis, "What Makes a Good Process?," *BP Trends*, November 2009, http://www.bptrends.com/publicationfiles/FIVE11-09-ART-Whatmakesagood process-BPTrends.pdf.
3. It should be reiterated that attempting to implement a mature risk process in an organization lacking risk maturity, whether in terms of understanding and awareness or capabilities and capacity, will not generally result in achieving the objectives noted.
4. EL in the credit risk context: "In statistical terms, the expected loss is the average credit loss that we would expect from an exposure or a portfolio over a given period of time," http://financetrain.com/expected-loss-unexpected-loss-and-loss-distribution/.
5. The risk appetite framework is a very important topic deserving focus. The framework needs to include not just appetite and clear limits but also capacity. It must be established within the context of strategy and recognizing organizational capabilities.
6. These often show up as stand-alone risk process diagrams. We believe they are fundamental to strategy formulation and execution and embed them in the larger strategy-risk-governance process.
7. An example of a tool used to identify the sources and direction of interest rate risks is a DV01 calculation. DV01 is the dollar value of a 1-basis point move. A specific underlying instrument price or yield can be moved by 1 (basis point or specified number of cents, if price based) and the portfolio value is recalculated to show the value affect. This approach is used across different market risk drivers. Another tool that is used to identify key drivers of performance outcomes is income statement decomposition. Unfortunately, accounting treatments can obscure the economics of the business performance although as mark to market and fair value accounting is increasingly used, the less this difficulty exists. This is an effective tool because losses flow through the income statement, and this is where risk outcomes are first experienced. Income statement decomposition is best used for high-frequency risk drivers affecting portfolios that are marked to market with a corresponding frequency. Risk registers are also a tool in general use. Revenue lines are affected by level of sales and changes in prices, in name two drivers and costs, and expenses are similarly affected by changes in prices. This type of analysis often does not go deep enough to identify specific strategic or reputation risk affects.

8. These sources include The World Economic Forum's Global Risk Report 2018, which is not strictly an emerging risks report, but it does provide excellent coverage of the following top five risks in terms of likelihood: extreme weather events, natural disasters, cyberattacks, data fraud or theft, and failure of climate change mitigation and adaptation. "Risks from Transformations and Emerging Technologies," February 18, 2020, http://www3.weforum.org/docs/WEF_GRR18_Report.pdf.
9. This important area is beginning to receive attention from management academics. See Cynthia Hardy and Steve Maguire, "Organizations, Risk Translation, and the Ecology of Risks: The Discursive Construction of a Novel Risk," *Academy of Management Journal* (2019).
10. This is another reason why breaking down silos is critical.
11. J.R.R. Tolkien, *The Fellowship of the Ring, The Lord of the Rings* (New York: HarperCollins, 2009).
12. This is discussed in Chapter 8.
13. Decision-making is increasingly a focus at McKinsey. See Aaron De Smet, Gregor Jost, and Leigh Weiss, "Three Keys to Faster Better Decisions," *McKinsey Quarterly* (May 2019) and Aaron De Smet, Gregor Jost, and Leigh Weiss, "Want a Better Decision? Plan a Better Meeting," *McKinsey Quarterly* (May 2019).
14. See Chris Seabury, "1979 Government Bailout of Chrysler: A Retrospective," June 25, 2019, https://www.investopedia.com/articles/economics/chrysler-bailout.asp.
15. Robert S. Kaplan and Anette Mikes, "Managing Risks: A New Framework," *Harvard Business Review* (June 2012).
16. We will say more about scenario planning and stress testing in Chapter 8.
17. Anette Mikes in David Champion, "Roundtable: Managing Risk in the New World," *Harvard Business Review* (October 2009).
18. https://www.theirm.org/knowledge-and-resources/thought-leadership/risk-culture.aspx.
19. Kevin Buehler, Andrew Freeman, and Ron Hulme, "Owning the Right Risks," *Harvard Business Review* (September 2008).
20. See the discussion in Chapter 4.
21. Kaplan and Mikes, "Managing Risks."
22. Kaplan and Mikes, "Managing Risks," 13.
23. See Lisa Meulbroek, "A Better Way to Manage Risk," *Harvard Business Review* (February 2001).
24. Increasingly, retail and commercial lending is undertaken through credit models that change the nature of the first and second lines of defense in credit risk.
25. Recall that emerging risks are those risks that are unknown or are known but changing in unexpected ways.
26. The Directors and Chief Risk Officers Group, "Qualified Risk Director Guidelines," September 19, 2019, https://img1.wsimg.com/blobby/go/6299e5c2-5f50-4421-b3c0-652e6c91f6e1/downloads/1cgrl807n_314439.pdf.

CHAPTER 6

Enterprise Risk Management and Competitive Advantage

Once the appropriate risk-governance framework and supporting processes are in place to identify, measure, assess, monitor, and report risks, the organization needs to decide which risks to keep. Clearly the risks that the firm should retain are the ones that are related to the value in its value proposition, which in turn links to its reputation and hence competitive advantage. Because the purchaser will compare the value proposition offered to competing offers, there is a market limitation on the price or the organization's downside risk that the customer will accept, as we discussed previously. Investors, however, are only prepared to accept limitations on the buffer against uncertainty. So, there is a market limitation on capital structure.[1] But for now, we simply want to recognize the importance of risk and uncertainty in creating value for the customer and the firm. As with many other topics in this book, value creation for the customer must be balanced against value claiming by the firm to compensate its stakeholders.

Although we recognize the importance of shareholders, we prefer the broader use of stakeholders because it recognizes the importance of the social license to operate that is essential to sustainable success and the importance of which is increasingly recognized by institutional investors, such as BlackRock founder and CEO, Larry Fink.[2] Moreover, consumers and customers are increasingly considering the stance of companies on social issues when making their purchase decisions.[3] Perhaps even more important, they are willing to pay up to 25% more according to the 2017 Edelman Earned Brand Study.[4]

This has important implications for the dialogue between risk managers and strategists. First, it expands the scope of risk management into reputation management, reinforcing our decision to employ the term *stakeholder* with its broader scope. Second, it fosters an approach to risk that embraces upside and downside potential. In our discussions of the pricing decision, we emphasized that expected loss (EL) sets a floor price and strategic efforts to differentiate try to get us as close as possible to the market-imposed ceiling. But, given the risk manager's role in managing reputation, which is essential to differentiation as much as the concrete product/service attributes, the roles of strategists and risk managers become more challenging as customers become more demanding in more dimensions of reputation.

But let us return to the simpler times when product/service attributes were hegemonic. However, before beginning our exploration into the origin of risk, we need to delineate different implications from different types of risk. Returning to either Royal Bank of Canada's risk pyramid or our modified one (Figures P.1 and 4.2), we call attention to the differences in the ability to control and influence risk. Following, we will explore differences in the ability to identify and manage risks and comment on the difficulty in controlling even what is listed as the "more controllable" financial risks. But even among the different financial risks, there are significant differences in the perception of risks that affect the management and cultures associated with the different types. Perhaps the easiest pair to contrast are credit risk and market risk. Credit risk is essentially the issue of borrower default, whereas market risk reflects changes in the portfolio of securities, such as stocks and bonds.[5] For credit risk, beyond contractual interest earned, there is an asymmetry of risk and return. There is virtually no upside to credit risk, only downside. To those familiar with portfolio theory, the purpose of diversification is to limit the bankruptcy tail; it really cannot be offset by gains from other parts of the portfolio.[6] Market risk, however, has an upside and a downside. Losses from some securities may be offset by gains from others. The essential point is that in the case of credit risk, we manage the negative by processes to protect against loss, but with market risk, we are as concerned about future gains as well as losses.

These differences promote different approaches to organizational design and culture. Anyone who is familiar with banks that have retail and investment banking arms will have noticed the very different cultures between the two. The retail side tends to be more heavily bureaucratic because it is concerned with loss prevention. The investment side tends to be a flatter organization and nimbler because it is structured to be able to act quickly on opportunities. It is not that one is right and one is wrong but rather that both are structured according to how risk/return is perceived and pursued. From a strategic point of view, we are concerned about seeing risk as opportunity, while recognizing the challenges.

Let us return to considering credit risk for the moment. Previously, we stressed that there was only downside to this form of risk. But is that true? Seen from the limited point of view of credit, yes, but from the view of the overall firm's strategy? And here we can generalize away from financial institutions (FIs) to all institutions. We grant credit and incur credit risk to grow our businesses. Although there is no upside to credit risk per se, it does create a relationship with the customer that helps us provide other products/services to the customer.[7] And though credit risk properly managed should be profitable on its own, it also shares a relationship with other products. It is this kind of thinking that shifts an organization from thinking about product profitability to managing customer profitability.[8] This is not to ignore product/service profitability but rather to put it into the more complex context of managing relationships. Risk management has a role to play even in customer-centricity. This calls attention to the enterprise-wide scope of risk management as a complement to strategic positioning.

So, when should we first start thinking about risk? As soon as we start formulating our value proposition, because that is when the risks that need to be identified and managed are created. Recall that we are seeing risk as opportunity and threat. Simply put, your value proposition *promises* to customers that you will meet a need or solve a problem for them.[9] You are taking over any uncertainty they had concerning this issue, and from this your risk is created. Whatever expectations your value proposition created, your product/service design and creation needs to deliver upon. We are now in the area of strategic risk that Deloitte has discussed thusly:

> *Strategic risk has become a major focus, with 81% of surveyed companies now explicitly managing strategic risk—rather than limiting their focus to traditional risk areas such as operational, financial and compliance risk. Also, many companies are taking a broad view of strategic risk that doesn't just focus on challenges that might cause a particular strategy to fail, but on any major risks that could affect a company's long-term positioning and performance.*[10]

This means breaking down silos.[11]

In accord with our general preference, we would add that strategic risk is also double-sided. Taking a strategic risk should have an upside and a downside, that is, it can succeed beyond expectations or fail beyond your worst nightmare. This takes us into an examination of some of the major assumptions that underlie the goals established in the strategic plan, for example, profitability and market share.[12] Because managing downside risk probably receives more attention, although often not enough, let us look at the areas that provide for greater upside potential and how to identify them.

A strategic risk that changes the game to your benefit is one such area. Progressive Insurance Company is one firm that has frequently secured competitive advantage through innovative strategic moves to change the game.[13] One of its more interesting decisions was to try to manage the volatility of its stock price through changing its disclosure strategy. Because Progressive refused to provide earnings guidance, analysts were often puzzled by the volatility of its earnings. This suggested that either other firms in the industry were managing earnings or that Progressive was not as good at risk management, meaning, setting prices for ELs, as their competitors. The resulting higher cost of capital put the firm at a competitive disadvantage despite impressive relative financial performance. This led the firm to reexamine the links among corporate strategy, financial goals, and reporting policies.[14]

To make clear that the volatility in Progressive's earnings were the result of volatility in the industry due to the unpredictable effects of weather, Progressive decided in 2001 to disclose its underwriting data on a monthly basis so that investors and analysts could see what was driving volatility. The result was to significantly reduce volatility in Progressive's share price and led to demands for greater transparency from its competitors. What is of interest is not only the success of the move, because it could have backfired, but how it leveraged the capabilities of the firm. Previously we discussed the risks created in managing the value chain. We suspect that many of you focused on the chain of the value-adding process to the product/service. Now we would like to focus on the role played by key components of the support activities: firm infrastructure, human resource management, and especially technology development.[15]

Many will be familiar with how competitive advantage can arise from primary activities, but the Progressive example reveals how support activities can also be leveraged for game-changing competitive advantage. Platform companies, such as Amazon and Uber, take this understanding to the next level. Progressive's history of innovation in serving higher-risk customers led it to develop state-of-the-art internal reporting systems believed to be ahead of its competitors. For Progressive, the costs of leveraging this capability via monthly disclosure was significantly less than for its competitors. If investors and analysts began to demand similar disclosure from rivals, Progressive would succeed in securing an advantage until its rivals caught up.[16] But if investors further came to believe that Progressive's results were more "trustworthy" because of its stance, the advantage could go from being temporary to longer term or sustainable. Progressive's Ethisphere award in 2013 as the world's most ethical company attests to the reputational advantage that Progressive has achieved.[17] The reputation is enhanced by a reputation with customers for "relentlessly improving performance."[18]

The Progressive story is important for revealing not only the importance of ethics to competitive advantage when reputation matters[19] but also the interconnectedness of the elements of a strategy. Progressive worried that if it employed earnings guidance it would lead the firm into managing to achieve these results. Smoothing earnings would come at the expense of customer service because claims might be delayed in order to hit the promised numbers. Meeting the new value proposition to investors would come at the expense of failing to meet its service value proposition to customers of speedy service. Progressive sought and found an innovative solution to the problem.

In fact, as Michael Hammer noted several years ago, the key to Progressive's success was that it outcompeted its rivals via organizational innovation. He elaborated by arguing that the practice is rooted in a culture that realizes that "leaving well enough alone is a principle with which the company is systematically uncomfortable."[20] This culture helps transform what could be a one-time innovation that will be copied into a sustainable advantage as the firm uses the new platform to create the opportunity for further innovation. Innovation is ongoing, not a one-time event.[21]

This is complemented by the company's approach to decentralization. The measurement system has been developed to give the product managers as much information as possible to improve the decision-making progress. The measurement system makes decentralization work. King explains:

> *Decentralization is a critical part of our strategy and our success. And since Stern Stewart is the former publisher of the* Journal of Applied Corporate Finance, *you'll probably be happy to hear that we think about decentralization in much the same way as Michael Jensen, one of your regular contributors. That is, we think in terms of the optimal assignment of "decision rights." We try hard to give those rights to the people in the organization who have the specific knowledge—the knowledge of local markets and conditions—necessary to make the best decisions.*[22]

Fundamental to Progressive's success was that it clearly articulated its goal to grow as fast as possible while making money on its core auto insurance business.[23] One of Progressive's innovations that differentiated it from the industry was when it moved to a new pricing approach: "One big success was our pioneering move away from underwriting to pricing. Underwriting means risk acceptance or rejection at a given price, whereas pricing means that there are no bad risks, only bad rates. We decided we could insure anything for the right price. And we were the first company to say that if you are a licensed driver, we'll quote you a price."[24]

Progressive was also one of the first players in its industry to recognize the potential of the digital transformation to improve customer service. In 1995 it launched its first website and has continued to be a leader in implementing digital technologies. However, to date, Progressive has decided to stay as a single business company in property and casualty insurance in a single country. And it has been very successful. But the next wave of digital innovators sees the world differently—they see the potential for platforms in the digital transformation. Just as Progressive leveraged its internal reporting systems for competitive advantage, Amazon is leveraging its predictive analytics and logistics capabilities to disrupt traditional retailing through recognizing the power of its "platform" to create an ecosystem.[25]

McKinsey offers the following definitions of what a platform is in the banking industry:

- Software-based digital environments with open infrastructures
- Matchmakers linking people, organizations, and resources
- Orchestrators of ecosystems extending across sectors without borders[26]
- Reducers of marginal costs to near zero
- Harnessers of network effects
- Foundations of combinatorial innovation[27]

But the new strategies adopted by the platform companies are even more challenging for incumbents. By creating a customer-centric, unified value proposition that extends beyond what users could previously obtain, digital pioneers are bridging the value chains of various industries to create ecosystems that reduce customers' costs, increase convenience, provide them with new experiences, and whet their appetites for more. Not only do they have exceptional data that they exploit with remarkable effectiveness but also, more worrisome for incumbents, they are often more central in the customer journeys that include big financial decisions.[28] Just an aside, the element of new experiences in creating emotional bonds with the customer should not be underplayed, as we shall see.

Although this discussion refers to banks, we can and should generalize it to other industries.[29] A prime example of a platform company is Amazon. Few new users of Amazon might recall that when Amazon started in 1994 it was an e-commerce site selling books. In hard copy. It was only in 2007 that Amazon introduced the Kindle and revolutionized the industry—for a second time. But the first glimmers of Bezos recognizing Amazon was a platform, not a bookseller, was clear by 1998 when he added CDs, but more importantly bought PlanetAll, an internet address service that facilitated people keeping in touch, and Junglee Corporation, which offered shopping for everything.[30] As Easter and Parish put it in their *LA Times* piece, Amazon became "The Everything Store."[31]

Amazon offers several compelling strategic lessons concerning digital transformation. Classic strategists with our economic roots often link value to uniqueness. The network effects of platform companies turn this around: the more ubiquitous, the better. Some of you may remember how Visa countered Amex's claim of "membership has its privileges," with Visa is "everywhere you want to be." Network industries turn uniqueness into a limitation and often an expense. In the same sense, digital transformations often force us to rethink truisms such as location, location, location in retailing. What was meant was convenience, convenience, convenience. This was brought home to one of us on a beach in St. Martin when ordering a new book from our beach chair. The location was great, and the convenience was great, but the two were decoupled. Disruptive technologies often reveal the real meaning of "truisms."

This leads us to ask the classic strategy question: what business is Amazon in? [32] Although it looks like a retailer, it is really in the information business. The more information Amazon collects on its users the more powerful its analytics becomes. The more it expands its product offerings the richer its database becomes. So, expansion into new areas creates a virtuous circle because the ability to acquire more information on customers' tastes and preferences drives into new business areas. This is a much more powerful logic for horizontal growth than has been seen previously.

The sharing economy has led to a different form of platform business, including Airbnb and Uber.[33] Years ago, many applauded Enron's asset-light strategy only to be shocked at its downfall. But at the risk of stereotyping the emergence of these new platform companies, they are transforming the hospitality and transportation industries by creating an infrastructure of everyday people to monetize their assets and thus create new supply. Without having to invest in physical assets, expansion is only limited by the cost of the IT architecture. Although there are significant quality control issues, the solution seems to be in market based rather than bureaucratic solutions. Riders rate drivers, and drivers rate passengers—an interesting take on the 360-degree evaluations common in the human resources world. It should be noted that this is similar to the practice of eBay and Amazon marketplace.

The success of these new platform companies does bring with it new forms of risk, starting with strategic risk. The affected incumbents, with their different cost structures, frequently argue for a regulatory response to bring the new competitors into the fold. In many ways this is an effort to force the disruptive business models into a cost structure more similar to the incumbents by making many safety, quality control, and employment conditions more similar. Although this will not end the threat, it is an attempt to diminish the cost advantage of the new business models.

We also see the importance of reputation risk. With novelty comes uncertainty in the minds of consumers. Here, again, network effects become important. The more people that try the service, the more providers of assets are drawn in. The change in supply should lead to greater choice and improved quality of service. Growth for platform firms solves more problems than it creates. Again, another sign of changing times for the incumbents.

HOW DOES STRATEGY AFFECT RANDOMNESS?

In our previous discussion of capacity planning it might be assumed that we would be basing these projections on historical experience and essentially assuming randomness.[34] Although the modelers may assume randomness as experience grows via interactions with customers, we can learn about customer behavior and even influence it. And though it may be random who will go into an unknown restaurant, the positioning of the restaurant alters this by allocating resources to communicate to the targeted segment. More important, once the targeted segment enters into the restaurant's delivery system the strategic opportunity arises to influence behavior. A good service representative who knows the customer and has built a relationship with the customer will be able to influence the customer's choice to enhance the experience. However, just as there is an upside, there are potential risks depending on the strategic goals and the execution. If the strategist accepts that the first premise of strategy is to create value for the customer, then the customer service representative will spend the time to learn more about the customer to enhance the dining experience. It is worth noting that in this case the waitstaff is likely motivated to take actions to please the customer because of the role that tips play in a server's compensation. It is always important to understand the relations between incentives and behavior.[35]

Alternatively, suppose that the waitstaff work in a kiosk that earns profits through high turnover. The incentives may be to push whatever is faster or in greater supply. The customer may still see value because the customer knows the commodity being purchased and is interested in saving time. Here operational risks to be identified are those that arise from too hasty preparation and so on. Incentives here need to be managed differently for food preparers who should not be totally compensated for speed and servers whose compensation should be weighted toward turnover.

Let us suppose for a moment that all did not go according to plan for our two entrepreneurs and they are on the verge of bankruptcy. Late one night they are discussing their plight with some wealthy customers. The customers—one an investment banker and the other a partner in a boutique management consulting firm offer to invest in the restaurant. Although the original two partners are in trouble, they are not so desperate that they immediately accept the offer; rather, they reply that they need to know the terms of the offer and also to consider the implications.[36] The two customers offer a loan that will be sufficient to carry the restaurant for a year in return for 50% ownership. Although the original partners see the strict financial terms as fair, they are very concerned about some of the positive and negative covenants in the deal because these would seem to affect the actual running of the restaurant. The two customers like much about the restaurant, but they believe its failure is rooted in food that is too exotic, which reflects the original partners desire to become a highly rated restaurant. The original goal of the restaurant was to earn a Michelin star or three, not just to generate a financial return.

The new potential investors see the economic goals as important as the "artistic" goals and are insisting on controls to align the positioning and operation of the restaurant with their financial goals. They also want to remind the original partners that they have not been able to generate sufficient economic returns to accomplish their goals, so a change of positioning is needed. We are not going to explore the decision of the two partners because what we want to highlight is how outside investors change the game of strategy and risk. Once you seek outside investment on an ownership basis, the game changes.

NOTES

1. This limitation is not absolute but is at least partly contingent on market conditions.
2. Larry Fink, "Larry Fink's Annual Letter to CEOs: A Sense of Purpose," 2018, https://www.blackrock.com/corporate/investor-relations/larry-fink-ceo-letter. The 2019 letter took an even stronger stance:

   > *Unnerved by fundamental economic changes and the failure of government to provide lasting solutions, society is increasingly looking to companies, both public and private, to address pressing social and economic issues. These issues range from protecting the environment to retirement to gender and racial inequality, among others. Fueled in part by social media, public pressures on corporations build faster and reach further than ever before. ("Larry Fink's 2019 Letter to CEOs," 2019, https://www.blackrock.com/corporate/investor-relations/larry-fink-ceo-letter?mod=article_inline)*

Also see Richard L. Priem, Ryan Krause, Caterina Tantalo, and Ann McFadyen, "Promoting Long-Term Shareholder Value by 'Competing' for Essential Stakeholders: A New Multi-Sided Market Logic for Top Managers," *Academy of Management Perspectives* (2019).

3. See David M. Bersoff, "The Ideological Shopping Cart," 2017, https://www.edelman.com/post/ideological-shopping-cart.
4. See Edelman, "2017 Earned Brank Study," July 18, 2018, https://www.slideshare.net/EdelmanInsights/2017-edelman-earned-brand?from_action=save.
5. We recognize that we are greatly simplifying the definition to make our point.
6. We do recognize that from a strategic perspective there may be an upside if scarce credit is rationed to customers who purchase more services. We will discuss building customer relationships in Chapter 9.
7. Similar to all generalizations, there are exceptions, such as Capital One showed in their subprime credit cards or an FI that we came across that demonstrated how proper management can provide excess returns. For example, it can lend money to companies with credit ratings, say BBB, that may actually be, if assessed correctly, better quality or the best of the BBBs. In this case, the organization may get lower risk than a BBB but BBB pricing. Harris Bank used this approach in the late 1990s and their ELs were BBB+ for that portfolio, but their interest rates were BBB.
8. This is not a simple task. Customers can be unprofitable even if they have extensive relationships. For insights into this issue and to manage unprofitable customers, see Robert S. Kaplan and Steven R. Anderson, *Time-Driven Activity-Based Costing: A Simpler and More Powerful Pat to Higher Profits* (Boston: Harvard Business Review Press, 2007), Appendix A.
9. We do recognize that sometimes firms create needs that are not socially beneficial but we'll leave that discussion to our corporate social responsibility colleagues for now. However, it should be recognized that with our stakeholder approach it is an issue that affects the firm.
10. Deloitte, "Exploring Strategic Risk," July 20, 2018, https://www2.deloitte.com/content/dam/Deloitte/global/Documents/Governance-Risk-Compliance/dttl-grc-exploring-strategic-risk.pdf.
11. A holistic approach to risk means not discussing risk culture per se but the role of risk awareness in the overall organizational culture.
12. In Chapter 8 we will discuss the importance of challenging assumptions in managing model risk and scenario planning in managing strategic risk.
13. https://www.progressive.com/about/firsts/. Also see "Ethisphere Institute Names Progressive as a 2013 World's Most Ethical Company," September 18, 2019, https://progressive.mediaroom.com/2013-04-03-Ethisphere-Institute-names-Progressive-as-a-2013-Worlds-Most-Ethical-Company.
14. See Amy Hutton, "Beyond Financial Reporting—An Integrated Approach to Disclosure," *Journal of Applied Corporate Finance* 16, no. 4 (2004): 8–16; Tom King, "Making Financial Goals and Reporting Policies Serve Corporate Strategy: The Case of Progressive Insurance," *Journal of Applied Corporate Finance* 16, no. 4 (2004): 17–27; "Roundtable on Corporate Governance," *Journal of Applied Corporate Finance* 16 no. 4 (2004): 36–62.

15. Michael E. Porter, *Competitive Advantage: Creating and Sustaining Superior Performance* (New York: Free Press, 1985).
16. Progressive's relative performance is enhanced not by increasing its margins in this case but by diminishing its competitors by forcing new costs on them.
17. "Ethisphere Institute Names Progressive as a 2013 World's Most Ethical Company." For the reputation of one rival, see David J. Berardinelli, *From Good Hands to Boxing Gloves: The Dark Side of Insurance* (Portland, OR: Trial Guides, 2009).
18. Michael Hammer, "Deep Change: How Operational Innovation Can Transform Your Company," *Harvard Business Review* (April 2004).
19. Clearly the competitive context matters. If consumers have little choice, a bad reputation is far less damaging to both sales and possible recruiting.
20. He also notes that Walmart and Dell competed in the same way. Hammer, "Deep Change."
21. This might cause some readers to recall how Steve Jobs knew that the iPhone would cannibalize the iPod, but the future was worth the risk. If Apple didn't do this, someone else would.
22. Tom King (Interview), "Making Financial Goals and Reporting Policies Serve Corporate Strategy: The Case of Progressive Insurance," *Journal of Applied Corporate Finance* 16, no. 4 (2004): 18.
23. The actual goal is to have a combined ratio of 96%. This is unusual in an industry where many players make their money by investing the premiums. King, "Making Financial Goals and Reporting Policies Serve Corporate Strategy," 17. One can see how Progressive sought to balance potentially competing strategic goals.
24. King, "Making Financial Goals and Reporting Policies Serve Corporate Strategy," 17. Emphasis added.
25. See Shannon Bond, "Amazon Takes Machine-Learning to the Masses," *Financial Times* (December 3, 2018). Peter Weill has discussed how this model will transform financial services. See "Leading the Next Generation Business: Increased Customer Intimacy & Digital Ecosystems," LATAM CXO & Government Forum, October 6 and 7, 2015, https://www.the-digital-insurer.com/wp-content/uploadfau:s/2016/01/640-Peter_Weill.pdf. Also see Miklos Dietz, Matthieu Lemerle, Asheet Mehta, Joydeep Sengupta, and Nicole Zhou, "Remaking the Bank for an Ecosystem World," *McKinsey & Company Report*, October 2017, https://www.mckinsey.com/industries/financial-services/our-insights/remaking-the-bank-for-an-ecosystem-world.
26. This is elaborated on in Barry Libert and Megan Beck, *The Network Imperative: How to Survive and Grow in the Age of Digital Business Models* (Boston: Harvard Business Review Press, 2016).
27. "Five Fifty," *McKinsey Quarterly*, July 24, 2018, https://www.mckinsey.com/business-functions/digital-mckinsey/our-insights/five-fifty-platform-plays. Al. Also see Libert and Beck, *The Network Imperative*.
28. Diet, Lemerle, Mehta, Sengupta, and Zhou, "Remaking the Bank for an Ecosystem World."

29. This is done in a masterful fashion by Geoffrey G. Parker, Marshall W. Van Alstyne, and Sangeet Paul Choudary, *Platform Revolution: How Networked Markets Are Transforming the Economy and How to Make Them Work for You* (New York: W. W. Norton, 2016) and Michael A. Cusumano, Annabelle Gawer, and David B. Yoffie, *The Business of Platforms: Strategy in the Age of Digital Competition, Innovation, and Power* (New York: HarperBusiness, 2019).
30. Saul Hansell, "Amazon.com Is Expanding Beyond Books," *New York Times*, August 5, 1998, https://www.nytimes.com/1998/08/05/business/amazoncom-is-expanding-beyond-books.html. But Amazon continues its expansion in the book industry. See Jeffrey A. Trachtenberg, "'They Own the System': Amazon Rewrites Book Industry by Marching into Publishing," *The Wall Street Journal* (January 16, 2019).
31. Makeda Eastera and Dave Paresh, "Remember When Amazon Only Sold Books?" *LA Times* (June18, 2017). See also "Five Fifty."
32. Amazon ranked number 1 in the "2018 Harris Reputation Quotient Rankings" and it was ranked number 1 in three of the six dimensions of corporate reputation: products and services, financial performance, and emotional appeal. We will explore this further in Chapter 6, particularly the emotional appeal dimension, which might strike you as strange. See the "2018 Harris Poll Reputation Quotient Rankings," July 24, 2018, https://theharrispoll.com/reputation-quotient/.
33. This is becoming an increasingly important focus of academic research. See Tomi Laamanen, Jeffrey Pfeffer, Ke Rong, Andrew Van de Ven, "Editors' Introduction: Business Models, Ecosystems, and Society in the Sharing Economy," *Academy of Management Discoveries* 4, no. 3 (2018) and the other articles in the special issue.
34. Assumptions about randomness play a major role in risk management. See, for example, Nassim Nicholas Taleb, *Fooled by Randomness,* 2nd updated ed. (New York: Random House, 2008) or *The Black Swan: The Impact of the Highly Improbable,* 2nd ed. (New York: Random House, 2010).
35. Readers may note the introduction of the agency issue, which has received considerable attention in the finance and governance literature. We will pick up on this topic in Chapter 10.
36. Finding the right investor is key to success. See Daniel Thomas and Alice Hancock, "Jeremy King Says Private Equity No Recipe for Restaurant Success," *Financial Times* (May 30, 2019).

CHAPTER 7

What Reputation Do We Want? With Whom?

In Chapter 6 we discussed the multiple dimensions of reputation risk. Old-style risk managers may think that if they manage all the risks below reputation risk on the risk pyramid that all is well. That is not so—it is necessary but not sufficient. It is table stakes. Reputation risk is important because it captures the entirety of how the organization's promises (value proposition) are met. The strategic questions are *what reputation do you want and with whom?* The desired reputation captures the content of your value proposition and your ability to deliver on it. The "who" identifies your target market and introduces the saliency of stakeholders. You can't be everything to everybody.[1] Strategy is about making choices, which is made clear when you focus on reputation management. And the threats to corporate reputations are increasing in this age of social media.[2]

Stephen Kehoe, Global Chair, Reputation at Edelman, of Edelman Trust Barometer fame, asserted the following: "Guided by the belief that increasing the level of trust in a company is the cornerstone of protecting reputations and strengthening relationships, we work in close partnership with corporate clients to engage employees, deepen customer relationships, attract investors and align government and public interests."[3] Although we recognize that trust and reputation are not the same things, we do believe they are highly correlated. Reputation means that a target group of stakeholders, potential customers, employees, suppliers, and regulators have expectations concerning how they will be treated. This relates to our overarching concern with uncertainty: although we do not know what the results of an interaction with an organization will be, we do have expectations. These expectations will either lessen or heighten our uncertainty about dealing with the organization. Once we realize the limitations of rational analysis, then we must accept the importance of emotions, such as trust. David R. Koenig makes this clear in connection to customers:

> *Articulating the meaning of trust is difficult, because trust is a feeling. Alex Todd, formerly the Chief Executive Officer of Canadian advisory firm Trust Enablement, defines trust both as "a person's willingness to accept (and/or increase) their vulnerability" and "acceptable uncertainty." In our Value Equation, acceptable uncertainty is quantified by the risk premium we demand in order to feel adequately compensated for the risk we perceive or for the lack of trust we feel. Our absolute and relative choices help us gauge how much trust exists in a given relationship.*[4]

Although the science of risk management may calculate the appropriate risk premium, the perception of risk by stakeholders is an important determinant of the premium, and reputation management is a basic element in managing the premium.

To understand the relationship between risk and strategy we need to provide a broader understanding of risks and their interactions. In Figure 7.1, shown previously as Figure 4.2, we have modified Royal Bank of Canada's risk pyramid because our concern now is less with control and more with inclusiveness of the thought process. So, although we can control to some extent the elements below "strategic" we need to consider uncertainty, or what we can't completely control.

Recall that we specifically chose the 2014 version over more recent versions because of the portrayal of how operational risk affects all the financial risks. The Basel Committee (2011) notes that "operational risk is inherent in all banking products, activities, processes and systems."[5] We hold that this is true for all corporate products, activities, and systems, not just banking, and that operational risk affects all other risks and, more important, is the area of risk that can be most easily associated with competitive advantage, as David Apgar has suggested.[6] Although superior risk management capabilities in the areas of financial risk may be the source of competitive advantage, the use of probability theory based on randomness limits their potential as learning areas.[7] This is not true for many areas of operational risk.

If we return to our restaurant story, the importance of operations and operational risk comes alive. The consistent excellence of the chef's food depends on her ability to manage a number of operational issues, from

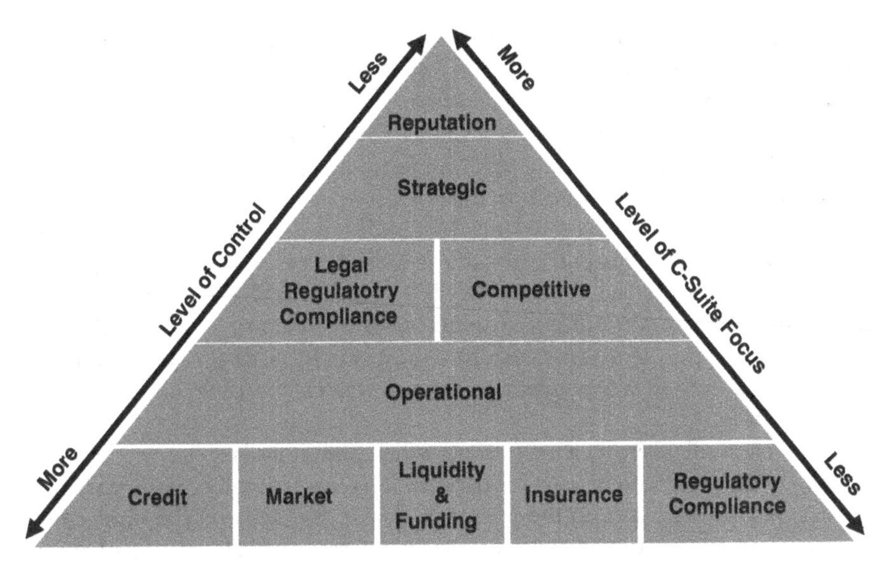

FIGURE 7.1 A Modified Strategy Risk Pyramid Emphasizing the Challenge of Strategy and Reputation Risk
Source: Royal Bank of Canada Annual Report 2014, The Royal Bank of Canada's Risk Governance Framework (2014), 49–50. © 2014, Royal Bank of Canada.

sourcing food to managing the kitchen staff to the appropriate standards of excellence and health.[8] Yet, it is important to understand that human skills will necessarily lead to some variation; the challenge is to keep those variations within an acceptable range—what we would call *risk tolerances*. But we also need to understand that there are other uncontrollable elements that can be monitored but are challenging. Agricultural items vary—it is part of what makes dining enjoyable. But it makes achieving consistency a challenge. But the challenge of the food is dwarfed by the challenge of maintaining a consistent environment. Certainly, the culture of the restaurant is manageable through the right human resource policies, but the ambience of a restaurant or most service organizations is affected by the customers. How do you deal with inappropriate customers?[9] Think of this as an example of uncontrollable or exogenous events.

In an increasingly polarized society, this is becoming an important issue. Remember what happened when Sarah Huckabee Sanders, then the White House press secretary for President Trump, was asked to leave the Red Hen restaurant in Lexington, Virginia, because the staff were uncomfortable serving her.[10] Whether one approves of this or not, it raises an important question of the relationship between stakeholder management and reputation. Suppose the owner insisted that Sanders be served. Would the kitchen or waitstaff put forward their best effort or not? Even worse, would they deliberately sabotage the meal? Let's give them the benefit of the doubt and accept that they would behave professionally, as going to the owner with their complaint demonstrated. If their heart isn't in it, wouldn't Sanders's experience be lower than the norm? So, Sanders is disappointed and decides not to return. But that isn't the end of the story for two reasons. First, potentially there would be the negative word of mouth from Sanders to her social circle. But more important, what would be the impact on the other diners? The restaurant may lose some customers and gain some new loyal customers, but the net gain/loss is dependent on the targeted customer segment and specific situation.[11]

We have all been in a restaurant when someone is behaving obnoxiously.[12] We have often seen owners address the situation with patience before occasionally asking the patron to leave. But what if the obnoxious customer is a regular and most of the other diners are from out of town attending a convention? Is the course of action the same? Whatever the decision, expect it to be amplified by social media. Social media turn local (private) events into global public ones.

This example clearly illustrates why reputation risk is less controllable than strategic risk: because of the connection to external stakeholders—with whom the organization may not directly interact. Although we are sympathetic to placing reputation and strategic response side by side because of the implicit recognition of reputation as a strategic asset, we also believe that in the age of social media the firm has less control over its reputation than it does its strategy—even given the challenges of competitive response in a highly interdependent world.[13] Complexity has certainly enhanced the strategic challenge.[14]

What is reputation risk? Consider this definition for the *Financial Times of London:*

> *A company's reputation is perhaps its most valuable asset. Reputational risk is the possible loss of the organisation's reputational capital. Imagine that the company has an account similar to a bank account that they are either filling up or depleting. Every time the company does something good, its reputational capital account goes up; every time the company does something bad, or is accused of doing something bad, the account goes down.*

> *The commercial bank examination, which is a supervisory manual published by the Federal Reserve Board in the US to provide guidance in bank inspections, defines reputational risk as the potential loss in reputational capital based on either real or perceived losses in reputational capital. In fact,* **the manual states very clearly that a company can lose its reputation whether allegations are true or not.**[15]

The last phrase is key—"whether allegations are true or not." This is an important factor in making reputation risk less controllable than many other risks. It would be unfair to the companies who have endured false accusations to list them here but we are certain all readers will have recollections of false accusations that drew considerable press, and the later, more truthful account barely got covered.[16] This also takes us back to the start of this chapter: we are less likely to believe negative reports about organizations we trust.

A primary reason for thinking that reputation risk is less controllable is the difficulty in knowing what is being said about you in the cyber world. A classic example is the Starbucks' and 9/11 incident when a Starbucks near the twin towers charged first responders $130 for three cases of water needed to treat victims.[17] It should be noted that Starbucks quickly apologized and did everything they could to redress the situation, but the rumor persisted. We want to use the Starbucks example to illustrate another dimension as to why reputation risk is so difficult to manage. Rules and procedures that are established to control discretionary behavior of employees in normal times can lead to disastrous behavior in abnormal times. Our very tools for managing operational risk are turned against us. And abnormal times are becoming increasingly common. Rumors arising from abnormal times are further exacerbated by increasing polarization. For example, the 2017 Harris Reputation Quotient (RQ)® Poll noted the polarization between Democrats and Republicans over which companies they admired.[18]

Although we will return to this polarization, it is important to first examine the different dimension of reputation and here the Harris Poll provides a very useful guide. The Harris Poll considers six dimensions and 20 attributes of reputation:

Social Responsibility

- Supports good causes
- Environmental responsibility
- Community responsibility

Products and Services

- High-quality products and services
- Innovative
- Good value for the money
- Stands behind products and services

Emotional Appeal

- Feel good about
- Trust
- Admire and respect

Vision and Leadership

- Market opportunities
- Excellent leadership
- Clear vision for the future

Financial Performance

- Outperforms competitors
- Record of profitability
- Low-risk investment
- Growth prospects

Workplace Environment[19]

- Rewards employees fairly
- Good place to work
- Has good employees

If you thought that delivering on your value proposition was all you needed to do to score high in the poll, you now know you were sadly mistaken. Emotional appeal, which makes buyers feel good and give you their trust because of their admiration and respect, is very important. The report notes these results:

- Only Wegmans and Chick-fil-A crack the top 10 on each of the six RQ dimensions.
- Notably, whereas 28 companies score an "excellent" rating (80+) for products and services, only 10 have an excellent rating for social responsibility.[20]

Reputation management takes you beyond the realm of products and services and even financial performance into areas often not considered in an organization's strategy and consequently not measured as frequently or by as many.

There is a danger in taking examples from one year, and one of the advantages of using the Harris Poll is it gives you a lengthy time series. However, it is worth noting that even reaching the top 10 on all six dimensions does not ensure overall leadership among the 14 companies that were rated excellent (a score of 80 or higher):

1. Amazon.com 83.22
2. Wegmans 82.75
3. Tesla Motors 81.96
4. Chick-fil-A 81.68
5. The Walt Disney Company 81.53
6. HEB Grocery* 81.14[21]
7. UPS 81.12
8. Publix Super Markets 80.81
9. Patagonia* 80.44
10. Aldi 80.43
11. Microsoft 80.42
12. Nike 80.24 13
13. The Kraft Heinz Company 80.15
14. Kellogg Company 80.00

The story of 2018 was the ascendancy of groceries and the fall of some tech companies, notably Apple and Google.[22] But what is also striking is the three dimensions in which Amazon placed first—products and services, emotional appeal, and financial performance. Although the classic dimensions are not enough, they are clearly very important. But what stands out to us is that Amazon led in emotional appeal.

We would have thought of an e-commerce site as being highly transactional, not usually a basis for emotional appeal. But on reflection, we realize that Amazon has made the transition so many firms are attempting—the transition from seller to advisor—or to put it differently, from a product focus to a relationship focus. Amazon doesn't sell; it advises you. It reminds you of what you want to purchase. The power of its predictive analytics not only increases sales but also forges an emotional appeal. Understanding how the emotional bond is forged takes us into an analysis of Amazon's competitive advantage: predictive analytics.

Amazon does not wait for you to experience a need or desire for a book or a DVD or increasingly anything; rather, it anticipates that you will be interested in books, movies, or items related to what you have purchased in the past or put on your wish list. It sends you a notice that the item is, or soon will be, available. It is like a friend advising you that one of your favorite authors has a new book. Over time, you stop searching for items and become reliant on Amazon. You save time on search costs, while Amazon solidifies its hold on you as a customer and reduces your price sensitivity. Repeat sales are not only more profitable but also the additional data enhance Amazon's competitive advantage over competitors. Another feature of Amazon's predictive analytics enables it to improve customer service too via "anticipatory shipping":

> *It was revealed recently that Amazon.com has obtained a patent for what it calls "anticipatory shipping"—a system of delivering products to customers before they place an order. As the Wall Street Journal reported, "Amazon says it may box and ship products it expects customers in a specific area will want—based on previous orders and other factors . . . According to the patent, the packages could wait at the shippers' hubs or on trucks until an order arrives." If implemented well, this strategy has the potential to take predictive analytics to the next level, allowing the data-savvy company to greatly expand its base of loyal customers.*[23]

Amazon's brilliance is shown in its ability to monetize its competitive advantage.[24] If you search the net for "Amazon and predictive analytics" you will quickly come to AWS (https://aws.Amazon.com/aml/).[25] Although AWS may be relatively new to you, this cloud business is growing fast and is responsible for most of Amazon's profits.[26] On this site, you can learn using Amazon Machine Learning to build your own predictive models. Not only does this monetize what would have been simply a cost center when others purchase the capability but also, by reducing the barriers for others to enter this high-tech world, it discourages others from building the capacity and become a competitor in this field.[27] It preempts the market and makes its competitive position sustainable.

What makes Amazon such a formidable competitor is how the various elements of its strategy are mutually reinforcing and revenue generating. Amazon doesn't pay to get information; it gains information by selling you ever more products that enable it to sell you ever more products and strengthen its competitive advantage at the same time. A brilliant strategy that clearly demonstrates how a platform strategy leads to a new approach to horizontal diversification.[28]

Ironically, Amazon's value proposition as advisor is potentially its weak spot. The more we "trust" Amazon to anticipate our wants and desires, the more damaging any failure to anticipate these becomes. Admittedly, the most likely cause of this would be in purchases of goods made outside the Amazon platform, which is of course a spur to horizontal expansion. But the other alternative is a family member using your account. Sharing an account does have certain advantages from the customer's perspective, but it does lead to a confusing person from Amazon's point of view. We are not thinking so much of embarrassing episodes such as Target's misstep in using predictive analytics to identify pregnant women and send them coupons for appropriate products.[29] The problem was that coupons were sent to a pregnant teen who had not informed her parents she was pregnant. The father was outraged and thought the coupons were encouraging his daughter to get pregnant. There are other potential problems, such as Amazon seeing customers as schizophrenic. Over time, artificial intelligence may be able to sort out how many individuals are using an account, but until it does, there is the potential for some embarrassing moments. Or, more important, the reason for some customers to doubt Amazon's recommendations. Although many will laugh and understand what has happened, will everyone?

MANAGING REPUTATION RISK

As was pointed out in 2007, to manage reputation risk it is necessary to objectively assess what your reputation is and consider the gap between the reputation you want and the reputation that you have.[30] This requires an appreciation of how you are perceived by the salient stakeholders. Note that we emphasize salient stakeholders, by which we mean those who have an impact on your strategy. This ties to the segments that you are targeting with your value proposition. It should also be noted that salience will be somewhat contingent because what matters can change from time to time, so you must manage reputation like everything else in a dynamic context. We also emphasize that it is essential to focus on the elements that differentiate you from your competitors because these facets will be key to your reputation.

Often reputation risk management is tied to disasters, so we want to stress the upside of reputation risk as an essential everyday task of strategic management.[31] Let us return to your value proposition. It is a promise to customers/clients that sets expectations about your performance. You manage your brand in an effort to set the appropriate expectations, but to some degree the perceptions of your (potential) customers are beyond your control. Remember how Royal Bank of Canada's risk pyramid has reputation risk as less controllable than many other risks. Events beyond your control can and will influence perceptions in the marketplace. For example, as we are writing this, trade battles are making the country of origin more important than they were before. Although this will damage some brands, it enhances others, such as local brands over imports.

To maximize the strategic value of reputation the firm must separate what are table stakes to what is differentiating for the firm's value proposition. Meeting the industry standards will not lead to an enhanced reputation or profits. What makes your offering valuable to a specific segment will. Subaru's emphasis on safety, Apple's ease of use, and Amazon's massive offerings all differentiate them from competitors. If you return to the 2018 Harris Poll, look at where Amazon excels—products and services, emotional appeal, and financial performance. Amazon's commitment to expanding its product offerings is key to the other two and further protects its position against rivals. Interestingly, it does not make the top 10 in social responsibility and is 10th in workplace environment. Amazon's customers care about the products and services and less so about social responsibility, including key stakeholders such as employees.[32]

Let us look at another interesting evolving class of reputations, one that is focused on trust: the battle between banks and technology companies. If you examine the 2018 Harris Poll[33] you will discover that the highest-ranked financial service company is USAA at 34, which is rated as having a very good reputation. The next highest group rated as good is American Express, ranked at 50, and JP Morgan Chase at 63. Then we have the group rated as fair—Citigroup (68) and AIG (84)—then a group labeled as having a poor reputation—Bank of America (85), Goldman Sachs (92), and Wells Fargo (97).

Yet, a recent study concerning whom people trust with their money by Bain & Company shows that although large tech companies are catching up to the banks in this area they still lag.[34] This takes us back to the critical questions of *trust whom, for what*? Although consumers may trust high-tech firms more than banks in general, they do not in the specific area of money management. But as Amazon has shown with its horizontal expansion, trust in one area can be a platform to grow into other areas, especially in times of disruption. Bain & Company articulate the problem well:

> *Many consumers are open to buying financial products from established tech firms . . . The greatest latent demand exists in countries where the bank branch experience is more time-consuming and cumbersome, such as India and Mexico; there, 91% and 81% of respondents, respectively, expressed a willingness to run their finances through major tech firms. By contrast, where banks have taken some of the pain out of banking by digitalizing most routine transactions, as in the Netherlands, they have inoculated themselves to some extent against the threat.*[35]

The point is clear, traditional banks have an advantage if they adjust to shifts in consumer preferences, but if they don't do it with reasonable speed, they will fall victims to firms with greater expertise in the new area or to firms that are timelier in making consumers aware of new products. Again, Bain found that consumers were open to offerings from other banks, especially via digital channels.[36] The lesson for banks is that reputation management is about the future. Counting stability rooted in the past in a time of disruption is a very risky strategy, as Bain points out:

> *Consumers' expectations keep rising as people grow accustomed to simple, convenient digital channels in other parts of their lives. If banks don't reorient their approach and radically accelerate their rate of progress, loyalty will suffer, and they will watch technology firms poach more business. Meanwhile, their economics will erode as too many routine transactions continue to flow through expensive branch and call-center networks.*[37]

We draw on banks because that is our area of greatest familiarity, but the lessons should be clear for all organizations. In an era of disruptive change, being slow to respond isn't damaging, it's fatal.

The focus in managing reputation risk is to understand the gap between performance and expectations. As Garry Honey has noted, it is quite possible that your performance exceeds expectations.[38] In this case, you have an underleveraged asset. That is what the success of Amazon Cash and growth in lending to small merchants demonstrate.[39] Generally, though, we suspect that executives suffer like Icarus and overestimate the reputations of their firms. For large firms, surveys such as the Harris Poll, or Edelman's Trust Barometer, offer a healthy corrective. But it must also be recognized that such broad measures may not be appropriate for every firm. But it is a starting point and disregarding them without careful analysis would be a mistake.

But the starting point must be to ask what reputation you want. What fits with your value proposition and what trade-offs will you have to make? How do you measure it? These are difficult decisions, but they can't be left to chance. If reputation is an important asset, then it must be managed, and risk-managed, like any other important asset.

NOTES

1. For some surprising aspects of reputation, see David Chandler, Francisco Polidoro Jr., and Wei Yang "When Is It Good to Be Bad? Contrasting Effects of Multiple Reputations for Bad Behavior on Media Coverage of Serious Organizational errors," *Academy of Management Journal* (2019).

2. According to McKinsey, more incidents are turning into full-blown crises. See Sanjay Kalavar and Mihir Mysore, "Are You Prepared for a Corporate Crisis," *McKinsey Quarterly* (April 2017).
3. Stephen Kehoe, "Corporate Reputation," Edelman, 2019, https://www.edelman.com/expertise/corporate-reputation.
4. David R. Koenig, *Governance Reimagined: Organizational Design, Risk, and Value Creation* (Northfield, MN: B Right Governance Publications, 2018), 108. "Trust Enabling Strategies," trustenablement.com (July 14, 2018).
5. Basel Committee on Banking Supervision, *Principles for the Sound Management of Operational Risk*, June 2011, http://www.bis.org/publ/bcbs195.pdf.
6. See David Apgar, *Risk Intelligence: Learning to Manage What We Don't Know* (Boston: Harvard Business Review Press, 2006).
7. See Nassim Nicholas Taleb, *Fooled by Randomness: The Hidden Role of Chance in Life and in the Markets (Incerto)*, updated (New York: Random House, 2008). There are, of course, exceptions, as Capital One in subprime credit cards, Wells Fargo in Small Business lending, or the mid-market lender discussed previously.
8. For those interested in this area, see Anthony Bourdain, *Kitchen Confidential* (New York: Bloomsbury USA, 2008).
9. This is an important issue for all organizations, see Vikas Mittal, Matthew Sarkees, and Feisal Murshed, "The Right Way to Manage Unprofitable Customers," *Harvard Business Review* (April 2008).
10. For those unfamiliar with the incident and its aftermath, see the opinion piece by the owner of the Red Hen, Stephanie Wilkinson: "I Own the Red Hen Restaurant That Asked Sarah Sanders to Leave. Resistance Isn't Futile," *The Washington Post*, May 14, 2019, https://www.washingtonpost.com/opinions/i-own-the-red-hen-restaurant-that-asked-sarah-sanders-to-leave-resistance-isnt-futile/2019/05/14/125b4742-75a8-11e9-b7ae-390de4259661_story.html.
11. A study conducted by the Jay H. Baker Retailing Initiative at Wharton found the following:

> *"Only 6% of shoppers who experienced a problem with a retailer contacted the company, but 31% went on to tell friends, family or colleagues what happened. Of those, 8% told one person, another 8% told two people, but 6% told six or more people. Even though these shoppers don't share their pain with the store, they do share their pain with other people, apparently quite a* few *other people," says Hoch. Overall, if 100 people have a bad experience, a retailer stands to lose between 32 and 36 current or potential customers, according to the study. (Knowledge@Wharton "Beware of Dissatisfied Consumers: They Like to Blab," March 8, 2006, http://knowledge.wharton.upenn.edu/article/beware-of-dissatisfied-consumers-they-like-to-blab/)*

One can only assume that the growth of social media has amplified these results since the study was done a decade and a half ago.
12. See Mittal, Sarkees, and Murshed, "The Right Way to Manage Unprofitable Customers."

13. See Jessica Brown, "How Social Media Could Ruin Your Business," BBC News, July 9, 2019, https://www.bbc.com/news/business-48871456.
14. See Rick Nason, *It's Not Complicated: The Art and Science of Complexity for Business Success* (Toronto: Rotman University of Toronto Press, 2017).
15. Emphasis added. http://markets.ft.com/research/Lexicon/Term?term=reputational-risk.
16. See Ronald J. Alsop, *The 18 Immutable Laws of Corporate Reputation: Creating, Protecting and Repairing Your Most Valuable Asset* (New York: Free Press, 2004) for how certain false claims were impossible to refute.
17. See *The Guardian*, "Starbucks Charged Rescuers for Water" (September 26, 2001).
18. PR Newswire, "Harris Poll: Corporate Reputation Politically Polarized as Companies Wrestle with Taking a Stand for Their Values," August 3, 2018, https://www.prnewswire.com/news-releases/harris-poll-corporate-reputation-politically-polarized-as-companies-wrestle-with-taking-a-stand-for-their-values-300404867.html.
19. See the Harris Poll, August 3, 2018, https://theharrispoll.com/wp-content/uploads/2018/07/2018-HARRIS-POLL-RQ_2-Summary-Report_FNL.pdf.
20. The Harris Poll, 16.
21. HEB is a privately owned grocery chain out of San Antonio. See https://www.heb.com/. Asterisks (*) indicate that the company is new to the most visible list in 2018.
22. See Stephen Nellis, "Apple, Google See Reputation of Corporate Brands Tumble in Survey," Reuters, March 13, 2018, https://www.google.ca/webhp?hl=en&sa=X&ved=0ahUKEwiQ9LbmndHcAhVp9IMKHbMUAzAQPAgD.
23. Praveen Kopalle, "Why Amazon's Anticipatory Shipping Is Pure Genius," *Forbes*, January 28, 2014, https://www.forbes.com/sites/onmarketing/2014/01/28/why-amazons-anticipatory-shipping-is-pure-genius/#3151652f4605.
24. See Lara O'Reilly and Laura Stevens, "Amazon, with Little Fanfare, Emerges as an Advertising Giant," *The Wall Street Journal* (November 27, 2018).
25. See Amazon Machine Learning, https://aws.amazon.com/aml/.
26. See Lex, "Amazon: AWSome," *The Financial Times* (December 5, 2018) and O'Reilly and Stevens, "Amazon, with Little Fanfare, Emerges as an Advertising Giant."
27. See Shannon Bond, "Amazon Takes Machine-Learning to the Masses," *Financial Times* (December 3, 2018).
28. Rather than challenging any of Richard Rumelt's findings in his classic piece, it is more correct to see how the meaning of *relatedness* is changed or expanded. See, for example, Richard Rumelt, "Strategy, Structure, and Economic Performance," *Journal of Behavioral Economics* (June 1975) and "Diversification Strategy and Profitability," *Strategic Management Journal* 3, no. 4 (1982). Amazon has further capitalized on this by expanding into advertising. See O'Reilly and Stevens, "Amazon, with Little Fanfare, Emerges as an Advertising Giant" and Suzanne Vranica, "Amazon's Rise in Ad Searches Dents Google's Dominance," *The Wall Street Journal* (April 4, 2019).

29. See Charles Duhigg, "How Companies Learn Your Secrets," *New York Times Magazine*, February 16, 2012, https://www.nytimes.com/2012/02/19/magazine/shopping-habits.html.
30. Robert G. Eccles, Scott C. Newquist, and Roland Schatz, "Reputation and Its Risks," *Harvard Business Review* (February 2007).
31. For a recent focus on reputation and disasters, see Anthony Fitzsimmons and Derek Atkins, *Rethinking Reputational Risk: How to Manage the Risks That Can Ruin Your Business, Your Reputation and You* (London: Kogan Page, 2017). We do not underestimate the importance of responding to disasters but prefer to focus on anticipating and avoiding these incidents.
32. Whether treatment of employees will have a greater impact on service quality when labor markets loosen and better employees have choices remains to be seen. As always, market conditions matter. See Michael Sainato, "Exploited Amazon Workers Need a Union. When Will They Get One?" *The Guardian*, July 8, 2018, https://www.theguardian.com/commentisfree/2018/jul/08/amazon-jeff-bezos-unionize-working-conditions. Michael Sainato, "Accidents at Amazon: Workers Left to Suffer after Warehouse Injuries," *The Guardian,* July 30, 2018, https://www.theguardian.com/technology/2018/jul/30/accidents-at-amazon-workers-left-to-suffer-after-warehouse-injuries. Also see Susan Adams, "How People Who Work for Amazon Really Feel," *Forbes,* August 18, 2015, https://www.forbes.com/sites/susanadams/2015/08/18/how-people-who-work-for-amazon-really-feel/#647da3bb3305.
33. Gerard Du Toit and Maureen Burns, "Evolving the Customer Experience in Banking," Bain & Company (2017): 1, http://www.bain.de/Images/BAIN_REPORT_Evolving_the_Customer_Experience_in_Banking.pdf.
34. See Gerard Du Toit and Maureen Burns, "Why Consumers Trust Amazon Almost as Much as Banks," Bain & Company (November 2017). This originally appeared on Forbes.com, https://www.bain.com/insights/why-consumers-trust-amazon-almost-as-much-as-banks-forbes/.
35. Du Toit and Burns, "Evolving the Customer Experience in Banking," 1.
36. Du Toit and Burns, "Evolving the Customer Experience in Banking," 31–34.
37. Du Toit and Burns, "Evolving the Customer Experience in Banking," 7.
38. Garry Honey, "Reputation Risk: Challenges for the Insurance Market," Emerging Risks Workshop, AIRIC Conference, June 12, 2012, https://pdfs.semanticscholar.org/presentation/1e97/fc83566acb3c585aa453ce1919c9e95226f2.pdf.
39. Du Toit and Burns, "Evolving the Customer Experience in Banking," 1.

CHAPTER 8

Uncertainty, Scenario Planning, and Real Options

There are few things we know about the future, except that it is uncertain. Although we may in our daily lives forecast a future that looks pretty much like today, the existence of surprises and black swans is a warning not to place too much confidence in these linear projections.[1] The art of strategy is not just about the best positioning for today but the best positioning for the long term. In the highly interconnected world in which we live and develop our plans, shocks are the new normal. As we are writing this, forecasters are concerned how the US-Iran dispute will affect myriad previously loosely correlated events. The 2018 murder of Jamal Khashoggi, a Saudi citizen living in self-imposed exile, sent shock waves into Middle East relations. Khashoggi was a columnist for the *Washington Post* and a critic of the Saudi regime who was murdered after being lured into the Saudi Consulate in Istanbul. A United Nations special rapporteur concluded that Khashoggi was "the victim of a deliberated, premeditated execution, an extrajudicial killing for which the state of Saudi Arabia is responsible."[2] More recently, in the aftermath of the US killing Qasem Soleimani in a drone attack in Baghdad, Iranian forces shot down a Ukrainian passenger jet killing 176 people. Now, it is unclear what the geopolitical situation is. However, globalization, which has created an increasingly interdependent world, has led to interactions that are increasingly difficult, if not impossible, to predict and hence difficult to prepare for, as pandemics clearly show.[3] *But the inability to predict is not the same as being ill-prepared.*

One of us remembers taking a course on economic forecasting and the statement by the learned professor about forecasting. The one thing you know for certain is you will be wrong. However, the process of going through building a forecast forces you to consider various possible interactions. Moreover, when you test your forecast against possible changes in key variables, you will learn what your forecast is sensitive to and what it is not. Given that it is impossible to include all variables and interactions, the process of selecting the variables and interactions is a learning process. If it is carried out in a group or team setting, a deeper understanding of what will drive the future should emerge. As we stress to the executive groups we work with, try to determine which forces are relatively stable and which are volatile or potentially volatile. This approach gives you the weft and warp of possible futures.

Events that heighten previously loosely correlated events may give us a window into emerging risks. The identification of emerging risks relies on these considerations:

- Deep, broad, and multidisciplinary learning and experience
- Combined analytical and intuitive thinking
- Multiple perspectives—in-out, macro-micro, past-present-future
- Knowledge of diverse human behaviors at a practical level
- Thinking about entanglements and connections rather than isolates
- Willingness to take contrarian views

The assessment following the identification requires a similar skill set, which can deal with these issues:

- No recognizable patterns, uncertain significance, ambiguous consequences, and implications
- Unknown unknowns—you only know ex post what you needed to know ex ante
- Complex interactions and interconnectedness, which require enterprise and risk-wide perspective
- Effects that may be systemic and outside of organization sightlines and control

Preparing for emerging risk is akin to preparing for uncertainty. The framework most suited for this is scenario planning, and it requires a process very similar to what we discussed in the identification and assessment of emerging risks. A pioneer of scenario planning, Pierre Wack of Shell, provides insight into the starting point for scenarios:

> *Wack identified three essential starting points for corporate strategy: global scenarios, competitive positioning, and strategic vision.*

> *The first represents the world of possibility, the second the world of relativity, and the third the world of creativity. The challenge in effective scenario work is to go beyond the usual strategic focus on current trends and competitive positioning.*[4]

As this makes clear, scenario planning is an integrative and complex process. Wack describes a process that assumes change—the future—will not mirror the past and thus calls for a creative response. The positioning theme makes clear the importance of analysis, but given it is impossible to have data about the future, analysis can never get us all the way there. There must be creativity.

In terms of creativity, or "the vision thing," as it has been somewhat derisively labeled, vision is meant to be inclusive. Others can participate in a vision, as Steve Jobs and Apple clearly have demonstrated. And it is this inclusiveness that can give power to the process. However, this demands authenticity on the part of leadership to offset the potential pitfalls of groupthink or the official company history.[5] It also involves making fundamental methodological assumptions, as Wack did:

> *Credit for originating scenario planning often goes to the American game theorist and futurist Herman Kahn. However, a form of the practice emerged simultaneously in France in the work of Gaston Berger, Bertrand de Jouvenel, and others. The American approach came to emphasize probability, with degrees of likelihood assigned to various outcomes, while the French approach focused more on what should happen. Newland and Wack, aware of both, steered clear of probabilistic forecasts and normative statements and instead insisted that scenarios should first and foremost be plausible.*

The appeal of Wack's approach is that it is pragmatic. Just as we mentioned the issues that arise from the asymptotic nature of the normal curve, there is little point in worrying about events that are linked to unexpected losses that will bankrupt the firm. Or is there? The use of probabilities is a topic we need to return to later in this chapter.

The value of scenario planning lies primarily in how it can stimulate conversations in an organization. For most companies, scenario planning is essential in creating the base case for the long-term budget. A fascinating dialogue between Peter Schwartz and Kees van der Hijden elaborates on the process aspect of scenario planning. By bringing different players to the table it is possible to have a conversation that serves to integrate the diverse parts of an organization.[6] Arie de Geus stressed that this was possible because "scenarios help to create language and language creates reality

(Wittgenstein)."[7] The common language is the precursor to developing the content, which becomes the strategy. The crux of the problem is getting the process right because this is essential to produce the necessary output. As Peter Schwartz has commented, this facilitates a reframing of the uncertainties and brings the underlying structural interconnections to the fore.[8]

Schwartz outlines the conditions for holding a strategic conversation in a section entitled "User's Guide: How to Hold a Strategic Conversation":

1. Create a hospitable climate.
2. Establish an initial group including key decision-makers and outsiders.
   a. Outsiders can promote diversity of views and knowledge.
3. Include outside information and people.
4. Look ahead far in advance of decisions.
   a. Focus on decisions.
   b. The process takes time to develop.
   c. Instill learning orientation.
5. Begin by looking at the present and past.
   a. Identify drivers of change and how they have and are behaving—demography, consumer tastes, and so on.
6. Conduct preliminary work in smaller groups.
   a. Work on diversity and consensus (paradox mirroring centralization-decentralization tension).
   b. Consider diversity of views; decision point forces convergence.
7. Play out the conversation.
   a. Ask, "What are we going to do as an organization?" This links formulation and implementation.
   b. Diffuse the process to tap into expertise.
8. Live in a permanent strategic conversation.
   a. Embed strategic and risk thinking in the organization.
   b. Constantly challenge the "official future."
   c. Promote diversity without divergence.
   d. Balance the forces of continuity and discontinuity.[9]

Interestingly and importantly, step 1 states the necessary organizational context—a hospitable climate. But what does this mean? He means an organizational culture that is open to diverse views, where people are not overpowered by the dominant views of the organization. In a sense it means being open to having your ideas rejected but being taken seriously. Without the right culture, the second and third steps of inviting key decision-makers and outsiders won't work. And outsiders are important to countering excessive optimism or hubris of senior executives. They might show up once, but not too often if their views are not contributing to the discussion. Daniel Kahneman,[10] the Nobel Prize–winning psychologist and economist, has emphasized the importance of the "outside view" as a corrective to optimistic bias in forecasts.[11] The outside view is a necessary corrective to flawed decision processes that account for many business failures:

> *We don't believe that the high number of business failures is best explained as the result of rational choices gone wrong. Rather, we see it as a consequence of flawed decision making. When forecasting the outcomes of risky projects, executives all too easily fall victim to what psychologists call the planning fallacy. In its grip, managers make decisions based on delusional optimism rather than on a rational weighting of gains, losses, and probabilities.*

In step 2, note the word *initial*—the initiation of the process demands the participation of senior executives to show that this is a significant undertaking, not just a feel-good session. It is this group that can identify the appropriate outsiders and have the connections or know-how to identify and attract them. The inclusion of outsiders in step 3 demonstrates a willingness to challenge the official views, but just as importantly it emphasizes the need to have access to all the necessary inputs. Again, the word *initial* is significant because as the process unfolds the need for more and different inputs will become clear.

The time frame is long because this is not a process that can be rushed. Developing the inaugural scenario will especially take considerable time. A tight deadline would be in conflict with the hospitable climate because people may limit diversity in a rush to get to consensus. In the fourth step, the focus on decisions helps to determine the parameters for what is significant in the past and present. Recognizing that you can't assemble all the data, it is imperative to have a screening device for what is the relevant starting point. We emphasize starting point, because these parameters can change. Although the steps appear linear, in reality, you must see that the open nature of the conversations could and should lead to a looping back to earlier decisions. Smaller groups are generally more conducive to encouraging diverse voices. So, the small groups need a diverse composition in order not to just get back specific siloed views reflecting one part of the organization. The decision point sets a focal point for convergence as the diverse groups understand how the decision will affect them. This naturally facilitates a smoother implementation via the seventh step: play out the conversation.

The final step institutionalizes the process into the organization. It embeds a dynamic future orientation that links strategy and risk management by recognizing how uncertainty is a constant in the environment. It creates a focus on the changing environment and the need for ongoing learning to be prepared. It does not mean that you are constantly changing, but rather that you have a framework that enables you to monitor important changes and be prepared to act. It can also assist you in understanding what abilities you have to shape the changing environment via the timing of your actions. The initial group now resembles a stone thrown into a pond as the open and future-oriented model of discussion radiates out. The acceptance of diverse views leads to a convergence in action. You have moved from compliance to commitment.[12]

Once the context for the process is clear, then Peter Schwartz lays out the steps for developing the content of the scenarios:

1. Identify focal issue or decision.
2. Identify key forces in the local environment.
3. Identify the driving forces.
4. Rank the first three items by importance and uncertainty.
5. Select scenario logics.
6. Flesh out the scenarios.
7. Find implications.
8. Select leading indicators and signposts.[13]

By starting at the focal point or decision, we are creating the point of convergence of the diverse points of view and reinforcing the importance of the process. The focal points are invariably important decisions for the organization. Next, we set the initial parameter in the immediate environment as we move from the more known to the currently unknown and possibly unknowable with certainty. Often, we see key forces as something to put into a checklist, which may have the unfortunate effect of making them static. The challenge is to make them dynamic and that is accomplished by identifying and projecting the driving forces. A fundamental goal and achievement of the scenario-planning process is to make strategy dynamic by taking account of the inherent uncertainty of the future. Although we may deal with it via subjective probabilities, it is essential that we do not fool ourselves into thinking these probabilities are as solid as those related to the past or natural events.

This description, of course, is scenario planning in an ideal world, or one that doesn't exist. Although the process may be pure, human interactions lead to a much more rough-and-tumble process. This is to be expected and welcomed, not rejected because of some purity tests. Scenario planning becomes robust by promoting thinking and dialogue. Even if the focal point is precisely correct, it does not follow that the thoughts it inspires will lead to a clear, linear process. Rather, the promotion of dialogue, if it is properly inclusive, has the potential to be messy. But then uncertainty is a messy concept for most of us, so this is a necessary part of the process.

The crux of step 4 is to identify what is most important and most uncertain because that is the focus. In selecting the logics of the scenarios, we may think of how to get to the story we want to tell. Schwartz explains:

> *The results of this ranking exercise are, in effect, the axes along which the eventual scenarios will differ. Determining these axes is among the most important steps in the entire scenario-generating process. The goal is to end up with just a few scenarios whose differences make a difference to performance and are recognized by decision-makers. If the scenarios are to function as useful learning tools, the lessons they teach must be based on issues basic to the success of the focal decisions. And those "scenario drivers" must be few in number in order to avoid a proliferation of scenarios around every possible uncertainty.*[14]

For example, if market share is a key determinant of the decision, the market share would be one axis going from low to high, where low would lead to a negative decision and high an investment decision. Now the key uncertainty, say if we were looking at entering a foreign market, could be the reaction of competitors. The strength of their reaction, for example in cost cutting, could be a determinant of the profitability of the venture.

Figure 8.1 presents a simple matrix with story titles. It is the construction of the story that really develops the scenario. This is a generic set of considerations for virtually any business enterprise, although many service businesses would use the term *partner* over distributor. But the essential dynamics are to identify the axes and give a title to the story line. We will elaborate on each narrative that would be used to facilitate the process of coming to an entry decision.

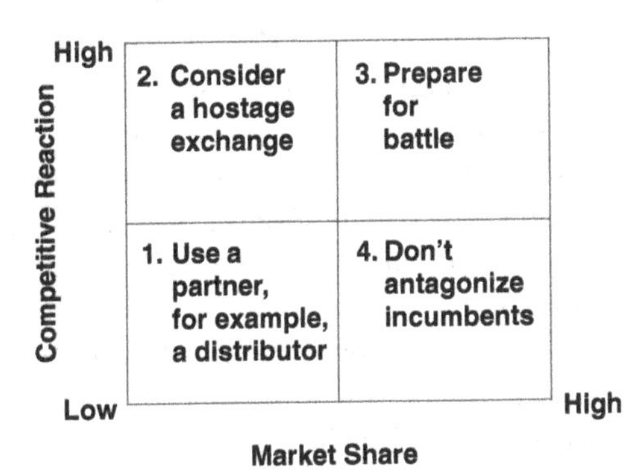

FIGURE 8.1 Illustration of a Scenario Matrix for Entering a Foreign Market

Cell 1 is straightforward: the market has been determined to be reasonably attractive, competitive reaction will not make it less attractive, but the potential gains are low. So, it is worthwhile to explore, but not to commit, major resources. Hence, the best risk return structure is to use local resources. Although this may limit potential upside, it also limits potential downside. It is important to recognize that although this lowers risk, it also changes the risks. Partner selection will create new risks. For example, if the distributor has unfair or unsafe labor practices, this will taint your reputation not only in that market but also potentially in your home market. A globalized world with social media means news spreads fast. Therefore, partner selection becomes a key skill in implementing this scenario. Given that in some markets there may be a limited number of potential appropriate partners, some markets may be preempted. This is a clear example of the importance of timing and windows of opportunity.

Cell 2 recognizes that a strong competitive response may make the market unattractive. If this is the case, then is the competitor vulnerable in another market? In this scenario, an important consideration is that rivals could use high returns in their home markets to subsidize an attack on you in your home market. If the rival is content with the current state of rivalry, it may be best to abandon plans for that market. Alternatively, if the rival is considering entering your market, an attack may be needed as a warning. A different approach may be to take the battle to a third market where the rival may not be as powerful. In fleshing out this scenario, there is a full examination of offensive and defensive strategies. What trade-offs are you willing to make?

Cell 3 offers the potential for significant gains but also an intense battle for market share. What are your competitive advantages against the rival? What happens if price competition breaks out? What will be the nature of your commitment to this market—for how long are losses sustainable? Might the rival choose to attack you in your home market or a third market so as not to engage in intense competition in the home market? The focus on one market must be put into the context of global rivalries and not limited to the new market.

Cell 4 suggests that you as a new entrant can gain significant share but probably will grow the market at the same time. You can differentiate your product without directly attacking the incumbent. This leaves incumbents content with their positions. In this scenario, aggressive efforts will destabilize the market and leave everyone worse off. How can you use signaling to suggest the future of a duopoly is best for everyone?

REAL OPTIONS

We could take a different resolution to the alternatives presented in the scenario by using real options. The examination of real options in strategy has a history going back to Edward H. Bowman and Dileep Hurry in 1993.[15] By real options we mean investments in real assets, not financial options. Interest in real options seems to increase when uncertainty increases, so interest is gaining again. But the real options approach also indicates a very different style of strategic thinking. In many strategy books, the emphasis is on using power to improve performance, but real options thinking stresses flexibility. And, going back to Bowman and Hurry, such an approach has a different benefit. Options can be seen as learning investments because they create a preferential access to an opportunity. The approach also has direct ties to financial theorists such as Merton by noting that a portfolio of options is more valuable than an option on a portfolio.[16] So the firm's growth prospects are evaluated according to its portfolio of real options.[17]

Because options convey the right, but not the obligation, to exercise on an opportunity they allow some uncertainty to clarify as it plays out in time. Simply put, if we buy an option at time (0) but don't have to exercise it until time (5), we will have gained more knowledge with the passage of time. The opportunity will typically be either more or less attractive. Going back to the example we discussed, suppose that the organization is considering several markets for growth; does it need to immediately decide on one or is there a way to maximize the allocation of resources? Rather than making a substantial investment in one market, could the firm set up distributors, or even enter into agreements with global retailers who are in all those markets? By pursuing this real-option approach, the downside risk is limited as is the upside, and the quality of the investment decision is improved by increased market knowledge. Depending on how sales go, the extent of the investment can be scaled up or down.

The calculation of the value of real options although painstaking is much simpler than for financial options. Rather than using complex mathematics, real options are best calculated using a Bayesian approach that follows a familiar decision tree logic.[18]

The crux is to manage a multistage approach. Think about a firm considering whether or not to build a factory to supply the new market. Rather than build or rent a factory now, they would scan for an appropriate location and purchase an option to either lease or buy the property at some date. One would expect the longer the length of the option, the greater the opportunity to see the future unfold, but it will also increase the cost of the option. In any event, the expiry conditions or expiry date of the option are the trigger points for when the firm will decide whether or not the opportunity merits further investment. If it does, the lease is signed, or the property is purchased. But that does not mean that the factory will be built. Depending on how many decision points there are, that is how many times options will be exercised or not.

At the heart of this approach is the estimation of asset values at various times. This involves estimations of what will happen in the future and emphasizes a key difference from financial options, where volatility can be calculated and the value, or strike price, is set.[19] Real options are about a future reality and that forces us to deal with uncertainty. How can this be done? One way is to move from mathematical certainty to subjective probabilities. Some may find this an overly formal term for guestimates, but what are the other options? So, we need to find a way to maximize the value of subjective estimates. Some will suggest the use of "experts," or the Delphi panel method[20]—a forecasting process that employs multiple rounds of questionnaires to experts. After each round the responses are aggregated and shared allowing the group to move to consensus. Although the answer varies in contexts, for our purposes we want to tie it to Schwartz's process for holding a strategic conversation—so let's start with a key group of players—including outsiders. Depending on the level of granularity that is desired, it may be easiest to start with high, medium, and low. Or alternatively, highly probable, likely, and improbable. This initiates the discussion, and it is important not to get hung up on false precision. The point is to have discussion that generates ranges. The dialogue is not just about generating numbers but creating a learning opportunity for all involved in the discussion. Given the level of uncertainty it must be recognized that there will be a certain arbitrariness to the assignment of specific probabilities needed for calculations. This was the approach our partners in the restaurant venture employed, as shown in Figure 8.2. Suppose the partners manage uncertainty by obtaining options on two very different locations. They then use their experience gained from observations at the two sites and dialogue with local experts and potential customers to generate what the expected net incomes may be. This confirms their hunch that the more expensive, busy location is the way to go and they take a lease on that location. To further the use of real options and help reduce uncertainty, they could take a short-term, renewable lease on the expensive location and maintain the option on the second location. If the first location works, the option on the second location would be allowed to expire unexercised. However, if the first does not work as expected, the partners could transfer much of the capital investment in restaurant equipment to the second location and try again.

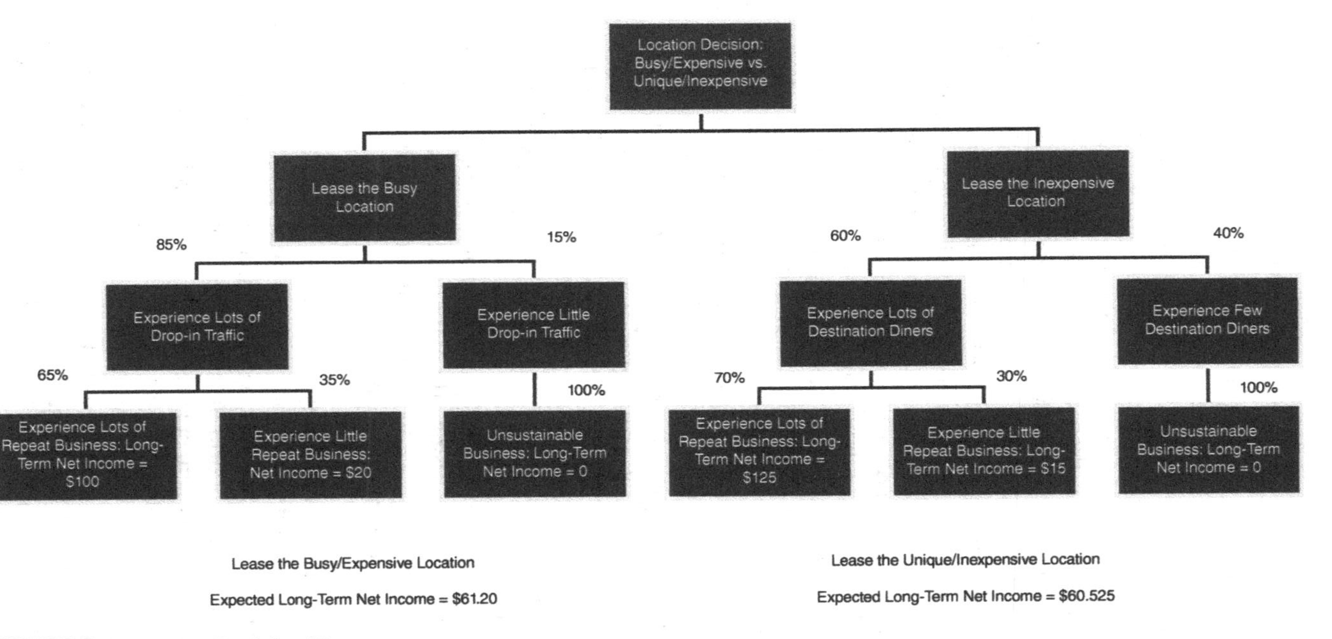

FIGURE 8.2 Location Decision Tree

CONCLUSION

Although some may be uncomfortable with the arbitrariness of assigning the necessary probabilities, it is the price we pay for dealing with uncertainty. In this process, it is imperative to identify assumptions, drivers of performance/risk, and inflection points to create a positive feedback loop. To offset concerns with the generation of probabilities it needs to be emphasized from the beginning that this is the start of a nonlinear process. The specific probabilities will be returned to as time unfolds and more information becomes available. Efforts to get it exactly right are a waste of time. What is a good use of time is setting up a framework for future learning and refinement. If time is spent on getting the process right good results should emerge. In this scenario there is an assumption of convergence, so we need to consider what happens when there is polarization of likelihoods.

Again, Schwartz's guidance on conversations comes into play. Go into small groups and have them fully explore each option. Then reconvene to see if convergence emerges. Whatever the outcome, you will be better prepared for the future because both sides should have become aware of fundamental assumptions in their thinking. The surfacing of these assumptions advances the risk identification in the face of uncertainty. In practice, the promise of scenario planning has not always lived up to its promise as Drew Erdman, Bernardo Sichel, and Luk Yeung of McKinsey point out. They identify the biases that need to be combatted in effective scenario planning:

1. *Availability bias:* fight the urge to make decisions based on what you already know.
2. *Probability neglect:* beware of giving too much weight to unlikely events.
3. *Stability bias:* don't assume the future will look like the past.
4. *Overconfidence bias:* combat overconfidence and excessive optimism.
5. *Social bias:* encourage free and open debate.[21]

Point 1 recognizes the reality of the problem we all have in dealing with uncertainty. It is frightening, and the temptation is to retreat into what we know, or as point 3 makes clear, what we think we know. Although this may be a more comfortable world, it is not one in which the fundamental challenge of strategic management is being met. Point 5 relates to Schwartz's first condition of creating a hospitable climate. Only a culture that encourages participation from all levels will allow participants with firsthand knowledge of some issues to come forward. If the official history or future is not to lead to groupthink this is essential.

We are not quite as certain about point 2—Probability neglect—for a few reasons. As we have argued, to some degree you can ignore uncertainty because markets may not allow you to protect against highly improbable events. But there is another dimension to this problem. Is it possible to prepare for highly unlikely events with minimal cost? Isn't this the role for business continuity planning and even succession planning? The fashion designer Laura Ashley is a case in point. There were plans to take the company public in November 1985. Unfortunately, Laura Ashley fell down the stairs at her daughter's house and died in September of that year. Now it can't be said that her death was highly unlikely because death is a certainty for all, but the timing of her death was certainly unexpected. But the IPO was wildly successful because succession planning had created a strong company. This is an example of resiliency.

In general, the McKinsey folks are right—focus your resources on what is likely. Their comment really reinforces Pierre Wack's admonition that scenarios should be plausible.[22] In other words, don't waste your time or risk losing legitimacy by going down rabbit holes. But there are times when it is worthwhile to consider improbable events, especially if the likelihood of improbable events, or at least the perception of such, is rooted in overconfidence.[23] Overconfidence leads to what Pankaj Ghemawat has labeled "lock-in," which, simply put leads to throwing good money after bad to accomplish what was sanctified by flawed forecasts.[24]

NOTES

1. One way to counter overconfidence could be the use of premortems. See Gary Klein, Tim Koller, and Dan Lovallo, "Premortems: Being Smart at the Start," *McKinsey Quarterly* (March 2019).
2. BBC News, "Jamal Khashoggi: All You Need to Know about Saudi Journalist's Death," September 16, 2019, https://www.bbc.com/news/world-europe-45812399.
3. See Rick Nason, *It's Not Complicated: The Art and Science of Complexity for Business Success* (Toronto: Rotman University of Toronto Press, 2017).
4. Angela Wilkinson and Roland Kupers, "Living in the Futures: How Scenario Planning Changed Corporate Strategy," *Harvard Business Review* (May 2013).
5. See, for example, "Survey—Mastering Risk 2: The Official Future, Self-Delusion and the Value of Scenarios," *Financial Times* (May 2, 2000).
6. Kees van der Heijden, *Scenarios: The Art of Strategic Conversation*, 2nd ed. (Hoboken NJ: Wiley, 2005), Preface.
7. Arie de Geus, "Scenarios and Decision-Taking," Oxford Futures Forum, October 2005, https://www.ariedegeus.com/usr/library/documents/main/oxford_futures_forum.pdf. Recall the importance of creating a common language to promote a common understanding of key concepts in risk management.
8. van der Heijden, *Scenarios*, Preface.

9. Peter Schwartz, *The Art of the Long View: Planning for the Future of an Uncertain World* (New York: Doubleday, 1991); Howard Leyda, "Be Strategic, Plan for Uncertainty." LinkedIn, June 25, 2018, https://www.linkedin.com/pulse/strategic-plan-uncertainty-william-howard-leyda-jr-/.
10. Daniel Kahneman became a best-selling author for his *Thinking, Fast and Slow* (New York: Penguin 2011). We both saw this book on many executives' desks over the years.
11. See Heidi Grant Halvorson and David Rock, "Beyond Bias: Neuroscience Research Show How New Organizational Practices Can Shift Ingrained Thinking," *strategy + business* 80, Autumn 2019, https://www.strategy-business.com/article/00345?gko=d11ee. Dan Lovallo and Daniel Kahneman, "Delusions of Success: How Optimism Undermines Executives' Decisions," *Harvard Business Review* (July 200)3; Tobias Baer, Sven Heilgtag, and Hamid Samandari, "The Business Logic in Debiasing," McKinsey & Co., May 2017, https://www.mckinsey.com/business-functions/risk/our-insights/the-business-logic-in-debiasing; Bill Javetski and Tim Koller, "Debiasing the Corporation: An Interview with Nobel Laureate Richard Thaler," *McKinsey Corporate Finance Practice* (May 2017); and Tim Koller and Dan Lovallo, "Taking the 'Outside View,'" *Bias Busters*, 2018, https://www.mckinsey.com/business-functions/strategy-and-corporate-finance/our-insights/bias-busters-taking-the-outside-view.
12. For the origin of this debate, see Richard E. Walton, "From Control to Commitment in the Workplace," *Harvard Business Review* (March 1985).
13. Schwartz, *The Art of the Long View,* Appendix: Step to Developing Scenarios.
14. Peter Schwartz, *The Art of the Long View,* Appendix: Step to Developing Scenarios.
15. Edward H. Bowman and Dileep Hurry, "Strategy through the Option Lens: An Integrated View of Resource Investments and the Incremental-Choice Process, " *Academy of Management Review* 18 (1993): 760–82.
16. Bowman and Hurry, "Strategy through the Option Lens." Also see Timothy A. Luehrman, "Strategy as a Portfolio of Real Options," *Harvard Business Review* (September–October 1998) and Lenos Trigeorgis and Jeffrey J. Reuer, "Real Options in Strategic Management," *Strategic Management Journal* 38 (2017): 42–63.
17. Tom Copeland and Peter Tufano, "A Real-World Way to Manage Real Options," *Harvard Business Review* (March 2004).
18. See Copeland and Tufano, "A Real-World Way to Manage Real Options" or Nelson Ferreira, Jayanti Kar, and Lenos Trigeorgis, "Option Games: The Key to Competing in Capital-Intensive Industries," *Harvard Business Review* (March 2009) for good examples of the approach.
19. Copeland and Tufano, "A Real-World Way to Manage Real Options," Choosing the Right Model section.
20. Alexandra Twin, "Delphi Method," Investopedia, September 16, 2019, https://www.investopedia.com/terms/d/delphi-method.asp.
21. Drew Erdman, Bernardo Sichel, and Luk Yeung, "Overcoming Obstacles to Effective Scenario Planning," McKinsey & Company, June 2015, https://www

.mckinsey.com/business-functions/strategy-and-corporate-finance/our-insights/overcoming-obstacles-to-effective-scenario-planning. A behavioral science unit may be useful in this context. See Anna Guntner, Kinstantin Lucks, and Julia Sperling-Magro, "Lessons from the Front Line of Corporate Nudging," *McKinsey Quarterly* (January 2019).

22. Angela Wilkinson and Roland Kupers, "Living in the Futures: How Scenario Planning Changed Corporate Strategy," *Harvard Business Review* (May 2013).
23. The ties to the discussion of risk homeostasis should be clear.
24. See Pankaj Ghemawat, *Commitment: The Dynamic of Strategy* (New York: Free Press, 1991). "Lock-in" may be exacerbated by another dimension of commitment—inertia—a complex set of forces that keep organizations doing what they are doing.

CHAPTER 9

Risk Culture and Ethics

Can You Have Excellence and Consistency at the Same Time?

In the competitive landscape of today's financial institutions and many other service industries the articulated value propositions are depressingly similar. Yet, some organizations succeed in the battle for customers and others fall by the wayside. Why is this so? The answer lies in the successful execution of the strategy, which in turn is the result of the nurturing of the appropriate organizational culture.[1] On the positive side, there is plenty of evidence that although a toxic culture destroys value, a strong and resilient culture fully championed and embodied by the very top of the organization (read: CEOs and directors) can and will add long-term sustainable value to the company's reputation and financial bottom line.[2] Although many have focused on the role of culture for the successful execution of strategies, fewer have focused on the links between ethics and integrated, enterprise risk management, which must fit with the appropriate culture. To understand this, we must focus on the term *value* in value proposition.

Strategies succeed when they produce superior value for customers with a cost structure that ensures appropriate returns.[3] We argue that for service industries the role of the provider, or advisor, at the moment of truth makes the organizational culture especially critical in the successful delivery of customer value.[4] We are certain that many serious readers will flinch at the cliché term "moments of truth," but we argue that this catchy term popularized in the business press actually is based on an important reality. For customers to emotionally connect with the firm's value proposition at the moment of truth, the advisor must make decisions that the customers believe are in their best interest. This has become especially timely as the Edelman Trust Barometer documents changing attitudes toward "trust." More and more employees are trusting their CEOs to have their best interests at heart, and this trust must be mirrored in their relationships with customers.[5]

It goes without saying that the customer must believe the advisor is qualified. In 2019, GE Capital ran a series of television commercials that stressed capability as a differentiator, but we would suggest that most financial institutions (FIs) have or can develop similar capabilities, as the current rush into wealth management shows. But this is an example of a general situation. Let us return to our restaurant. When the waitstaff recommends the special, is it to avoid wastage or because it will delight the customer? To make a recommendation the waitstaff must learn about customers' tastes and then seek to educate them about choices.

This leads us to consider situations in which the customers' primary concern is that the advisor has their best interests at heart. For example, if a customer is seeking to buy a commodity item, her primary concern will be price. In this assessment we are not limited solely to the price of the item but a broader consideration of costs, including search and other costs. We are primarily interested in situations where the customer and the provider are interested in establishing and building longer-term relationships, which they hope lead to repeat sales. The following analysis, then, focuses on multiple dimensions in addition to price that affect a relationship strategy for value creation. One encounter in this context is especially interesting: the granting of credit. The reason for selecting this encounter is the built-in asymmetry of the risk-return decision. In general, depending on the specific transaction, the potential loss to the creditor far exceeds the potential gain. Consequently, most incentive systems will lead to a built-in bias to turn down the request because the punishment for a bad loan exceeds the rewards for a good loan.

Let us now call attention to some important aspects of this interaction. First, robotic decisions based solely on big data may limit interaction and transactions costs, but in a way that limits interaction and hence the opportunity to forge a relationship.[6] Second, we argue that there are always exceptions to the general rule and such exceptions may be the basis for building exceptional, rather than average, customer experiences. Excellent service is a differentiator. Third, the bias toward "no" may not be profit maximizing. Modern risk management is not about limiting losses but identifying and managing risks for competitive advantage. A prime example is the memory one of us has when his father's company acquired a company with zero bad debts. The sellers had not realized the capacity that this reflected for revenue growth if a higher risk of bad debt was accepted and managed well. The experience of Capital One in the subprime credit card space is another example. Capital One identified an underserved market in credit cards—the subprime borrower. And just as Progressive did in the property and casualty market, it developed the skills to grow and develop this market successfully.[7] The ideal amount of loss is unlikely to be zero because zero is more likely to indicate that the business is turning down profitable business possibilities. The negative word of mouth created by such practices is also profit limiting because it might deter customers from entering into a relationship with you.

There is a similar yet opposite logic taking place in many sales situations. Superior knowledge of the product/service gives the salesperson power. To some degree, no matter how much research you have done, advisors are critical in matching your needs to the right product. If advisors are on commission, they are highly incented to oversell—especially if this is an infrequent purchase. Yet, from the store's perspective, this is the wrong thing to do if you are trying to create customer loyalty. The problem is to align the two interests.

We need to be clear that we are not suggesting that the customer is always right; in fact, because the customer may be wrong, there is a need for individual judgment or discretion in the process. This is a complicating factor when the service delivery system must deliver consistently. Second, if one is managing to be exceptional, then there will be failures. How are failures managed? These factors demand that customers believe that the advisors are authentic in their concern for the customers' best interests.[8] For this to occur, the organization must manage the paradox of being centralized and decentralized: centralized to promote a strong ethical culture and decentralized to promote strong individual ethics. A strong ethical culture is the necessary condition for this to be managed effectively in a cost-efficient manner and to promote consistency in delivery of the value proposition, whereas strong individual ethics are necessary to promote customer confidence in the customer service representative (CSR). This is supported by no less than Warren Buffet of Berkshire Hathaway fame, who has asserted that "integrity is the most important trait to hire for."[9]

The question arises: how do we assess integrity? We can't see the organizational culture nor the motivation of the advisor. What we see is behavior. The value of a strong ethical culture lies in how it affects the behavior of the advisor at times of discretionary behavior. It is especially important in a decentralized structure that the right values guide behaviors. And this is why organizational culture becomes a critical differentiator in service-based industries.[10]

THE ADVISOR-CUSTOMER ENCOUNTER

Many customers have insecurities when they are making a purchase and this creates a degree of reliance on the salesperson, who in effect becomes an advisor. This is rooted in the knowledge, which sometimes may be more of a belief, that the salesperson or the person providing the service, has superior knowledge. This creates a form of dependency. When we are seeking a loan, we feel like a teenager asking a parent to borrow the car. We may have similar trepidations when buying clothes or getting our hair cut, and this may especially be the case when we are making a major purchase. Now we recognize that sometimes the customer may be, or believe they are, more knowledgeable than the salesperson. But that is not what we are interested in.

As should be clear by now, one of us has a penchant for fine dining and especially tasting menus at renowned restaurants. Let us explore one such experience. The restaurant's specialty is customizing the meal for every individual diner. To that end, the waitperson asks you a number of questions about likes and dislikes. Then, the waitperson goes to the kitchen and puts together a unique meal limited only by what is on hand. Now think for a moment about the dynamics of this encounter. The diner wants to appear knowledgeable about food and wine; otherwise, why is that person spending so much? But for the waitperson to prepare the best possible experience for the diner, the diner may have to admit knowledge limitations and the diner can't possibly know as much about the chef's capability as the waitperson. The diner must recognize the limitations of her knowledge while the waitperson must create an ambience in which the diner feels able to expose her hopes for the meal. She needs to expose her true self, not project the persona of a classic foodie. Only then can the waitperson make the appropriate choices for the diner. This may even involve educating the diner.

However, if the diner feels that the waitperson is promoting what the kitchen wants to move to avoid wastage, then she will not allow herself to be educated about the capabilities of the restaurant. Rather, she will take control of the situation and educate the waitperson about what she wants. This will be a suboptimal experience. And it will all be for naught if she is wrong about the waitstaff. Perceptions matter as much as reality in this encounter.

This situation is complicated because it can be viewed as a win-lose scenario, but we will argue that it should be also be viewed as a win-win situation. We can gain insight into this situation by comparing it to the classic prisoner's dilemma as analyzed by Axelrod, in which the nature of the payoffs differ due to different asymmetries of outcomes and both situations share the need for cooperation and the possibility of mutual gain: the customer gets what she wants or perhaps more importantly needs and the restaurant creates a valuable relationship.[11] The distinction between "wants" and "needs" is critical. Many diners may "want" to appear more knowledgeable than they are, but this immediate ego gratification will only lead to long-term pain for both sides of the transaction. Consequently, the evolution of cooperation, the win-win, can only occur when the relationship is sustainable, and this requires that only choices with an acceptable degree of probability of being enjoyable will be made. This outcome may require a modification of the original request and not a simple yes or no.

For the relationship to develop in this encounter, the classic tit-for-tat negotiation strategy must take place; however, unlike most formulations of the prisoner's dilemma, it is clear that because the diner may expose herself to a stressful situation, it is essential that the advisor make the first appropriate disclosures to promote the needed aura of transparency. The possible outcomes are shown in Figure 9.1 based on differences between promoting and educating or alternatively monologue and dialogue. What we mean by promoting is that the advisor has the answer and is actively engaged in a monologue to convince the customer by highlighting the advantages and hiding the risks. The objective of the encounter from the advisor's viewpoint is to close the deal. When the customer is promoting, she is highlighting the positive and hiding the negative. By advising, we are trying to capture a dialogue in which the customer is working to present her needs and capacities in a way that the advisor understands. When the advisor is educating, she is paying attention to the verbal and nonverbal clues emanating from the customer. The purpose from the advisor's viewpoint is to get to know the customer so that the advisor can develop the answer that is correct for the customer. In order to do this, the customer must be sufficiently comfortable that she is able to express herself and that means she must perceive the advisor as authentic.

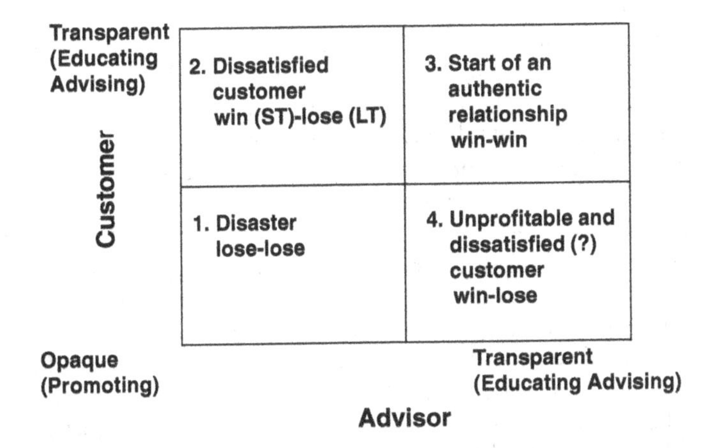

FIGURE 9.1 The Moment of Truth

Quadrants 2 and 4 are the classic win-lose scenarios. In quadrant 2, the waitperson convinces the customer to order the special, but the resulting meal leads to a dissatisfied customer. Although the customer may stay with the meal and even say how wonderful it is as she leaves a generous tip, the restaurant has earned considerable negative comments by the customer—this may be especially harmful in the age of social media, for example, Yelp—so the short-term win is actually a long-term loss.

Quadrant 4 is especially interesting and merits additional comment on the possible dynamic. Further elaboration of the diner may bring clarity to the situation. Consider a foodie who is well known on social media and comes to the restaurant. She wants to be known and known for her expertise and the waitperson knows the chef's ego will want to win her over. So, she wants (demands) to order off menu. But this order does not fit with what food is best (freshest) in the kitchen nor well with the chef's skills. This leads to a distribution of possible outcomes ranging from the smug winning customer to the distressed diner who blames the waitperson for lack of stewardship. The restaurant damages its reputation because it will be portrayed as lacking in expertise or lacking in concern for its customer (ethics). Quadrant 1 is the lose-lose scenario because the restaurant would seem to get what it wants but does not because the customer gamed the system. We can only say a pox on both their houses in this quadrant where greed meets greed in this transactionally motivated encounter.

Quadrant 3 is the win-win quadrant and is built on the exchange of information that allows for the development of first understanding and then trust. Because the customer is the vulnerable party, it is incumbent on the advisor to create the environment of openness that facilitates the series of interactions that will allow understanding and eventually trust to develop. At the risk of caricature, think about how this relationship may change. It could start out with the diner as supplicant approaching the all-powerful advisor only to be transformed into an appreciative client who is seeking advice from a trusted adviser. The relationship then becomes sustainable because the client has a memorable dining experience and every desire to repeat it. There is little incentive to incur the high switching costs of establishing a relationship with a new restaurant.

Credit risk isn't especially important in the restaurant industry, although more in demand restaurants are realizing the value of space and demanding nonrefundable deposits for reservations. But for any industry in which credit losses can be large, such as construction or financial services, one more aspect needs to be added. Consider the case of a client who wants to take on too high a mortgage.[12] We will leave it to the reader to play out the different cells, but there is an additional aspect to the decision. It is not just the ability of the applicant to repay, but the willingness to repay. It is a fact of human nature that some people in declaring bankruptcy will do everything possible to protect themselves, and others will do everything to preserve their reputations and make their best efforts to make the creditors whole. Assessing the willingness to repay does not affect the probability of default, but it does materially affect the potential loss given default. Consequently, the advisor's assessment of the applicant's willingness to repay will not only affect the yes/no of the credit decision but also the pricing and conditions placed on the loan. The pricing and conditions will have a significant impact on the applicant's perception of the encounter and therefore of the FI.

- The delivery system must be properly designed to facilitate the interaction.
- Given that no system can ever anticipate every element of the interaction, the advisor must be empowered to make decisions to align the customer's interest with the organization's value proposition.
- The customer must believe that the advisor is acting in the customer's interest.

We recognize that if the interaction is a one-off and the relationship between the customer and the organization is infrequent, then the possibility exists for acting skills to replace authenticity, but especially if the interactions are important and/or frequent and meant to cultivate a relationship, then the customer must believe that the advisor is authentic in her concern for the customer's best interests. To put it succinctly, there must be truth in the moment of truth and this demands authenticity of the advisor and then the customer, if the cooperation needed to elicit the necessary information is to emerge. This is why we have added the term *educating:* the customer must believe that the advisor has answers to her problems and will give the answers that are best for her. And for this to occur, the organization must manage the paradox of being centralized and decentralized.

CONTROL SYSTEMS, DISCRETION, AND ETHICS

To extend the discussion, we need to consider the role of the control systems needed for good risk management. Since the classic work on decentralization by Richard F. Vancil in 1979,[13] it has been recognized that managers need to use influence to achieve appropriate levels of control to achieve strategic objectives in ambiguous situations. Culture must be recognized as a key influencer at the organizational level and, consequently, successful implementation of good risk management in a service organization's strategy demands the appropriate culture.[14]

It has been previously noted that leading-edge ERM firms seek to balance the forces of centralization and decentralization using policies and limits to influence the discretion of decision-makers to achieve consistency.[15] This is especially important for how the organization manages the strategic risk of delivering on its value proposition. McKinsey & Co. noted the importance of consistency in a recent article, "The Three Cs of Customer Satisfaction: Consistency, Consistency, Consistency."[16] The quest for consistency brings to the fore many of the most-demanding challenges in management:

- Balancing centralization and decentralization
- Reconciling the quest for consistency and excellence
- Dealing with failure

Let us explore the organizational tools that can ensure consistency in the credit decision. Going back to Henry Mintzberg, one classic choice is the professional bureaucracy.[17] As is often the case with classic thinking, the core is relevant, but adjustments to a changed environment are needed: specifically, the manner in which data and decision support systems require centralization to complement the training in "indoctrination" to ensure consistency. This, of course, is in keeping with the bureaucratic nature of the organization. Richard E. Walton wrote very insightfully on the relationship between centralization via information technology and operations in the late 1980s.[18] Moreover, he hit on a theme that is especially relevant for managing empowerment and consistency in service organizations: commitment. Walton discusses the shift from "imposing control and securing compliance" to "eliciting commitment." If one thinks about a customer-centric organization the shift is of fundamental importance. Instead of using control systems to promote robotic consistency, commitment is to the organization's value of customer centricity. Rather than a prescribed content to the outcome, the desired outcome is measured by the customer's satisfaction, and this introduces a significant element of variability. Walton delineates the differences between compliance and commitment effects. Some of the most important commitment effects arise from dispersing power and information to promote self-supervision and increase the importance of individual skill and internal motivation.[19] In a sense, compliance with its strict monitoring robs the individual of contributing their individual knowledge to the organization, which leads to a lack of internal motivation.

We can understand how some readers may be questioning the link to risk management, so let us start with the most straightforward instance: operational risk. The Basel Committee defines operational risk as "the risk of loss resulting from inadequate or failed internal processes, people and systems or from external events. This definition includes legal risk but excludes strategic and reputational risk."[20] Although we believe that operational risk is intimately connected with reputational and strategic risk, we will focus on operational risk as defined for the moment.

As compared to a product, such as fast food, where consistency to a significant degree can be ensured via strict operational controls, the experience of dining in a fast food restaurant is partly affected by the attitude of the CSR. Anyone who has ever shopped in an Apple store is aware of the importance of the CSR sharing the values of the organization and its impact on not just behavior but attitude. The Apple CSR wants you to understand the value of Apple's products and share in the joy of the experience that the products bring. This forges a common experiential bond between customer and CSR.

Reflecting on these experiences leads us to consider the role of centralization—the values that the actions and attitudes of the CSR must embody. The strong centralized values of the culture limit the range of acceptable behaviors.[21] This brings us to the tension between excellence and consistency. It needs to be recognized that in some contexts the quest for excellence is the enemy of consistency. The quest for excellence often means pushing the boundary, but if one is pushing the boundary then one is moving further from the norm and hence increasing the gap between worst and best. For a service organization, this can be problematic. If one's first encounter is with the excellent outlier, then expectations for future encounters are set too high and the customer is doomed to be disappointed even if she is met with objectively excellent service because it fails in comparison to what was expected.

Yet, if one abandons the quest for excellence one risks creating a culture of complacency, and such a culture is very prone to deterioration and mediocrity. Consequently, it is imperative to balance the quest for excellence with the quest for consistency. This is accomplished by having a strong culture and empowered CSRs who can respond to different customers consistent with the values of the organization. This balancing act inevitably leads us to deal with the management of failure. Not all CSRs will perform as desired all the time. If an organization does not have failures, it is not challenging itself, so in a very important sense, failure may be a good thing. If that is true, then leaders must distinguish between different types of failures and manage the situation accordingly. For example, if a CSR responds to an inquiry, "that's not my job," that is unacceptable because she has failed to respond properly to the customer's problem. This CSR may not fit with the organization. However, if the CSR errs because she answers and is out of her depth, then we applaud the attitude, but need to engage in corrective action. There would be two paths. First, reassure the CSR that she can't know the answers to all questions, but she can consult a directory to properly direct the customer or even escort her to the appropriate person. Alternatively, the organization may realize that it has failed the CSR by putting her into a situation for which she has not been properly trained. The right attitude without the appropriate training can be a fertile ground for failure. Just as wins can be shared so too can failure. If failure is inevitable if one demands excellence, then it must be managed, and this demands the organization have the appropriate values.

And this leads us to the importance of culture—especially in the modern centralized-decentralized organization. James Lam offers the following definition of culture:

> *By "culture," I am referring to a set of repeated, observable patterns of a group's behavior. It is shaped by a broad spectrum of forces: leadership, shared values and beliefs, habit, and incentives, both positive and negative. Culture in turn drives human behavior, hence its value to risk management. In a typical risk culture, people will do the right thing when told what to do. In a poor one, people may actually do the* wrong *things even when rules are laid down. But when a powerful risk culture has taken root,* people are likely to do the right things even when they are not told what to do. *By embedding risk awareness and accountability into a positive corporate culture, managers needn't spend a lot of time brainstorming policies for every last risk situation but can instead allocate their resources elsewhere.*[22]

An appropriate organizational culture includes a recognition of risk: it has been argued that this included "the shared perceptions among employees of the relative priority given to risk management, including perceptions of the risk-related practices and behaviors that are expected, valued and supported."[23] Culture is another multidimensional concept that must promote a basic understanding of the different factors that drive organizational success. As such, when we discuss risk culture, it is meant as one essential dimension, comparable to ethics, in the overall organizational culture.

Financial institutions have become leaders in recognizing the importance of risk awareness in their organizational cultures. Unfortunately, this has not been because of idealism but rather the costs of failures rooted in the organizational cultures. We view this recognition at FIs as the proverbial canary in the coal mine. We believe that work done at banks on the importance of risk awareness in the organizational culture has lessons for all organizations. Sheedy and Griffin have been leaders in the empirical research on the appropriate attitudes toward risk in the culture and are creators of the Macquarie

Risk Culture Scale to assess this. They have identified four cultural factors three positive and one negative.

- Valued
  - Risk management is valued within the organization.
- Proactive
  - Risk issues and events are proactively identified and addressed.
- Avoidance
  - Risk issues and policy breaches are ignored, downplayed, or excused.
- Manager
  - The immediate manager is an effective role model for desirable risk management and behaviors.[24]

The empirical study helps us make concrete the study of this "softer" side of management by combining the talents of a risk manager, Sheedy, and a psychologist, Griffin. This also facilitates a more granular approach by distinguishing different cultures at the business unit level and the individual level.

The study differentiates the drivers at the organizational level and at the individual level to arrive at a risk culture in which the beliefs and values are shared across the organization and are consistent with the individual employee's perception of the risk culture. It is this harmonization that leads to the appropriate outcomes at the organizational level, because the employees are taking the appropriate actions to promote risk awareness.[25]

The studies have produced some interesting insights. Not surprisingly good risk structures support a strong risk culture, but there are some other important insights into what promotes and what hinders embedding risk values into the organizational culture:

- Senior staff tend to have a significantly more favorable perception of culture than junior staff. This highlights the importance of anonymous and independent risk culture assessments in which staff feel safe to reveal their true beliefs.[26]
- There are statistically significant differences between the risk cultures of the three large banks we have analyzed. That is, we can rank them meaningfully in terms of the average risk culture scores. This average comparison may be misleading, however, because variations exist within each of the three banks.[27]
- Contrary to the "tone-at-the-top" hypothesis, there were significant differences in risk culture factor scores between different business units even within the same bank. Rather, the data support the proposition that culture exists at the local level as staff interact with one another

and look to local management for guidance. The implication is that risk culture should be measured and managed at a subfirm level—whether that is best done in business units as in the current study or at lower team units is for further research to ascertain.[28]
- Overall, avoidance is the factor rated most negatively by staff. Moreover, avoidance was the factor showing the greatest difference between staff perceptions and the perceptions of the senior leaders. This finding highlights how independent and anonymous staff surveys are a useful tool to help senior leaders calibrate their understanding of staff perceptions. It also implies that more work is needed to build staff confidence that questions and issues will be taken seriously.[29]

In our experience organizations have a mirror-like quality. That is, if you want your CSRs to be attentive to your customers, you need to be attentive to your employees. In effect, the communication model inverts the authority hierarchy to improve customer service.[30]

You might notice that this is the second use of the term *pyramid* and wonder about the consistency in our discussion. There is an issue. The risk pyramid is about control; the inverted pyramid is about the connection between employee and customer satisfaction. There is no simple resolution between necessary controls to limit employee discretion and the flexibility that excellent customer experience may demand. Controls aim at consistency while the inverted pyramid aims at excellence. The issue is how to reconcile the two because both are important and needed.

The initial and more operationally oriented answer would be to look at the value-adding activities and decide in which cases the need for consistency outweigh the need for excellence. In this case, it may come down to your value proposition. There is the question of what is meant by excellence. Consider the policy of returns with no questions asked in major stores. This provides consistency and a form of excellence, but it doesn't promote excellence in limiting abuse by customers. The following example illustrates the conflict between excellence in taste and the need for consistency in health and safety standards. One of us frequently eats very rare hamburgers in France and select restaurants at home. The level of excellence in food preparation makes this safe. McDonald's, however, insists that its burgers be cooked to the correct temperature to guarantee bacteria is killed.[31] Given its target markets of children and older people who are more sensitive to disease, this is a wise decision. But the real takeaway is the relationship between operational controls (risk) and your value proposition. In these two cases, both restaurants are making the trade-off between consistency and excellence from the perspective of the expectations of customers established via their value propositions. Once again, the importance of judgment is made clear.

One factor that affects how people behave has not been addressed: incentives. An observation by strategy guru Richard Rumelt makes clear the importance of incentives as they related to the 2007–2008 financial crisis:

> *I guess the mystery for me as an academic is that we know this. We know that if you incent someone with a call option—and that could be a stock option where if it turns out badly you don't lose money, but if it turns out great you can become incredibly wealthy—if you set up that kind of an option (and most bonus systems for CEOs and top management work that way), then the person who owns that option is risk seeking. For them, it pays to take big risks. It pays to take uneconomic risks. I don't mean the kind of risks where performance wobbles around from month to month. I mean Hindenburg kind of risks. Because if you become the biggest zeppelin maker in the world, you become incredibly wealthy. And even if the thing blows up three years down the road, well, that's somebody else's problem. And yet we keep creating these incentive systems, as if they made sense. And they don't. And we know they don't.*[32]

As much as culture is important in controlling discretionary behavior, the structure of incentives may have a significant impact on culture. In the case of Jack in the Box in 1993 it is likely that you were incented to serve food fast—isn't that the raison d'etre of fast food restaurants?[33] However, speed can lead to undercooking, which leads to unsafe food. Yet, slow employees typically don't meet the evolutionary test of survival.

But we need to move away from the extreme example given to the everyday impact of incentives on the tension between excellence and consistency. A most interesting example of how incentives and value propositions interact can be seen in the policy that different restaurants take toward tipping. Before delving into the practice, let us note how private clubs generally do not allow tipping. If you have a regular customer base and you want a consistent degree of excellence, you need to prohibit incentives that would encourage favoritism. Hence, no tipping. But let us move on to commercial restaurants where conflicting factors come into play.[34]

Incentive policies have many aims, but let's agree that the starting point is to promote a holistic approach to the customer experience. Chef Amanda Cohen of New York restaurant Dirt Candy explains how tipping can be disruptive to a restaurant:

> *When Dirt Candy re-opens on Manhattan's Lower East Side in January, patrons won't need to leave gratuities. Instead, an administrative fee of around 20 percent will be added to each check, chef*

> *Amanda Cohen tells Eater, a move that will provide for more stable wages by letting the restaurant, not the guest, play the chief role in front-of-the-house compensation. There will be no line on the check to leave a tip.*
>
> *The admin fee will also let Cohen provide higher salaries for certain jobs. Unlike tips, which are required to be disbursed to waiters, runners, and bussers, Dirt Candy's surcharge will help pay line cooks, dishwashers and other employees that don't traditionally make as much as waiters. "I'm just redistributing so that there's not a huge discrepancy between the front of the house and back of the house," Cohen says. "I can't pay my cooks $10 [an hour] any more and expect them to live in New York."*[35]

This policy aims to align incentives on all factors affecting customer service. Tipping may also have other negative aspects related to discriminatory pay practice. Michael Lynn[36] has found that people of color receive lower tips than their white colleagues and Elizabeth Dunn points to another problem:

> *The system perpetuates sexual misconduct, because service workers feel compelled to tolerate sexual misconduct behavior from customers who hold financial power over them. As restaurant prices have risen, gratuities—which are tied to sales, as a percentage—have too, so that there is now a substantial and hard-to-defend disparity between the pay of the kitchen workers who prepare food and the servers who deliver it. It is perhaps telling that countries in which tipping is a social norm also tend to experience higher levels of corruption; what's the real distinction, after all, between a tip and a bribe?*[37]

As you can see, not only does Dunn reinforce Cohen's point but also makes clear how what many might view as a harmless social practice to be related to underlying attitudes that cause significant social issues. Moreover, the practice does not seem to achieve its desired outcome because studies have shown a relatively small correlation to service quality and tipping levels.[38]

Given the preceding, the abolition of tipping seems to absolutely be the right thing to do but note the title of Dunn's article: "The Limitations of American Restaurants' No-Tipping Experiment." The focus on the employees ignores another critical player: the customer. In her article Dunn recounts why restaurants abandoned their no-tipping policy:

- Customers seem to prefer "partitioned prices" to bundled prices because they see bundled prices are higher, even when their normal tipping practice would have led to a higher price.
- Customer ratings fell when restaurants instituted a mandatory charge—tipping should be optional.
- Upscale restaurants suffered less because it was conjectured that customers at higher-end restaurants are less price sensitive.

Despite the logic of a no-tipping regime, it seems that most restaurants would do so at their peril. Just as most customers wish to order a la carte and not have the waiter choose for them, even if they seek advice, they want their tip to the advisor to be at their option and not part of a service charge, which would allow restaurants to share the tips with all and be in compliance with labor laws.

CULTURE, ETHICS, PERFORMANCE, AND RISK MANAGEMENT

Our experience in organizational and risk leadership has increasingly emphasized the importance of culture and ethics in risk and performance outcomes. Culture, whether it be organizational culture or its subset, risk culture, is about the organization's norms, values, language, stories, heroes, decision-making processes, accepted behaviors, and even habits. Culture is "the way things are done around here."[39]

Ethics is what is considered right and wrong or good and bad.[40] Ethics captures values, which are also captured within culture. The two are intrinsically linked and, because culture is a broader phenomenon and a driver of behavior, culture is logically the force behind the ethics displayed within an organization.

Risk-taking and risk management are, or at least should be, about creating a strategy and business process that address environmental uncertainties (risks) in a manner that enables the firm to take the risks it can best manage and for which it can be paid. In this sense, risk management is about limiting probabilities of downside outcomes and amplifying probabilities of gain through the creation of risk knowledge and insight. In this way, risk management can become a competitive advantage.

Historically, risk management and oversight have focused on broad classes of risks, including credit, counterparty, liquidity, market and operational risks, and on proper identification, assessment/measurement, monitoring, reporting, and planning.[41] Increasingly, risk, culture, and ethics are being linked. ISO 31000 notes that risk management should "integrate the process for managing risk into the company's overall governance, strategy and planning, management, reporting processes, policies, values and culture."[42] Also increasingly, the need for strong internal compliance monitoring and reporting is being recognized. There is a growing recognition that people and reputation risks reflect and are driven by, respectively, behaviors within the organization.

Trading room participants, risk professionals, and readers of the financial press are familiar with unethical behaviors. Often these occur in organizations with strong statements of values, principles, and codes of conduct. This dichotomy highlights the need to differentiate between the formal expression of values and the informal reality of day-to-day operating values. The inconsistency between the formal and informal values may reflect the inconsistency between the formal values and the individual performance goals and metrics to which staff members are held. Unrealistic sales, profitability, growth, or expense control targets can result in unethical behavior outside of the firm's stated values and intended culture.

In November 2013, Bill Dudley, president of the Federal Reserve Bank of New York, captured the macro nature of this phenomenon through his announcement that "there is evidence of deep-seated cultural and ethical failures at many large financial institutions."[43] And, less than nine months later, in July 2014, Mark Carney, governor of the Bank of England, decried the manipulation of the LIBOR rate by participant banks and the ethical breaches involved.[44]

In September 2016, Wells Fargo announced that it had been assessed $185 million in fines for the creation of over two million unauthorized customer accounts. Articles in the press revealed that the pressure on employees to hit sales quotas was highly focused: hourly tracking, pressure from supervisors to engage in unethical behavior, and a compensation system based heavily on bonuses.

As you can see, if culture is a multidimensional concept it is imperative to have polices to unify the different elements to ensure performance. It is the role of governance to promote such alignment. This is the subject of the concluding Chapter 10.

NOTES

1. Many years ago, Charles Handy published *The Age of Paradox* (Boston: Harvard Business School Press, 1995).
2. Andrea Bonime-Blanc, "Part 1: Catalysts for Transforming Culture Risk into Culture Value," National Association of Corporate Directors, February 26, 2018, https://gecrisk.com/wp-content/uploads/2018/05/ABonimeBlanc-Culture-Governance-3-Part-Blog-May-2018.pdf.
3. This view has been most recently articulated by Roger Martin, "The Age of Customer Capitalism," *Harvard Business Review* (January 2010). The ERM may

have come back into vogue with Marc Beaujean, Jonathan Davidson, and Stacey Madge, "The 'Moment of Truth' in Customer Service: Focus on the Interactions That Are Important to Customers—and on the Way Frontline Employees Handle Those Interactions," *McKinsey Quarterly* (February 2006).

4. To the best of our knowledge the term first gained currency via Jan Carlzon who turned around Scandinavian Airlines System (SAS) in the 1980s. See Jan Carlzon, *Moments of Truth* (New York: Harper Business, 1989).
5. Edelman, "2019 Edelman Trust Barometer," March 19, 2019, https://www.edelman.com/sites/g/files/aatuss191/files/2019-03/2019_Edelman_Trust_Barometer_Global_Report.pdf?utm_source=website&utm_medium=global_report&utm_campaign=downloads.
6. See Rafe Sagarin, "Customer Service Needs to Be Either More or Less Robotic," *Harvard Business Review FAQ* (November 24, 2014).
7. Andrew R. Johnson, "Credit-Card Issuers Vie for Risky Business—Subprime Borrowers," *The Wall Street Journal* (October 17, 2011). Of course, it should be noted that serving this market can lead to certain reputational issues.
8. Of course, this does not apply to all customers. Some customers value only price and hence not relationships. It should also be noted that many of the beliefs concerning objectivity that form part of our notion of scientific inquiry do not really address the problem of subject-subject investigations where the intent of one subject is to deceive the other.
9. See page 40 for the implications of this. Marcel Schwantes, "Warren Buffet Says Integrity Is the Most Important Trait to Hire For. Ask These 12 Questions to Find it," *Inc.*, February 13, 2018, https://www.inc.com/marcel-schwantes/first-90-days-warren-buffetts-advice-for-hiring-based-on-3-traits.htm.
10. See Mary Crossan, Bill Furlong, Jeffrey Gandz, and Gerard Seuts, "Addressing Culture and Its Associated Risks in Financial Institutions: A Character-Infused Approach," *Global Risk Institute Research Report*, 2018, https://globalriskinstitute.org/publications/addressing-culture-and-its-associated-risks-in-financial-institutions-2/ and Kristy Hull, "Getting to the Critical Few Behaviors That Can Drive Cultural Change," *strategy + business, S+B Blogs*, May 22, 2017, https://www.strategy-business.com/blog/Getting-to-the-Critical-Few-Behaviors-That-Can-Drive-Cultural-Change?gko=463e5.
11. Robert Axelrod, *The Evolution of Cooperation* (New York: Basic Books, 1984).
12. We add this example not only because of our familiarity with the industry but also because the question of character in willingness to pay is an important component in the lending decision. The classic guide to granting a loan is summarized in the 5Cs of credit: character, capacity, capital, collateral, and conditions. There is a reason why character comes first, and it is the most important and relevant to our discussion because many of the others are subject to more stringent external validation, whereas assessment of character is largely dependent on the discretion of the advisor. Although there will be controls over the range of the advisor's discretion, the advisor's judgment is the first line of defense in this risk management decision.
13. Richard F. Vancil, *Decentralization: Managerial Ambiguity by Design* (Homewood, IL: Dow Jones-Irwin, 1979).

14. This topic is gaining increasing recognition among practitioners. See Alexis Krivkovich and Cindy Levy, "Managing the People Side of Risk," *Corporate Finance Practice*, May 2013, http://www.mckinsey.com/insights/risk_management/managing_the_people_side_of_risk.
15. David Weitzner and James Darroch, "The Limits of Strategic Rationality," *Journal of Business Ethics* (2009).
16. Alfonso Pulido, Dorian Stone, and John Strevel, "The Three Cs of Customer Satisfaction: Consistency, Consistency, Consistency," *McKinsey & Co. Insights and Publications*, August 27, 2018, http://www.mckinsey.com/insights/consumer_and_retail/the_three_cs_of_customer_satisfaction_consistency_consistency_consistency. For some service industries, consistency can be created via the design of the delivery system, as Theodore Levitt noted in his classic, "The Industrialization of Service," *Harvard Business Review* (September 1976).
17. Henry Mintzberg, "Structure in 5's: A Synthesis of the Research on Organizational Design," *Management Science* 26, no. 3 (March 1980): 322–41.
18. Richard E Walton, "From Control to Commitment in the Workplace," *Harvard Business Review* (March–April 1985) and *Up and Running* (Boston: Harvard Business School Press, 1989).
19. Walton, *Up and Running*.
20. Basel Committee on Banking Supervision, *Principles for the Sound Management of Operational Risk*, June 2011, http://www.bis.org/publ/bcbs195.pdf.
21. We realize that not all will buy in, but those who don't buy in will have to be replaced.
22. James Lam, *Implementing Enterprise Risk Management: From Methods to Applications* (Hoboken, NJ: Wiley, 2017), Chapter 6.
23. Elizabeth Sheedy and Barbara Griffin, "Risk Governance, Culture, and Behavior: A View from the Inside," *Corporate Governance: An International Review* 26 (2017): 4–22, https://doi.org/10.1111/corg.12200.
24. See Elizabeth Sheedy and Barbara Griffin, "Empirical Analysis of Risk Culture in Financial Institutions: Interim Report," Risk Culture Project, Macquarie University (November 2014): 9, http://www.lse.ac.uk/accounting/Assets/CARR/documents/Previous-Seminars/2014/Sheedy-Risk-Culture-Paper-Nov-14.pdf.
25. Sheedy and Griffin, "Empirical Analysis of Risk Culture in Financial Institutions."
26. Sheedy and Griffin, "Empirical Analysis of Risk Culture in Financial Institutions," 3.
27. Sheedy and Griffin, "Empirical Analysis of Risk Culture in Financial Institutions," 3.
28. Sheedy and Griffin, "Risk Governance, Culture, and Behavior," 20.
29. Sheedy and Griffin, "Risk Governance, Culture, and Behavior," 20.
30. Vineet Nayar, "It's Time to Invert the Management Pyramid," *Harvard Business Review* (October 2008).
31. See the 1993 Jack in the Box *E. coli* outbreak due to certain restaurants being overwhelmed and serving undercooked meat. "Company News; Jack in the Box's Worst Nightmare," *New York Times*, February 6, 1993, https://www.nytimes.com/1993/02/06/business/company-news-jack-in-the-box-s-worst-nightmare.html.

32. Allan P. Webb, "Management Lessons from the Financial Crisis: A Conversation with Lowell Bryan and Richard Rumelt," *McKinsey Quarterly* (June 2009).
33. Phaedra Cook, "Ten Lessons Chipotle Must Learn from Jack in the Box and Taco Bell," *Houston Press* (January 18, 2016).
34. See Elizabeth Dunn, "The Limitations of American Restaurants' No-Tipping Experiment," *The New Yorker* (February 24, 2018). In the article she cites the work of Michael Lynn, a foremost expert on tipping. His work can be found at http://www.tippingresearch.com/.
35. Ryan Sutton, "You Won't Have to Tip at Dirt Candy 2.0," *New York Eater*, November 21, 2014, https://ny.eater.com/2014/11/21/7256693/you-wont-have-to-tip-at-dirt-candy-2-0. If the issue wasn't complicated enough, it is important to note that there are labor law issues. Restaurant labor laws regard cash tips and check tips as 100% the property of the employee. Service charges are property of the establishment. Credit card tips, alas, are complicated and depend on state law, which may allow the deduction of the processing fee.
36. Elizabeth Dunn, "The Limitations of American Restaurants' No-Tipping Experiment."
37. Elizabeth Dunn, "The Limitations of American Restaurants' No-Tipping Experiment."
38. Excerpted from Elizabeth Dunn, "The Limitations of American Restaurants' No-Tipping Experiment."

> *A statistical model created by Ofer Azar, at the Ben-Gurion University of the Negev, found only a small correlation between tip size and service quality, leading him to conclude that servers were motivated mainly by other factors (such as opportunities for professional advancement or—wild idea—simply the satisfaction of doing a good job). Another study by Lynn showed that perceived service quality affected tip size by less than two percentage points. A female server, by contrast, can expect to hike her tips by an average of seventeen per cent if she wears a flower in her hair.*

39. Terence E. Deal and Allan A. Kennedy, *Corporate Cultures: The Rites and Rituals of Corporate Life*, rev. ed. (New York: Basic Books, 2000).
40. John Graham, "The Role of Corporate Culture in Business Ethics," Management Challenges in the 21st Century, Bratislava, Slovakia, conference paper (April 2013).
41. For information on the risk process, refer to Chapter 3.
42. International Organisation for Standardisation (ISO), *ISO: 31000, Risk Management—Principles and Guidelines, Final Draft* (Geneva, Switzerland: ISO, 2009).
43. Neil Irwin, "Why Can't the Banking Industry Solve Its Ethics Problems," *New York Times* (July 29, 2014).
44. Irwin, "Why Can't the Banking Industry Solve Its Ethics Problems."

CHAPTER 10

The Top of the Pyramid

The CEO as Integrator of Strategy and Risk and the Board as the Fourth Line of Defense

Previous discussions in this book have focused on a misalignment between the organization and its target market; consequently, it is important to focus on governance that strives for alignment of all organizational activities to achieve the goals of the organization.[1] Fundamental to the formal alignment is the allocation of decision rights. It is this allocation that achieves the delicate balance between the forces of centralization and decentralization. As noted previously, this balance is not static but dynamic—and, as has been noted to both of us many times, market forces matter. So do internal cultural and political forces. Achieving balance is a dynamic not a static problem. Put simply, although strategists balance risk and return, their fingers push the balance toward returns in conflicting situations, whereas risk managers push the balance toward pricing risk.

Maintaining this balance to achieve higher performance requires a culture that promotes dialogue and the recognition of the importance of differing views and roles. We are not Pollyannas saying that everyone will be happy: both of us have been parties to decisions with which we disagreed. But we could live with the decision, because we knew our voices had been heard and could understand why the decisions were made. It is the shared values of the organization that allow for diversity and commitment to consensus. Consequently, although getting the allocation of decision rights is critical, it is the first step and only works when it is supported by the appropriate culture and goal alignment.

We have focused on the dialectic between strategy and risk management to achieve alignment, and we are now moving on to consider the broad role of the board and governance in achieving this. A major goal for governance should be the alignment of the interests of the organization's stakeholders. A code of conduct that informs all members of the organization how to behave in order to maintain, or even enhance, the desired reputation of the organization is an important measure. The desired reputation should include policies on corporate social responsibility and appropriate levels of transparency in dealing with fellow employees, customers, and other stakeholders. The implementation of the strategy facilitates this by assigning tasks and resources to achieve those tasks to the appropriate parts of the organization. The pyramid/hierarchical structures we have shown elsewhere emphasize the need to have a framework that integrates the diverse parts of the organization. We are now concerned with the horizontal flows of information essential for the smooth functioning of the organization. It is the framework for integration that creates common goals and communication protocols that facilitate horizontal flows of information. Internal reporting is essential to ensure this flow and the Progressive case illustrates the essential link between internal and external reporting. Naturally, there will also be internal controls to ensure that the policies are enforced. It is important to recognize that the alignment of interests is a dynamic one that requires monitoring to ensure that compensation and information flows are appropriate to achieving the strategic goals of the organization. Figure 10.1 illustrates the important role of codes of conduct in creating common alignment for horizontal information flow.

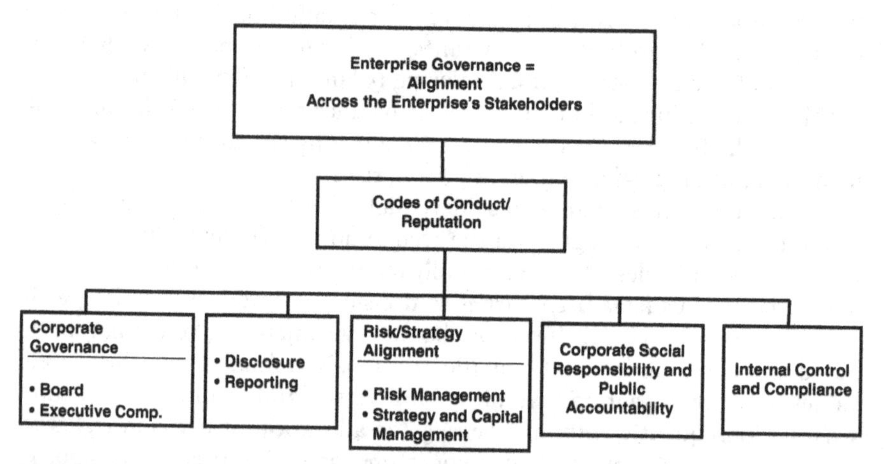

FIGURE 10.1 A High-Level Governance Map[2]
Source: James L. Darroch and Michel Maila.

Going back to the introduction, we strove to argue for how the addition of managing for stakeholders added dimensions to the goals of the corporation. But let us for now focus on one classic issue that faces all organizations that illustrates the need for balance: the tension between growth and profitability. To understand this issue, we further need to consider the competitive context. As mentioned, this is what makes maintaining the balance a dynamic problem. The role of subprime mortgages in the financial crisis provides exactly that.[3] Mortgage lenders at most financial institutions (FIs) see their compensation tied to growth of the mortgage portfolio. But it was becoming increasingly obvious, at least in the business press, that a credit problem was growing. *Bloomberg Business Week* had a cover story and podcast entitled "Nightmare Mortgages" on September 10, 2006.[4] And regulators were concerned, at least by July 2007.[5] Yet in July 2007, Chuck Prince, in an interview with the *Financial Times*, made an unfortunate and famous comment on the emerging bubble:

> *The Citigroup chief executive told the* Financial Times *that the party would end at some point but there was so much liquidity it would not be disrupted by the turmoil in the US subprime mortgage market.*
>
> . . .
>
> *"When the music stops, in terms of liquidity, things will be complicated. But as long as the music is playing, you've got to get up and dance. We're still dancing," he said in an interview with the* FT *in Japan.*[6]

It was only recently we have come to understand the importance of Prince's comment: How could Citi refuse to lend and not lose customers and even frighten shareholders in the short term? In retrospect, the comment looks foolish, but at the time it was reassuring to markets and a sign of confidence in the risk management capabilities of Citi. Alas, he was wrong, but you need to understand the competitive context of the time.[7]

If you are following the thread so far, then let us look at the likely conflict at Citi between the mortgage lenders and the central risk function, or the second line of defense, as it would be known now. The mortgage line of business perhaps even grudgingly could accept that risk was being underpriced in certain subprime mortgages because we know certain managers countered with arguments about the lifetime value of the customer or even said the risk can be transformed into market risk and sold off. No problem. Unless the FI was also buying the securitized products with infected mortgages. Let's assume the risk people held firm and the risk committee of the board supported them. How does this fight get resolved? Certainly, it could be settled by the CEO, but it may already be an issue for the board. Critics who blamed the risk departments of FIs did not understand that the conflict would have been raised beyond its level.[8]

One of us still recalls an experience with a mortgage business leader who proposed entry into the subprime mortgage business. The business case showed high returns even after adjusting for the risk assumed to exist. However, analysis by the risk team revealed many unstated risks and a lack of information to provide risk insights. It was clear that all the risks were not accounted for and that the returns could easily be compromised. The board relied on the business leader and the risk team to resolve the conflict. They couldn't, and the board ultimately turned down the opportunity to enter this business. Interestingly, the business leader promptly resigned to pursue this opportunity elsewhere.

Let us explore another contrary example provided by Kevin Buehler, Andrew Freeman, and Ron Hulme in a section of their article, "The New Arsenal of Risk Management," entitled "Risk as Culture: The Case of Goldman Sachs."[9] Goldman is interesting as the major investment bank that escaped from the 2007–2008 financial crisis in relatively good shape. Here is how David Viniar, chief financial officer of Goldman Sachs, described the markets in an August interview with the *Financial Times:* "We were seeing things that were 25-standard deviation moves, several days in a row. . . . There have been issues in some of the other quantitative spaces. But nothing like what we saw last week."[10] Seeing this turmoil, Goldman aggressively hedged its position in the subprime mortgage market.[11]

Now this raises an interesting question. If such dramatic moves were taking place in the market, why didn't others respond as Goldman did? One answer is that they lacked the same risk management skill and capability. That is probably correct, but the signals were sufficiently dramatic that even lesser risk functions should have been concerned. So, if you accept that they were aware of the unprecedented volatility, then why didn't they act? Was the root cause excessive confidence in the quant models? Recall our previous discussion of risk homeostasis. Our strong, sometimes too strong, belief in our capabilities causes us to perceive reality as what we want it to be, not what it is.[12]

Buehler et al. point to not only the technical skill at Goldman but their risk culture that promoted action. Four key areas are identified:

- Quantitative professionals
  - The analytic skills and mindset may offset the optimism that biases many organizational decision processes.

- Strong oversight
  - Jon Corzine restructured Goldman's risk control structure in 1994 when an unexpected rise in interest rates caused problems. Prominent were daily risk controls and weekly meetings of the firmwide risk committee.
- Partnership heritage
  - The partners were careful stewards of the firm's capital because it was their own. Goldman's most senior executives continue this heritage, and the fact that employees still own a significant portion of equity helps reinforce the partnership culture.[13]
- Business principles
  - Goldman's pride in its reputation reinforced the risk practices.

Without such a reinforcing culture, the most talented risk managers will find it challenging to succeed.

THE CEO: THE OPERATIONAL INTEGRATION OF STRATEGY AND RISK

The board delegates authority to the CEO to accomplish the strategy and maintain risk within a defined appetite and/or tolerance. The CEO is the first integrator of strategy and risk to drive competitive advantage and strong performance. It is the CEO's responsibility to effectively integrate risk capabilities within the strategic decision process to ensure that the organization takes only those risks it can understand, manage, track, and monitor and for which it can effectively plan.

The CEO must allocate resources to a number of oversight functions within the organization to ensure appropriate controls and processes are in place and effective. The CEO must also ensure that the risk oversight function has an appropriate profile within the organization and that the organizational culture has a strong risk presence.

THE BOARD: THE GOVERNANCE INTEGRATION OF STRATEGY AND RISK

The board is the ultimate line of defense as it is where disputes among different parties must be settled. Even if one holds to the fiction that the goal of the firm is to maximize profits, there will still be a dispute over how, or over what time frame. Somehow these conflicts over resource allocations must be settled and increasingly the board is playing a role. As it should. So, what should we expect from boards?

Remember Figure 4.1: Royal Bank of Canada's Risk-Governance Framework and especially the third line—independent assurance? As we noted at that time, internal audit has a role to play in ensuring that appropriate processes are in place to ensure data integrity. The only way you can have confidence in the output of a process is to have confidence in the process. The board's audit committee must ensure the internal audit is independent so that the data employed in strategic and risk decisions are objective. The *IIA Policy Paper,* "Independence and Objectivity" states the issue clearly: "They [internal audit] must have unrestricted access to all parts of the organization and operate free from interference or obstruction. Although it works closely with the executive, internal audit must be independent of the activities it is auditing, and its functional accountability must be to the board, either directly or through an audit committee."[14] It is this internal independent oversight that prevents the common statements on culture, ethics, and so on from being so much hot air.

Previously we noted conflicts between business lines and risk managers. This can be a healthy tension, but frequently incentives tied to growth lead to frictions. As the Chuck Prince quotation reveals and a previously discussed example illustrate, this tension is a governance issue and akin to the internal audit issue. The CRO reporting to the CFO or CEO worked at Goldman, but if other CROs did spot similar issues, then why was there no action? Did the incentive structures discussed by Rumelt lead to the CRO's warnings falling on deaf ears? If this was the case, then so much for the independence of the risk function. At the very least, as boards become more involved with strategic planning and risk is recognized as the other side of the coin, then the boards must become more involved with risk. But this raises the question, is this an issue for the risk committee as it is for the audit committee or is it an issue for the entire board? Consistent with our position is that it is an issue for the entire board; otherwise, the board is only getting half the picture.

THE BOARD PROVIDES MORE THAN OVERSIGHT

But we can expect more from the board. Paul Cantor discussed the role of oversight and insight.[15] Oversight primarily means that the board fulfils its legal responsibilities to ensure that the firm is doing what it is supposed to do. Collectively the board must vet management decisions to ensure that the goals of the firm are being achieved within appropriate risk capacity and limits. This is essentially the long-standing view of governance. But in recent years, the role of the board is changing and becoming more involved in giving advice to managerial decisions. Cantor provides the following definition:

> *Insight is untamed. It requires a different mindset from oversight. If oversight comes from the reasoning side of the brain, insight comes from the intuitive side of the brain. Insight is how a board adds value. Insight is giving advice, not direction. Insight sounds like the phrase: "This is what you could do."*
>
> *Setting risk limits is a dose of oversight, while spotting black swans is a gift of insight.*[16]

David R. Koenig provides an example of an insight he offered to a board member of a not-for-profit providing food and clothing to families in need. An endowment had been raised and the question was how to invest the funds. One board member had suggested equities because equities provided the best returns in the long run. Another board member who was uncomfortable with this suggestion asked Koenig for his advice. He responded:

> *The assets suggested by his colleague were exactly "wrong-way." In other words, if the stock market crashed, so too would the value of their endowment, just as demand for the organization's services would increase. Such an event with stocks dominant in the portfolio would force the institution to begin external fundraising at a time when everyone else was experiencing a decline in their assets and might be fearing for their own situation. At that point, they would be less able to fund the nonprofit's needs.*[17]

This is the type of risk insight that should be expected from risk-aware directors.

But not all insights are as clear. Spotting black swans is a rare insight, but it reminds us that strategic and risk management are an art and a science. As we saw in *The Big Short*,[18] science can spot potential black swans, but it takes courage and insight to act on them. It takes insight to not blindly follow the crowd because that is often the safe course of action.[19]

It is insight that supplements scenario planning and other techniques for challenging implicit assumptions of strategies and acts as a check on risk homeostasis. It forces us to challenge our own predispositions on how the world is. It protects the long-term view of the organization. Strategy and risk management are about the future, and the future is inherently uncertain. We need to refine the science of strategy and risk, but we must never forget about the art. The art tempers our confidence in our plans and enhances the probability not only of long-term success but also survival.

NOTES

1. See Chapter 8 in James Lam, *Implementing Enterprise Risk Management: From Methods to Applications* (Hoboken, NJ: Wiley, 2017) for an interesting adaptation of the three lines of defense model to examine the role of the board. Accomplishing what we suggest may require innovation at the board level. This is challenging. See Matthew Semadini and Ryan Krause, "Innovation in the Board Room," *Academy of Management Perspectives* (2019).
2. Our thanks to Michel Maila, who was instrumental in the development of this graphic.
3. There is a lengthy literature on the causes of the 2007–2008 financial crisis and we are not asserting that subprime lending was the sole, or even the primary, cause. We want to focus on a classic dispute between business lines and the second line of defense, the risk function.
4. Mara Der Hovanesian, "Nightmare Mortgages," *BusinessWeek*, September 10, 2006, https://www.bloomberg.com/news/articles/2006–09–10/nightmare-mortgages. The article focuses on the option adjustable rate mortgage (ARM) and how payments were about to skyrocket. This was the trigger far more than subprime itself.
5. See Office of the Comptroller of the Currency, "OCC Bulletin 2007–26: Subprime Mortgage Lending," October 12, 2018, https://www.occ.treas.gov/news-issuances/bulletins/2007/bulletin-2007–26.html.
6. Michiyo Nakamoto and David Wighton, "Citigroup Chief Stays Bullish on Buy-Outs," July 9, 2007, https://www.ft.com/content/80e2987a-2e50–11dc-821c-0000779fd2ac.
7. This, by the way, calls attention to the need for postmortems of major decisions, not just when things go wrong but all the time. The review is not meant to point fingers, but rather to improve performance. Hence, it is not about allocating blame but identifying weaknesses. Reviewing both good and bad outcomes helps avoid stigma being attached to the process.
8. We are not contending that this happened at all FIs, but we know it happened at some.
9. Kevin Buehler, Andrew Freeman, and Ron Hulme, "The New Arsenal of Risk Management," *Harvard Business Review* (September 2008).
10. Peter Thai Larsen, "Goldman Pays the Price of Being Big," *Financial Times* (August 13, 2007).
11. Buehler, Freeman, and Hulme, "The New Arsenal of Risk Management."
12. Michelle Wucker, *The Gray Rhino: How to Recognize and Act On the Obvious Dangers We Ignore* (New York: St. Martin's Press, 2016), Chapter 1 provides an insightful analysis of why this occurred.
13. Buehler, Freeman, and Hulme, "The New Arsenal of Risk Management." Not all would agree with this discussion of Goldman's reputation, not at the time of the crisis or now. See Nicole Hong, Liz Hoffman, and Bradley Hope, "Justice Department Charges Ex-Goldman Bankers in Malaysia 1MDB Scandal," *Wall Street Journal* (November 1, 2018).

14. See Chartered Institute of Internal Auditors, "Independence and Objectivity," *IIA Policy Paper,* March 2015, https://www.iia.org.uk/resources/delivering-internal-audit/position-paper-independence-and-objectivity/.
15. Paul Cantor, "Oversight and Insight: Building Blocks Enhanced Board Effectiveness," *Director Journal* 163 (September 2012).
16. Cantor, "Oversight and Insight," 5.
17. David R. Koenig, *Governance Reimagined: Organizational Design, Risk, and Value Creation* (Northfield, MN: B Right Governance Publications, 2018).
18. Michael Lewis, *The Big Short: Inside the Doomsday Machine* (New York: W. W. Norton, 2010).
19. All should read Charles Mackay, *Extraordinary Popular Delusions and the Madness of Crowds* (London: Richard Bentley, 1841) as a reminder of certain timeless elements of human behavior.

Epilogue

Decision-Making at the Restaurant

Creating and Executing a Risk-Aware Strategy

Let us finish by returning to our two partners and consider the decisions they made and will be making as conditions evolve. The strategic positioning statement to be a fine dining establishment set the frame for all the other decisions that had to be made. You may recall that earlier they recognized that to some degree they would be price takers. Having accepted that constraint, but with no desire to compromise their positioning as a fine dining restaurant providing an excellent dining experience, they began to attack the Gordian knot of decisions that had to be made. They quickly realized that one of the first decisions would be location. From their experience they had a sense of the demographics and psychographics of their target customer base and decided it would be smart to locate in an area where their customer base resided. They identified a potential spot in an urban location with thriving businesses and a rapidly developing residential market. Many of the residents were singles who walked to work while others were younger families and empty nesters who had moved into the vibrant area. Cranes were everywhere, cultural facilities were growing, and complementary businesses were booming. And people enjoyed walking in good weather.

They did not want to rush into a decision but started to attend local meetings of various business groups and social gatherings to better understand the market. In these networking events they were able to test various ideas and create some buzz about what they were doing. Rather than try to be a point of destination, they would bring their vision into a hospitable locale. Rather than wait to have an opening event, they were creating expectations and learning what was important to the target market. They were attempting to identify risks and take only those risks they could manage effectively and use to create competitive advantage.

The downside of this decision was, of course, finding a place at an affordable price. Alas, the price was higher than initially planned, which led to a change in their hours of operation. Initially they had hoped to balance work and family life by being open only at dinner. The cost of real estate required stronger cash flows, which required greater capacity utilization. This meant being open for lunch and having the option for outdoor service in appropriate weather. They also benefitted from their business networking as they realized that they could add capacity by doing catering. This was an especially attractive option because catering was always ordered in advance and enabled them to expand capacity without putting too much stress on normal operating times. The catering menu would only provide food whose quality would not suffer in delivery and damage their reputation. The location also enticed local businesspeople at lunch and after work for drinks.

The next step was to plan the menu, but the partners realized that planning the menu would benefit from more local knowledge. They looked to hire an assistant manager who had experience working in a fine dining establishment in the area. They found one. Attracting the right person was also expensive, but they realized that in general you get what you pay for. They increased risk as noted previously, but they also reduced risk—creating a different risk profile that reflects their risk appetite and ability to take risk to create value. Because the partners were concerned about control, they offered a percentage of the gross rather than an equity stake. This decision was guided by the fact that an experienced person would know that a share of profits in a start-up would be meager and the partners realized that they didn't want the relationship soured by complicated accounting issues. So, go simple. A deal was struck.

The assistant manager explained that the area was very diverse so that it would be open to new and adventurous cuisine, but that there was also a market for health-conscious people and classic meat and potatoes. The chef saw this as a challenge rather than a limitation on his imagination. Careful discussion with the assistant manager helped create a portfolio menu that was limited but was structured to cater to those with adventurous taste and would allow them to bring more traditionally oriented partners. The challenge was to provide a novel take on classic dishes without frightening the more conservative. Part of the answer was to provide more exotic sauces served separately to be added at the customer's discretion. The assistant manager was also good at spreading the word via social media to former customers that the chef was pleased to accommodate diners by adjusting when possible. Although this did complicate preparation, it was consistent with fostering the customer experience. The chef recognized the need for trade-offs and the businesspeople recognized the need for the chef to limit what accommodations made sense.

This complication affected the selection and training of the waitstaff. It was important for them to be educated about the food and what could be changed. They were a crucial link in matching the customer to the chef's artistry. It was imperative that they be able to explain why some accommodations were possible but not others. All recognized that this would not fit all customers, but the decision was made that it was better to lose a customer than to have a dissatisfied customer who would poison the environment for other diners. To that end, it was essential that the waitstaff were helpful and accommodating not only to the diners they were serving but also the other diners. It was hoped that the menu portfolio would be diverse enough that everyone in the target segment would find something. All recognized that the aim was a moving target that would benefit from more information to enhance the menu to improve the dining experience, attract more customers, and reduce waste.

Waste was a particular concern because fresh food is best and it only stays fresh for a limited time. Although careful menu planning could reduce this, it couldn't eliminate it. Careful storage and planning specials ahead of time to use existing supplies while they were still fresh was a must. This meant that the kitchen staff had to be carefully trained to manage the food stock to preserve it at its best for as long as possible. In this context the decision to be open for lunch was a bonus.

The choice of an urban location had a positive impact on wine and liquor sales. A high proportion of the clientele were able to walk from their homes to the restaurant. This was especially beneficial for those desiring a romantic evening with wine. The desire to build a wine cellar was recognized to be a long-term dream. Although the partners could have attracted new investors that would have hastened the process, they preferred to keep control and build slowly. For that reason, they focused on wines in the lower to mid-price range that offered good value. As they developed a strong local customer base, they were able to introduce their clientele to new wines but also kept stock knowing what would move. Again, balance was important.

Given the aspiration level of the pair, they did spend on the appropriate wine infrastructure. This meant not only correct storage but also the elegant stemware appropriate for the different types of wine. This was an expensive, but important, signal to their wealthier clientele who were purchasing the more expensive wines. However, the vagaries of oenophiles were managed by charging a fairly low corkage fee. Oenophiles could bring their favorite vintages and know that they would be properly served. The decanting and serving of these wines also encouraged others to ask questions about the different wines and possibly to order lower-priced wines from the same regions. To encourage this, the partners introduced a bring your favorite wine on Monday evenings, traditionally a slow night, and sold from their own cellar at a significant reduction to encourage people to try better wines. This let customers experiment with higher-priced vintages and provided additional information to the sommelier about what to stock. Customers educating customers created a positive feedback loop. Over time, more expensive wines came to be a higher percentage of the cellar.

The after-work crowd demanded that a mixologist be hired to staff the bar. In addition to knowing all the classic cocktails the mixologist was encouraged to develop a house cocktail and work on seasonal specialties. This extended to serving beer from local craft breweries. The challenge was to be part of the neighborhood while also taking the dining experience into new realms.

You may have noticed how virtually every decision made to ensure attracting and maintaining customers changed the risks and drove up expenses. The strategic positioning decision demanded attracting experienced waitstaff and kitchen staff, and given the uncertainty surrounding a new restaurant, the partners had to offer financial incentives above the average in the area. Because the waitstaff could not count on tips, the partners had to pay more—in essence, driving up their fixed costs. The situation of being a price taker on both the customer and supplier sides forced the partners to think about the link between expected and unexpected losses. In order to reach the target for expected losses they chose to open in late spring when a patio could increase capacity and more people would be walking by. This was one way of taking advantage of their location.

The partners also engaged in scenario planning in order to determine how much of a contingency fund they needed to reach breakeven. Obviously, this was not a certainty, but it rather helped them be confident they had the financial resources to survive. This exercise combatted excessive optimism and prepared them to deal with unexpected losses. It would be nice to conclude this with telling you all was a success—but that would be at odds with our emphasis on uncertainty. The partners recognized that there was no way to guarantee success, but they also realized that careful planning enhanced the probability of success. Financial resources allowed them time to reduce uncertainty by learning about their customers and employees. This process enhanced the fit of the restaurant with its environment.

The partners realized that they could not provide the desired dining experience for customers if they did not have employees creating the right ambience. To that end they practiced a leadership style that was open. They did not shoot the messenger but rather made it clear that employees who failed to point out flaws as soon as they noticed them would not be part of the team if they didn't change their ways. Early on they established the practice of post mortems not to point fingers, but rather to focus on what could be done better. This became a weekly practice as the partners strove for continuous improvement. Employee recognition awards were instituted to reward those who made helpful suggestions.

All of these programs led to staff retention, which was in harmony with building a loyal customer base. Moreover, it led to being the place where the best CSRs wanted to work. Staff turnover is inevitable in this business, so it is important to market to staff as well as customers. For kitchen staff the goal was to be a place where you could develop your skills in a creative and demanding environment. During slack time the chef was generous in supporting his staff. People realized that working here was something they wanted on their résumé because it opened other doors.

Despite their best efforts, the partners could not identify and anticipate all eventualities, but they had done the best to prepare themselves to be resilient in the face of uncertainty. There were good days and very bad days. And even the very good days—the ones with heavy demand—created stress. There were very loyal customers and customers you hoped never to see again. But they had created a foundation that allowed them to pursue their dream. The trust of their employees and customers created the space to become ever-more adventurous, and the respect of the partners for their employees and customers ensured that they would preserve the favorites during change. Managing the menu portfolio was a dynamic challenge that benefitted from the increased management capacity developed through learning. Essential to the learning was listening to diverse stakeholders—customers, staff, suppliers, and others. The partners realized that identifying relevant risks required being open to other viewpoints. This enhanced not only risk recognition but also the ability to manage risks through the diverse skill sets. Uncertainty was a constant, but it was bounded by their enhanced risk management capability.

Appendix I

Risk Transformation and the Need for an Integrated Risk Approach

We have stated that risks cannot be eliminated, are interconnected, and that management must determine which risks to keep and manage. This results in the need to manage risks from an integrated point of view.

The oft-stated, standard risk management techniques include acceptance, mitigation, avoidance, and transference. The first two techniques recognize that risks can be central to a business's strategy and operations. The key in acceptance is to fully understand, monitor, manage, and get paid appropriately for the risks. Mitigation focuses on reducing the risks to manageable levels that do not threaten the business sustainability in the normal course or foreseeable stresses and still requires the abilities noted for acceptance. For both, it is important to follow the risk process.

The final two techniques, avoidance and transference, imply that risks can be eliminated or dramatically reduced. On the surface, this may appear to be true, but a deeper examination shows that the risks to the business are transformed, not eliminated.

Avoidance seems to be the most likely to eliminate risk. A firm can avoid the risks associated by entering a new market, developing new capabilities, or adapting a new technology or process, but in doing so, the company also eliminates the upside of each of these. The cost of loss avoidance is the loss of revenue opportunities and risk avoidance transforms the risks of these activities into, for example, the risk of losing competitiveness over time.

The simplest example of risk transfer is the purchase of insurance. The insurer becomes responsible for losses over a certain deductible level and within certain limitations depending on the policy purchased; the risk seems to be eliminated. However, the insured takes on fixed costs, which increases operational leverage and reduces risk capacity, remains responsible for effective business management to avoid negligence provisions in the policy, and takes on the risk of the insurer's continued solvency. The risk is transformed, not eliminated. This is still a very powerful risk management technique that allows the business to transfer the insured risk to an organization better able to create the necessary diversification and reserves to fund any losses. Cyber policies covering the losses due to cyber breaches and data loss are very popular for many industries.

A final note on risk transfer is the recognition that the risk is still within the economic system and may return in unexpected ways to jeopardize a firm's sustainability. This was most clearly seen during the 2007–2008 financial crisis. Many financial firms sourced and packaged risks inherent in the housing, particularly the subprime mortgage, market and sold these risks to others. These risks were eventually realized with significant costs to the economy, businesses, and individuals. These risks also become opaque to those ultimately affected by them.

The process of risk management is not the only way in which risks are transformed within and between organizations. Risks change as time progresses due to changes in economic conditions, emerging technologies and business processes, and sociopolitical trends. The very concept of emerging risks, risks that are new or that are changing in unexpected ways, confirms that business and risk managers recognize this reality. The strategic process is an ongoing review of key business drivers for the firm and, as such, it clearly recognizes that changes and transformations in key strategic factors and risks are ongoing.

All of this leads to the requirement to view the risks in the business and its environment as a portfolio of possible outcomes rather than a series of isolates. An integrated view of risks is essential. In fact, an integrated view of risks and strategic opportunities is a critical element in converting risk management from compliance and simple governance into a strategic and competitive advantage.

In other sections of this book we introduce the risk process and economic capital, both of which are necessary to integrate risk with strategy and create value. The risk process does not obviously consider risks from a portfolio perspective, but the identification element and the need to identify risk drivers and not simply risks leads to this approach. Risk drivers affect performance and, through income statement, cash flow statement, and balance sheet decomposition,[1] can be monitored for changes in effect. Some drivers may diminish in impact, others may increase, and still others may emerge. Sensitivity and stability analyses[2] also provide the opportunity to monitor key risk and performance drivers to quickly recognize how changes in underlying factors affect performance. In this way and using these techniques, the risk process enables a risk portfolio approach closely tied to the strategic and business decision processes.

Economic capital is the only measure of capital that captures risk and all other economic factors needed to create an understanding of required capital levels. Importantly, the risk-based element of economic capital not only aggregates risks in a fungible manner but also, in combination with scenario analysis, allows for risk trade-offs to be identified and for business decisions to be based on a full recognition of how risks and performance may be affected.

The final element in creating competitive analysis from risk understanding and integration with the strategic process is the proactive response and planning element within the risk process. This element focuses on creating effective business plans, including contingency plans, to address exposures and the underlying risk and performance drivers and the critical business vulnerabilities. This preparedness enables the firm to recover quickly from risk events and, perhaps, position itself to compete more effectively and gain market share and/or profitability.

NOTES

1. Income statement decomposition is the analytical technique of tracking each movement on the income statement, revenues, costs, and expenses to underlying factors affecting them.
2. Sensitivity and stability analyses are the analytical techniques of assessing the stability or volatility of the performance/risk drivers and the impact each has on performance. If performance is very sensitive to highly volatile drivers, the business is necessarily higher risk.

Appendix II
Resiliency

Resiliency has long been of interest to those in the disaster recovery and business continuity fields and is critical to considering strategy and risk management. The Organization for Economic Co-operation and Development (OECD) defines resiliency as "the ability of households, communities and nations to absorb and recover from shocks, whilst positively adapting and transforming their structures and means for living in the face of long-term stresses, change and uncertainty. Resilience is about addressing the root causes of crises while strengthening the capacities and resources of a system in order to cope with risks, stresses and shocks."[1]

Throughout this book, the concept of resiliency has been introduced in a few ways. Financial and operational leverage were noted as were the five forces in the Porter model. Every strategic model approach considers resiliency even if it is as simple as the SWOT (strengths, weaknesses, opportunities, and threats) model. A key element of the risk process is proactive response and planning to create and sustain resiliency. This points to a critical integration point between strategy and risk—both are focused on creating a sustainable business operation; an operation resilient to market dynamics, competitor and other stakeholder actions, and sociopolitical trends.

In the financial institution risk world, particularly in the regulatory approach, resiliency was originally focused on capital adequacy, and this is still a dominant view. International regulators, led by the Bank for International Settlements, created capital requirements for risk positions. The first Basel Accord dealt with credit risk capital requirements and subsequent versions added market risk and operational risk capital requirements, as well as systemic risk buffers for financial institutions deemed to be globally or domestically systemically important. The introduction of Pillar II[2] to the Basel approach[3] offered an overall assessment of risks that included quantitative and qualitative approaches. Pillar II introduced many key concepts including the need for appropriate capital planning and adequacy assessments clearly linked to the strategic planning process. Coupled with this is the concept that capital should be maintained above the minimums required in the Pillar I approach. This additional capital buffer needs to consider market competition, business operations and cycles, costs of raising capital (particularly in difficult conditions), consequences of failing to meet capital requirements, and idiosyncratic risks not considered in the Pillar I requirements. Pillar II risks are now often identified as strategic, reputation, and other[4] risks.

This still focuses on resiliency as a capital issue and requires a consideration of economic capital. There are different definitions of economic capital, such as this one from Investopedia: "Economic capital is the amount of capital that a firm, usually in financial services, needs to ensure that the company stays solvent. Economic capital is calculated internally and is the amount of capital the firm should have to support any risks it takes on."[5]

This definition is very narrow to the financial services sector and indicates that the only factor of interest is risk and the capital it requires. In the past and for most financial institutions, this was a very good approximation of the economic capital needed by the firm. Financial institutions are in the business of taking risks, and, as such, risk dominates any capital considerations. However, for current day financial institutions and most companies a broader definition is needed, one that must consider all the capital required for a firm to remain solvent. Many firms hold assets not directly affected by the standard risk categories (credit, market, and operational risk) or the introduced Pillar II risks. These assets include infrastructure assets such as buildings, IT systems, digital platforms, and, if they are critical to the success of the firm, they must be in place and the capital to support them must be available or the firm cannot exist.

Economic capital is defined here as the capital required by a firm to fund all assets whether risk-based or foundational such as infrastructure as well as the capital needed to support the strategic and reputational risk implicit in the firm's strategic plans. Implicit in this is the level of financial leverage. Economic capital does not include debt financing. Different industries have different levels of appropriate financial leverage depending on the level of risk associated with the business operations. The greater the risk, the lower the possible financial leverage. Similarly, the higher the financial leverage, the lower the capacity for risk-taking.

Risk capital is defined as a forward-looking estimate of the maximum unexpected loss in market value that an asset, portfolio, or line of business could incur over a specified time interval with a defined confidence level due to any and all types of quantifiable risks (credit, market, and operational risk). This can be seen in the Figure AII.1, which shows simulated possible future losses and the resulting expected loss and unexpected loss, resulting

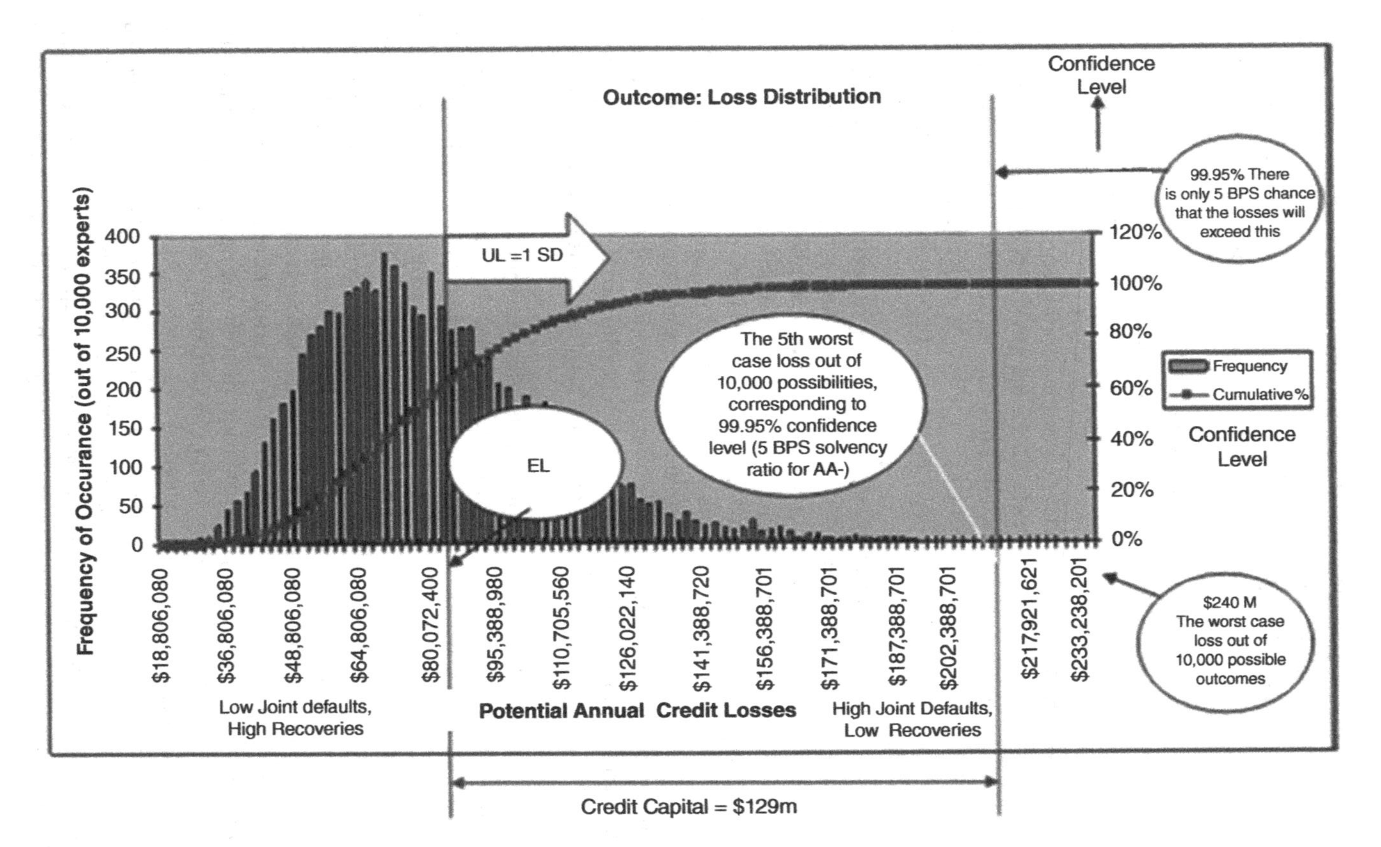

FIGURE AII.1 Credit Loss Distribution and Capital

in the capital requirement for credit risk. Similar calculations can be done for the other quantifiable risks.

Figure AII.1 reflects normal market conditions and the risk capital required under these conditions. Risk capital also includes the necessary capital given stress or extreme conditions. Firms need sufficient capital to weather the conditions in market downturns and recessions, sometimes for protracted periods of time. Our restauranteurs may need to sustain losses over time if the economy is weak and their usual patrons eat out less often or not at all.

Infrastructure capital is defined as the capital required, over a specified time interval, to fund, net of debt financing, any assets critical to the success of the company. These can include buildings, equipment, IT systems, or any other asset required to be owned for the firm to exist and survive. For our restauranteurs, capital may be required to support tables and chairs or the wine cellar previously noted.

The need to sustain business operations in difficult periods and the different capital requirements point to the quality and fungibility of capital. It is important to consider the quality of capital available for financing operations in good times and in bad. Financial institutions are familiar with the quality of capital issue in part through the regulatory definitions of the different tiers of capital. In simple terms, the highest quality capital in these definitions is shareholder equity including retained earnings. The quality of capital degrades as the capital funding moves toward equity-debt hybrids, including types of preferred shares and subordinated debt. Capital quality is determined largely based on how sticky it is, on whether it will exist when needed the most.

Capital, in its simplest form, is assets minus liabilities. Returning to our restauranteurs, their business could be financed with their equity contributions augmented with debt financing. The total funding would finance the purchase of any necessary cooking equipment and premise improvements and furnishings, current assets to be converted into sales, as well as several months of start-up costs (liquid asset reserves) to bridge the establishment of the restaurant to the point of profitability. The fungible capital in this scenario are current assets to be liquidated through the sales process and the liquid assets, whether they are cash or short-term marketable securities. If start-up costs (supplies, rent, salaries, debt financing costs, etc.) and the need to replenish the current assets exhaust these reserves, the restauranteurs will need more funding, whether from increased equity contributions or increased debt financing. Neither of these may be available when needed. Selling any of the capital investments would compromise the ability of the restaurant to function and attract patrons. The capital in these assets is generally not available in the scenario described here. These are foundational assets.

Underlying the fungibility of capital is the concept of liquidity, another key element in resiliency. The financial crisis of 2007–2008 brought liquidity into greater focus as a resiliency issue for those who had forgotten Metallgesellschaft[6] and the many "flights to quality" through time. One of us has liquidity concerns deeply etched in his consciousness after having experienced the rescue of Continental Bank of Canada, a Canadian, largely wholesale funded bank in the mid-1980s. Due to a loss in depositor confidence, several small banks experienced a rapid disappearance of wholesale funds. Continental needed to be rescued and was taken over by Lloyds Bank plc. Continental had assets exceeding its liabilities but was not liquid. The often-noted market truth at that time was, "the markets can stay irrational longer than you can stay liquid." This was true then and remains true today.

The preceding material illustrates the need for adequate capital and liquidity to support the business in both normal market conditions and the inevitable times of stress. But what can be forgotten is that too much of either can compromise resiliency in competitive environments. Idle capital, or capital in excess of the amount needed, does not earn a return appropriate to the business, but the business must still pay the return demanded by the market or investors. Idle capital can support increased liquidity, but liquid assets are low-return assets. Excess capital and liquidity result in lower returns and, in a public company, possibly shareholder dissatisfaction and disruption. In today's world of activist investors low returns can be very disruptive to a company's governance and operations.[7]

In considering resiliency, future capital or the ability to generate capital through earnings is also a key element. The previous section dealt primarily with the company's balance sheet—the contribution of assets and liabilities to capital, the quality of the capital, and the liquidity of the assets available for sale. In determining the level of resiliency, the nature and timing of earnings must be considered. The nature of earnings is dependent on the composition of earnings with respect to the proportion that is stable or "safe" even in difficult conditions and the proportion that is "hot" or unreliable. For a restaurant this could be the difference between strong neighborhood patronage and short-term social media–driven surges in popularity. For every industry there is the possibility of core stable earnings that can be considered in the company's resiliency to downturns or shifts in popularity.

Another income statement item is the nature of the cost structure of the business. This was previously introduced as operational leverage. The greater the fixed costs in the business, everything else being the same, the lower the resilience to a risk event and, therefore, the lower the level of risk that can be taken. However, a low operational leverage firm is not necessarily more resilient if the nature of the variable costs is not understood.

For example, one of us had the benefit of working for a financial services firm that behaved and performed more like a consumer marketing firm. This company had high variable costs centered on marketing, promotion, and sales. Part of the strategic and operational planning at this company involved analysis of the effect of reducing or completely suspending spending on these elements in its cost structure. The process enabled the company management to know how sensitive the company's sales were to spending in these areas. This enabled the company to know how long spending could be cut before its brand and market presence were compromised and, therefore, how much income and, ultimately, capital-consuming expenses could be eliminated and for how long. Many firms rely on cutting employment costs to weather market downturns. This may be a very successful approach if the full impact on ongoing and future business operations of such cuts is well understood.

NOTES

1. http://www.oecd.org/dac/conflict-fragility-resilience/risk-resilience/.
2. In the Basel Capital Accord, known as Basel II, Pillar I deals with minimum capital requirements, Pillar II with requirements governing supervisory reviews, and Pillar III with disclosure requirements and market discipline. Pillar II provided supervisory guidance and tools for regulators to better deal with strategic and reputation risks as well as systemic risk, concentration risk, pension risk, liquidity risk, and legal risk. This grouping of risks has become known as Pillar II risks.
3. The New Basel Capital Accord, Bank for International Settlements, April 2003, https://www.bis.org/bcbs/bcbscp3.pdf.
4. A single exposure or group of exposures that have the potential to produce losses large enough to jeopardize the solvency of the firm. An example for a nonfinancial institution may be a restaurant in a single company or industry town. The company or industry slows down or fails, and the restaurant business may become unsustainable. The New Basel Capital Accord, Bank for International Settlements.
5. http://www.investopedia.com/termss/e/economic-capital.asp.
6. Metallgesellschaft AG was a large German industrial firm involved in mining and related industries, including commodity trading. The firm sold using forward contracts and hedged the resulting exposures using the futures markets. However, market movements created the need to meet margin calls on the futures contracts and resulted in a liquidity issue. In 1993, the firm suffered losses, but the lack of liquidity, the shortage of cash to meet the margin calls, and not the losses drove Metallgesellschaft to the verge of bankruptcy.
7. We do recognize that an organization may keep a strategic war chest as a guard against strategic uncertainty.

Bibliography

Adams, Susan. "How People Who Work For Amazon Really Feel." *Forbes*. August 18, 2015. https://www.forbes.com/sites/susanadams/2015/08/18/how-people-who-work-for-amazon-really-feel/?sh=be7712833059.

Agg, Jen. *I Hear She's a Real Bitch*. New York: Doubleday Canada, 2017.

Alsop, Ronald J. *The 18 Immutable Laws of Corporate Reputation: Creating, Protecting and Repairing Your Most Valuable Asset*. New York: Free Press, 2004.

Alvarez, S., A. Afuah, and C. Gibson. "Editors' Comments: Should Management Theories Take Uncertainty Seriously?" *Academy of Management Review* 43 (2018): 169–72.

Apgar, David. *Risk Intelligence: Learning to Manage What We Don't Know*. Boston: Harvard Business Review Press, 2006.

Axelrod, Robert. *The Evolution of Cooperation*. New York: Basic Books, 1984.

Baer, Tobias, Sven Heilgtag, and Hamid Samandari "The Business Logic In Debiasing." McKinsey & Co. May 2017. https://www.mckinsey.com/business-functions/risk/our-insights/the-business-logic-in-debiasing.

Bank for International Settlements. "The New Basel Capital Accord." April 2003. https://www.bis.org/bcbs/bcbscp3.pdf.

Bank for International Settlements. "Cyber-resilience: Range of Practices." December 2018. https://www.bis.org/bcbs/publ/d454.pdf.

Barney, Jay B. Measuring Firm Performance in a Way That Is Consistent With Strategic Management Theory. *Academy of Management Discoveries* 6:1 (2020): 5–7.

Barton, Dominic, Dezso Horvath, and Matthias Kipping, eds. *Re-Imagining Capitalism*. New York: Oxford University Press, 2016.

Barton, Dominic, and Mark Wiseman. "Focusing Capital on the Long Term." *Harvard Business Review* (January–February 2014).

Barton, Dominic, and Mark Wiseman. "Where Boards Fall Short." *Harvard Business Review* (January–February 2015).

Basel Committee on Banking Supervision. *Principles for the Sound Management of Operational Risk*. June 2011. https://www.bis.org/publ/bcbs195.pdf.

Basel Committee on Banking Supervision. "Basel Committee on Banking Supervision Reforms – Basel III." Accessed November 26, 2018. https://www.bis.org/bcbs/basel3/b3_bank_sup_reforms.pdf.

Battilania, Jullie, Anne-Claire Pache, Metin Sengul, and Marissa Kimsey. "The Dual-Purpose Playbook." *Harvard Business Review* (March–April 2019).

BBC News. "Jamal Khashoggi: All You Need to Know about Saudi Journalist's Death." *September* 16, 2019. https://www.bbc.com/news/world-europe-45812399.

Beaujean, Marc, Jonathan Davidson, and Stacey Madge. "The 'Moment of Truth' in Customer Service." *McKinsey Quarterly*. February 2006.

Bersoff, David M. "The Ideological Shopping Cart." 2017. https://www.edelman.com/post/ideological-shopping-cart.

Bettis, Richard A. "Risk Considerations in Modeling Corporate Strategy." *Academy of Management Proceedings* 1 (1982).

Bevan, Oliver, Jim Boehm, Merlina Manocaran, and Rolf Riemenschnitter. "Cybersecurity and the Risk Function." *McKinsey & Company Risk Practice*. November 2018. https://www.mckinsey.com/business-functions/risk/our-insights/cybersecurity-and-the-risk-function.

Bevan, Oliver, Matthew Freiman, Kanika Pasricha, Hamid Samandari, and Olivia White. "Transforming Risk Efficiency and Effectiveness." *McKinsey & Company Risk Practice. April* 25, 2019. https://www.mckinsey.com/business-functions/risk/our-insights/transforming-risk-efficiency-and-effectiveness.

Bevan, Oliver, Piotr Kaminski, Ida Kristensen, Thomas Poppensieker, and Azra Pravdic. "The Compliance Function at an Inflection Point." *McKinsey & Company Risk Practice*. January 2019. https://www.mckinsey.com/business-functions/risk/our-insights/the-compliance-function-at-an-inflection-point.

Boehm, Jim, Peter Merrath, Thomas Poppensieker, Rolf Riemenschnitter, and Tobias Stahle. "Cyber Risk Measurement and the Holistic Cybersecurity Approach." *McKinsey Quarterly*. November 2018. https://www.mckinsey.com/~/media/McKinsey/Business%20Functions/Risk/Our%20Insights/Cyber%20risk%20measurement%20and%20the%20holistic%20cybersecurity%20approach/Cyber-risk-measurement-and-the-holistic-cybersecurity-approach-vf.ashx.

Bond, Shannon "Amazon Takes Machine-Learning to the Masses." *Financial Times*. December 3, 2018.

Bonime-Blanc, Andrea. "Part 1: Catalysts for Transforming Culture Risk into Culture Value." National Association of Corporate Directors. February 26, 2018. https://gecrisk.com/wp-content/uploads/2018/05/ABonimeBlanc-Culture-Governance-3-Part-Blog-May-2018.pdf.

Bose, Partha P. "Commitment: An Interview with Pankaj Ghemawat of the Harvard Business School on New Directions in Strategic Thinking." *McKinsey Quarterly* 3 (Summer 1992).

Bourdain, Anthony. *Kitchen Confidential*. New York: Bloomsbury USA, 2008.

Bowman, Edward H., and Dileep Hurry. "Strategy through the Option Lens: An Integrated View of Resource Investments and the Incremental-Choice Process." *Academy of Management Review* 18 (1993): 760–82.

Bradley, Chris, Martin Hirt, and Sven Smit. "Have You Tested Your Strategy Lately." *McKinsey Quarterly*. January 2011.

Bradley, Chris, Martin Hirt, and Sven Smit. "How to Confront Uncertainty in Your Strategy." *McKinsey Quarterly*. March 2018.

Bradley, Chris, Martin Hirt, and Sven Smit. *Strategy beyond the Hockey Stick*. Hoboken, NJ: Wiley, 2018.

Bradley, Chris, Martin Hirt, and Sven Smit. "Strategy to Beat the Odds." *McKinsey Quarterly*. February 2018.

Brandenburger, Adam. "Strategy Needs Creativity." *Harvard Business Review* (March 2019).

Brodeur, Andre, Kevin Buehler, Michael Patsalos-Fox, and Martin Pergler. "A Board Perspective on Enterprise Risk Management." *McKinsey Working Paper on Risk*. November 18, 2010. https://www.mckinsey.com/~/media/mckinsey/dotcom/client_service/Risk/Working%20papers/18_A_Board_perspective_on_enterprise_risk_management.ashx.

Brown, Jessica. "How Social Media Could Ruin Your Business." *BBC News*. July 9, 2019. https://www.bbc.com/news/business-48871456.

Buehler, Kevin, Andrew Freeman, and Ron Hulme. "The New Arsenal of Risk Management." *Harvard Business Review* (September 2008).

Buehler, Kevin, Andrew Freeman, and Ron Hulme. "Owning the Right Risks." *Harvard Business Review* (September 2008).

Bughin, Jacques, Tanguy Catlin, and Miklos Dietz. "The Right Digital-Platform Strategy." *McKinsey Quarterly*. May 2019.

Business Roundtable. "Statement on the Purpose of a Corporation." *August* 10, 2019. https://opportunity.businessroundtable.org/ourcommitment/.

Cable, Dan, and Freek Vermeulen. "Making Work Meaningful: A Leader's Guide," *McKinsey Quarterly*. October 2018.

Canavan, Hillary Dixler. "Why Chefs 'Give Back' Their Michelin Stars." *Eater*. September 21, 2017. https://www.eater.com/2017/9/21/16345242/chefs-give-back-michelin-stars.

Cantor, Paul. "Oversight and Insight: Building Blocks Enhanced Board Effectiveness." *Director Journal* 163 (September 2012).

Casciaro, Tiziana, Amy C. Edmondson, and Sujin Jang. "Cross Silo Leadership." *Harvard Business Review* (May–June 2019).

Chandler, David, Francisco Polidoro Jr., and Wei Yang. "When Is It Good to Be Bad? Contrasting Effects of Multiple Reputations for Bad Behavior on Media Coverage of Serious Organizational Errors." *Academy of Management Journal* 63:4 (2020): 1236–1265.

Champion, David. (moderator). "Roundtable: Managing Risk in the New World." *Harvard Business Review* (October 2009).

Chartered Institute of Internal Auditors. "Independence and Objectivity." *IIA Policy Paper* (March 2015).

Chew, Don. (moderator). "Roundtable on Corporate Disclosure." *Journal of Applied Corporate Finance* 16, no. 4 (2004): 36–62.

Coalition for Inclusive Capitalism. *Embankment Project for Inclusive Capitalism*. December 31, 2019. https://www.epic-value.com/#report.

Cohn, Alain, Ernst Fehr, and Michel Andre Marechal. "Business Culture and Dishonesty in the Banking Industry." *Nature* 516, no. 7529 (December 4, 2014).

Collis, David J., and Michael G. Rukstad. "Can You Say What Your Strategy Is?" *Harvard Business Review* (April 2008).

Committee of Sponsoring Organizations of the Treadway Commission (COSO). *Enterprise Risk Management – Integrated Framework*. September 2004.

"Company News: Jack in the Box's Worst Nightmare." *New York Times*. February 6, 1993. https://www.nytimes.com/1993/02/06/business/company-news-jack-in-the-box-s-worst-nightmare.html.

Cook, Phaedra. "Ten Lessons Chipotle Must Learn from Jack in the Box and Taco Bell." *Houston Press*. January 18, 2016.

Copeland, Tom, and Peter Tufano. "A Real-World Way to Manage Real Options." *Harvard Business Review* (March 2004).

Crossan, Mary, Bill Furlong, Jeffrey Gandz, and Gerard Seuts. "Addressing Culture and Its Associated Risks in Financial Institutions: A Character-Infused Approachs." *Global Risk Institute Research Report*. Accessed 2018. https://globalriskinstitute.org/publications/addressing-culture-and-its-associated-risks-in-financial-institutions-2/.

Cusumano, Michael A., Annabelle Gawer, and David B. Yoffie. *The Business of Platforms: Strategy in the Age of Digital Competition, Innovation, and Power*. New York: HarperBusiness, 2019.

Damaruju, Naga Lakshmi, Jay B. Barney, and Anil K. Makhija. "Real Options in Divestment Alternatives." *Strategic Management Journal* 36, no. 5 (2015): 728–44.

Davis, Rob. "What Makes a Good Process?" *BP Trends*. November 2009. http://www.bptrends.com/publicationfiles/FIVE11-09-ART-Whatmakesagoodprocess-BPTrends.pdf.

Davis, Stephen, Jon Lukomnik, and David Pitt-Watson. *The New Capitalists: How Citizen Investors Are Reshaping the Corporate Agenda*. Boston: Harvard Business School Press, 2006.

Dawarm, Niraj, and Charan K. Baggam. "A Better Way to Map Brand Strategy." *Harvard Business Review* (June 2015).

Deal, Terrence E. and Allan A. Kennedy. *Corporate Cultures: The Rites and Rituals of Corporate Life*, rev. ed. New York: Basic Books, 2001.

de Geus, Arie. "Scenarios and Decision-Taking." Oxford Futures Forum. October 2015. https://www.ariedegeus.com/usr/library/documents/main/oxford_futures_forum.pdf.

de Jong, Marc, and Menno van Dijk. "Disrupting Beliefs: A New Approach to Business Model Innovation." *McKinsey Quarterly* (July 2015).

De Smet, Aaron, Gregor Jost, and Leigh Weiss. "Three Keys to Faster Better Decisions." *McKinsey Quarterly* (May 2019).

De Smet, Aaron, Gregor Jost, and Leigh Weiss. "Want a Better Decision? Plan a Better Meeting." *McKinsey Quarterly*. May 2019.

Deloitte. "Developing an Effective Governance Model: A Guide for Financial Services Boards and Management Teams." 2013. https://www2.deloitte.com/content/dam/Deloitte/global/Documents/Financial-Services/dttl-fsi-US-FSI-Developinganeffectivegovernance-031913.pdf.

Deloitte. "Exploring Strategic Risk." 2013. https://www2.deloitte.com/global/en/pages/governance-risk-and-compliance/articles/exploring-strategic-risk.html.

Deloitte. "Good Governance Driving Corporate Performance? A Meta-Analysis of Academic Research & Invitation to Engage in the Dialogue." 2016. https://www2.deloitte.com/content/dam/Deloitte/nl/Documents/risk/deloitte-nl-risk-good-governance-driving-corporate-performance.pdf.

Der Hovanesian, Mara. "Nightmare Mortgages." *BusinessWeek*. September 10, 2006. https://www.bloomberg.com/news/articles/2006-09-10/nightmare-mortgages.

Diaz, Alejandro, Kayvaun Rowshankish, and Tamim Saleh. "Why Data Culture Matters." *McKinsey Quarterly*. September 2018.

Dietz, Miklos, Matthieu Lemerle, Asheet Mehta, Joydeep Sengupta, and Nicole Zhou. "Remaking the Bank for an Ecosystem World." *McKinsey & Company Report*. October 2017. https://www.mckinsey.com/industries/financial-services/our-insights/remaking-the-bank-for-an-ecosystem-world.

The Directors and Chief Risk Officers Group (DCRO). "Qualified Risk Director Guidelines." Accessed February 15, 2019. https://img1.wsimg.com/blobby/go/6299e5c2-5f50-4421-b3c0-652e6c91f6e1/downloads/1cgrl807n_314439.pdf.

Duhigg, Charles. "How Companies Learn Your Secrets." *New York Times Magazine. February* 16, 2012.https://www.nytimes.com/2012/02/19/magazine/shopping-habits.html.

Dunn, Elizabeth. "The Limitations of American Restaurants' No-Tipping Experiment." *The New Yorker*, February 24, 2018.

Du Toit, Gerard, and Maureen Burns. "Evolving the Customer Experience in Banking." Bain & Company. 2017. http://www.bain.de/Images/BAIN_REPORT_Evolving_the_Customer_Experience_in_Banking.pdf.

Du Toit, Gerard, and Maureen Burns. "Why Consumers Trust Amazon Almost as Much as Banks." Bain & Company. November 2017. This originally appeared on Forbes.com. https://www.bain.com/insights/why-consumers-trust-Amazon-almost-as-much-as-banks-forbes/.

Easter, Makeda, and Dave Paresh. "Remember When Amazon Only Sold Books?" *LA Times*. June 18, 2017.

"Five Fifty." *McKinsey Quarterly*. Accessed July 24, 2018. https://www.mckinsey.com/business-functions/digital-mckinsey/our-insights/five-fifty-platform-plays.

Eccles, Robert G., Scott C. Newquist, and Roland Schatz. "Reputation and Its Risks." *Harvard Business Review* (February 2007).

Eceiza, Joseba, Piotr Kaminski, and Thomas Poppensieker. "Nonfinancial Risk Today: Getting Risk and the Business Aligned." McKinsey & Company. January 2017.

Edelman. "2017 Earned Brand Study." 2017. https://www.slideshare.net/EdelmanInsights/2017-edelman-earned-brand?from_action=save.

Edelman. "2019 Edelman Trust Barometer." 2019. https://www.edelman.com/sites/g/files/aatuss191/files/2019-03/2019_Edelman_Trust_Barometer_Global_Report.pdf?utm_source=website&utm_medium=global_report&utm_campaign=downloads.

Ehrhart, Mark G., Benjamin Schneider, and William H. Macey. *Organizational Climate and Culture: An Introduction to Theory, Research, and Practice*. New York: Routledge, 2014.

Epley, Nicholas, and Amit Kumar. "How to Design an Ethical Organization." *Harvard Business Review* (May–June 2019).

Erdman, Drew, Bernardo Sichel, and Luk Yeung. "Overcoming Obstacles to Effective Scenario Planning." McKinsey & Company. June 2015. https://www.mckinsey.com/business-functions/strategy-and-corporate-finance/our-insights/overcoming-obstacles-to-effective-scenario-planning.

Fearn-Banks, Kathleen. *Crisis Communications: A Casebook Approach*. Mahwah, NJ: Lawrence Erlbaum, 2002.

Ferreira, Nelson, Jayanti Kar, and Lenos Trigeorgis. "Option Games: The Key to Competing in Capital-Intensive Industries." *Harvard Business Review* (March 2009).

Financial Stability Board. "Principles for an Effective Risk Appetite Framework." *November* 18, 2013. http://www.fsb.org/wp-content/uploads/r_131118.pdf.

Financial Stability Board. "Thematic Review on Risk Governance." February 2014. file:///C:/Users/jdarroch/Documents/2017-2018%20James/Risk%20strategy%20project/FSB%20Thematic%20Review%20of%20Risk%20Governance%202013.pdf.

Financial Times. "Survey – Mastering Risk 2: The Official Future, Self-Delusion and the Value of Scenarios." *Financial Times*. May 2, 2000.

Fink, Larry. "Larry Fink's Annual Letter to CEOs: A Sense of Purpose." 2018. https://www.blackrock.com/corporate/investor-relations/larry-fink-ceo-letter.

Fink, Larry. "Larry Fink's 2019 Letter to CEOs: Purpose & Profit." 2019. https://www.blackrock.com/corporate/investor-relations/larry-fink-ceo-letter?mod=article_inline.

Fitzsimmons, Anthony, and Derek Atkins. *Rethinking Reputational Risk: How to Manage the Risks That Can Ruin Your Business, Your Reputation and You*. London: Kogan Page, 2017.

"Five Fifty." *McKinsey Quarterly*. 2018. https://www.mckinsey.com/business-functions/digital-mckinsey/our-insights/five-fifty-platform-plays.

Fraser, John R. S., Betty J. Simkins, and Kristina Narvaez, eds. *Implementing Enterprise Risk Management: Case Studies and Best Practices*. Hoboken, NJ: Wiley, 2015.

Freeman, R. Edward. *Strategic Management: A Stakeholder Approach*. Boston: Pitman, 1984.

Freeman, R. Edward, Jeffrey S. Harrison, Andrew C. Hicks, Bidhan L. Parmar, and Simone De Colle. *Stakeholder Theory: The State of the Art*. Cambridge, UK: Cambridge University Press, 2010.

Genereux, Claude, Eric Lamarre, and Thomas-Olivier Leautier. "The Special Challenge of Measuring Industrial Company Risk," *McKinsey on Finance* 6 (2003). https://www.mckinsey.com/client_service/corporate_finance/latest_thinking/mckinsey_on_finance/~/media/C5BAB75D838B403582F1FB87B5E24A7F.ashx.

Gergaud, Olivier, and Victor Ginsburgh. "Natural Endowments, Production Technologies, Quality of Wines in Bordeaux. Is It Possible to Produce Wine on Paved Roads?" *American Association of Wine Economists Working Paper* 2 (2007). https://ideas.repec.org/p/ags/aawewp/37294.html.

Germano, Sara. "Acknowledge, Apologize, Investigate: How Big Brands Combat Online Outrage." *The Wall Street Journal*. February 19, 2019.

Ghemawat, Pankaj. *Commitment: The Dynamic of Strategy*. New York: Free Press, 1991.

Ghemawat, Pankaj, and Patricio del Sol. "Commitment versus Flexibility." *California Management Review* 40, no. 4 (1998).

Gius, Daniela, Jean-Christophe Mieszala, Ernesto Panayiotou, and Thomas Poppensieker. "Value and Resilience through Better Risk Management." *McKinsey & Company Risk Practice*. October 2018. https://www.mckinsey.com/business-functions/risk/our-insights/value-and-resilience-through-better-risk-management.

Goedhart, Marc, Tim Koller, and David Wessels. "The Real Business of Business." McKinsey & Company, March 2015. *Corporate Finance Practice*. March.

Graham, John. "*The Role of Corporate Culture in Business Ethics*." Conference paper. April 2013.

Grasshoff, Gerold, Matteo Coppola, Thomas Pfuhler, Norbert Gittfried, Stefan Bochtler, Volker Vonhoff, and Carsten Wiegand. "Global Risk 2019: Creating a More Digital Resilient Bank." Boston Consulting Group. 2019. https://image-src.bcg.com/Images/BCG-Creating-a-More-Digital-Resilient-Bank-Mar-2019_tcm9-217187.pdf.

Groysberg, Boris, Jeremiah Lee, Jesse Price, and J. Yo-Jud Cheng. "The Leader's Guide to Corporate Culture." *Harvard Business Review* 96, no. 1 (January).

Guardian Staff and Agencies. "Tesla Car That Crashed and Killed Driver Was Running on Autopilot, Firm Says." *The Guardian*. March 31, 2018. https://www.theguardian.com/technology/2018/mar/31/tesla-car-crash-autopilot-mountain-view.

Guntner, Anna, Kinstantin Lucks, and Julia Sperling-Magro. "Lessons from the Front Line of Corporate Nudging." *McKinsey Quarterly*. January 2019.

Halvorson, Heidi Grant, and David Rock. "Beyond Bias: Neuroscience Research Show How New Organizational Practices Can Shift Ingrained Thinking." *strategy + business 80* (2019). https://www.strategy-business.com/article/00345?gko=d11ee.

Hammer, Michael. "Deep Change: How Operational Innovation Can Transform Your Company." *Harvard Business Review* (April 2004).

Hansell, Saul. "Amazon.com Is Expanding Beyond Books." *New York Times. August* 5, 1998.

Hardy, Cynthia, and Steve Maguire. "Organizations, Risk Translation, and the Ecology of Risks: The Discursive Construction of a Novel Risk." *Academy of Management Journal* 63:3 (2020): 685–716.

Harris "The 2018 Harris Poll RQ© Summary Report." March 2018. https://theharrispoll.com/wp-content/uploads/2018/12/2018-HARRIS-POLL-RQ_2-Summary-Report_FNL.pdf.

Heiligtag, Sven, Florian Kuhn, Florian Kuster, and Joscha Schabram. "Merchant Risk Management: The New Frontier in Renewables." McKinsey & Company. April 2018. https://www.mckinsey.com/mm/our-insights/merchant-risk-management-the-new-frontier-in-renewables.

Heiligtag, Sven, Susanne Maurenbrecher, and Niklas Niemann. "From Scenario Planning to Stress Testing: The Next Step for Energy Companies." McKinsey

& Co. February 2017. https://www.mckinsey.com/business-functions/risk/our-insights/from-scenario-planning-to-stress-testing-the-next-step-for-energy-companies.

Hernandes, Exequiel, and Anoop Menon. "Corporate Strategy and Network Change." *Academy of Management Review* 46:1 (2021): 80–107.

Hill, Kashmir. "How Target Figured Out a Teen Girl Was Pregnant before Her Father Did." *Forbes* February 16, 2012. https://www.forbes.com/sites/kashmirhill/2012/02/16/how-target-figured-out-a-teen-girl-was-pregnant-before-her-father-did/#5a79de076668.

Honey, Garry. "Reputation Risk: Challenges for the Insurance Market." Emerging Risks Workshop, AIRIC Conference. June 12, 2012. https://docplayer.net/15545478-Reputation-risk-challenges-for-the-insurance-market-emerging-risks-workshop-airmic-conference-12-june-2012-prof-garry-honey-chiron.html.

Honey, Garry. *A Short Guide to Reputation Risk.* New York: Routledge, 2017.

Hong, Nicole, Liz Hoffman, and Bradley Hope. "Justice Department Charges Ex-Goldman Bankers in Malaysia 1MDB Scandal." *Wall Street Journal. November* 1, 2018.

Hoppe, Hans-Hermann. "The Limits of Numerical Probability: Frank H. Knight and Ludqig von Mises and the Frequency Interpretation." *The Quarterly Journal of Austrian Economics* X, no. 1 (2007): 1–20.

Hutton, Amy. "Beyond Financial Reporting – An Integrated Approach to Disclosure." *Journal of Applied Corporate Finance* 16, no. 4, (2004): 8–16.

Ignatius, Adi. "Profit and Purpose." *Harvard Business Review* (March 2019).

International Organisation for Standardisation (ISO). *ISO: 31000, Risk Management – Principles and Guidelines, Final Draft.* Geneva, Switzerland: ISO, 2009.

Irwin, Neil. "Why Can't the Banking Industry Solve Its Ethics Problems?" *New York Times.* July 29, 2014.

Jackson, Patricia. "Risk Appetite and Risk Responsibilities." 2015. https://www.ey.com/Publication/vwLUAssets/ey-risk-governance-2020-risk-appetite-and-risk-responsibilities/$FILE/ey-risk-governance-2020-risk-appetite-and-risk-responsibilities.pdf.

Jargon, Julie. "How Restaurants Are Using Big Data as a Competitive Tool." *Wall Street Journal.* October 2, 2018.

Javetski, Bill, and Tim Koller. "Debiasing the Corporation: An Interview with Nobel Laureate Richard Thaler." *McKinsey Corporate Finance Practice.* May 2017. https://assets.mckinsey.com/~/media/70B0411CF4524543B396B4AE2B44A827.ashx.

Jensen, Michael C. and William H. Meckling. "Specific and General Knowledge, and Organizational Structure." In Lars Werin and Hans Wijkander, eds. *Contract Economics.* Oxford, UK: Blackwell, 1990. https://papers.ssrn.com/sol3/papers.cfm?abstract_id=6658.

Johnson, Andrew R. "Credit-Card Issuers Vie for Risky Business—Subprime Borrowers." *The Wall Street Journal.* October 17, 2011.

Kahneman, Daniel. *Thinking Fast and Slow.* New York: Penguin, 2011.

Kahneman, Daniel, and Gary Klein. "Strategic Decisions: When Can You Trust Your Gut?" *McKinsey Quarterly,* March 2010.

Kahneman, Daniel, Dan Lovallo, and Oliver Sibony. "A Structured Approach to Strategic Decisions." *MIT Sloan Management Review Spring* (2019).

Kahneman, Daniel, and Amos Tversky. "Prospect Theory: An Analysis of Decision under Risk." *Econometrica* 47 (1979) 263–91.

Kalavar, Sanjay, and Mihir Mysore. "Are You Prepared for a Corporate Crisis?" *McKinsey Quarterly*. April 2017.

Kaplan, Robert S., and Steven R. Anderson. *Time-Driven Activity-Based Costing: A Simpler and More Powerful Pat to Higher Profits*. Boston: Harvard Business Review Press, 2007.

Kaplan, Robert S., and Anette Mikes. "Managing Risks: A New Framework." *Harvard Business Review* (June 2012).

Kehoe, Stephen. "Corporate Reputation." Edelman. 2019. https://www.edelman.com/expertise/corporate-reputation.

Kilduf, Gavin J. "Interfirm Relational Rivalry: Implications for Competitive Strategy." *Academy of Management Review* 44:4(2019): 775–799.

King, Tom. (Interview). "Making Financial Goals and Reporting Policies Serve Corporate Strategy: The Case of Progressive Insurance." *Journal of Applied Corporate Finance* 16, no. 4 (2004): 17–27.

Klein, Gary, Tim Koller, and Dan Lovallo. "Premortems: Being Smart at the Start." *McKinsey Quarterly*. March 2019.

Klingsbiel, Ronald, and Ron Adner. "Real Options Logic Revisited: The Performance Effects of Alternative Resource Allocation Regimes." *Academy of Management Journal* 58:1 (2015): 221–41.

Knight, Frank H. *Risk, Uncertainty and Profit*, 2nd ed. New York: Reprints of Economic Classics, 1964. https://mises.org/profile/frank-h-knight.

Knowledge@Wharton. "Beware of Dissatisfied Consumers: They Like to Blab." March 8, 2006. http://knowledge.wharton.upenn.edu/article/beware-of-dissatisfied-consumers-they-like-to-blab/.

Koenig, David R. *Governance Reimagined: Organizational Design, Risk, and Value Creation*. Northfield, MN: B Right Governance Publications, 2018.

Koenig, David R. *The Board Member's Guide to Risk*. Northfield, MN: B Right Governance Publications, 2020.

Koller, Tim, and Dan Lovallo. "Taking the "Outside View." *Bias Busters*. McKinsey & Co. (2018). https://www.mckinsey.com/business-functions/strategy-and-corporate-finance/our-insights/bias-busters-taking-the-outside-view.

Kopalle, Praveen. "Why Amazon's Anticipatory Shipping Is Pure Genius." *Forbes*. January 28, 2014. https://www.forbes.com/sites/onmarketing/2014/01/28/why-amazons-anticipatory-shipping-is-pure-genius/?sh=63b2f29e4605.

Kose, John, Sara De Masi, and Andrea Paci. "Corporate Governance in Banks." *Corporate Governance: An International Review* 24, no. 3 (2016): 303–21.

KPMG. "Internal Audit: Audit Committee Handbook, Chapter 5, Part 2." *Audit Committee News*. Edition 54/Q3 2016/Corporate Governance. 2016. https://home.kpmg.com/content/dam/kpmg/pdf/2016/06/ch-ac-news-54-article-03-en.pdf.

Krivkovich, Alexis, and Cindy Levy. "Managing the People Side of Risk." *Corporate Finance Practice*. McKinsey Company. May 2013. https://www.mckinsey.com/business-functions/risk/our-insights/managing-the-people-side-of-risk.

Laamanen, Tomi, Jeffrey Pfeffer, Ke Rong, and Andrew Van de Ven. "Editors' Introduction: Business Models, Ecosystems, and Society in the Sharing Economy." *Academy of Management Discoveries* 4:3 (2018).

Lam, James. *Enterprise Risk Management from Incentives to Controls*. Hoboken, NJ: Wiley, 2003.

Lam, James. "Implementing an Effective Risk Appetite." *IMA*. August 2015. https://www.imanet.org/-/media/8150b134bafd42aaaf5267bf49d6d2a3.ashx.

Lam, James. *Implementing Enterprise Risk Management: From Methods to Applications*. Hoboken, NJ: Wiley, 2017.

Lamarre, Eric, Martin Pergler, and Gregory Vaibert. "Reducing Risk in Your Manufacturing Footprint." *McKinsey Quarterly*. April 2009.

Langlois, Richard N., and Metin M. Cosgel. "Frank Knight on Risk, Uncertainty, and the Firm." *Economic Inquiry* XXXI (1993): 456–65.

Larsen, Peter Thai. "Goldman Pays the Price of Being Big." *Financial Times*. August 13, 2007.

Le Conte, Marie. "Vive l'indifference: Why Rude French Waiters Should Be Celebrated." *The Guardian*. March 27, 2018.

Lev, Baruch, and Feng Gu. *The End of Accounting and the Path Forward for Investors and Managers*. Hoboken, NJ: Wiley, 2016)

Levitt, Theodore. "Production-Line Approach to Service." *Harvard Business Review* (September 1972).

Levitt, Theodore. "The Industrialization of Service." *Harvard Business Review* (September 1976).

Lewis, Michael. *The Big Short: Inside the Doomsday Machine*. New York: W.W. Norton, 2010.

Lex. "Amazon: AWSome." *The Financial Times*. December 5, 2018.

Libert, Barry, and Megan Beck, *The Network Imperative: How to Survive and Grow in the Age of Digital Business Models*. Boston: Harvard Business Review Press, 2016.

Liu, Wilson, and Martin Pergler. "Concrete Steps for CFOs to Improve Strategic Risk Management." *McKinsey Working Papers on Risk* 44 (2013). https://www.mckinsey.com/business-functions/risk/our-insights/concrete-steps-for-cfos-to-improve-strategic-risk-management.

Lovallo, Dan, and Daniel Kahneman. "Delusions of Success: How Optimism Undermines Executives' Decisions." *Harvard Business Review* (July 2003).

Luehrman, Timothy A. "Strategy as a Portfolio of Real Options." *Harvard Business Review* (September–October 1998).

Luft, Joseph, and Harriet Ingham. "The Johari Window, A Graphic Model of Interpersonal Awareness." *Proceedings of the Western Training Laboratory in Group Development*. Los Angeles: University of California, Los Angeles, 1955.

Mackay, Charles. *Extraordinary Popular Delusions and the Madness of Crowds*. London, Richard Bentley, 1841.

MacKessy, John. "The Hierarchy of Risk: A New Approach to Risk Management." *The Finance Professionals' Post*. May 14, 2010. http://post.nyssa.org/nyssa-news/2010/05/the-hierarchy-of-risk-a-new-approach-to-risk-management .html.

Mackintosh, James. "A Davos Debate: What Is Finance for?" *The Wall Street Journal*. January 24, 2019.

Martin, Roger. "The Age of Customer Capitalism." *Harvard Business Review* (January–February 2010).

McAfee, Andrew, and Erik Brynjolfsson. *Machine, Platform Crowd: Harnessing Our Digital Future*. New York: W. W. Norton, 2017.

McGrath, Rita Gunther. "A Real Options Logic for Initiating Technology Positioning Investments." *Academy of Management Review* 22:4 (1997): 974–96.

McGrath, Rita Gunther. "Falling Forward: Real Options Reasoning and Entrepreneurial Failure." *Academy of Management Review* 24:1 (1999): 13–30.

McGrath, Rita Gunther. "Industry Analysis Is Out of Date." *Harvard Business Review*. HBR.org. September 27, 2012.

McKinsey & Company. "Decision Making in the Age of Urgency." *Organization Practice*. April 2019. https://www.mckinsey.com/business-functions/organization /our-insights/decision-making-in-the-age-of-urgency.

McKinsey Strategy and Corporate Finance Practice. "The New CFO Mandate: Prioritize, Transform, Repeat." November 2018. https://www.mckinsey.com/ business-functions/strategy-and-corporate-finance/our-insights/the-new-cfo-mandate-prioritize-transform-repeat.

McLaughlin, Katy, and Natalia V. Osipova. "A Reckoning with the Dark Side of the Restaurant Industry." *The Wall Street Journal*. November 12, 2018.

Merton, Robert C. "You Have More Capital Than You Think." *Harvard Business Review* (November 2005).

Meulbroek, Lisa. "A Better Way to Manage Risk." *Harvard Business Review* (February 2001).

Meulbroek, Lisa K. "Integrated Risk Management for the Firm: A Senior Manager's Guide." February 26, 2002. https://papers.ssrn.com/sol3/papers.cfm?abstract_ id=301331.

Michelin Guide. "9 Top Female Chefs to Celebrate This International Women's Day.") https://guide.michelin.com/hk/en/hong-kong-macau/features/世界頂尖女主廚/news.

Miller, Kent D., and H. Gregory Waller. "Scenarios, Real Options and Integrated Risk Management." *Long Range Planning* 36 (2003): 93–107.

Mintzberg, Henry. "Structure in 5's: A Synthesis of the Research on Organizational Design." *Management Science* 26, no. 3 (March 1980): 322–41.

Mintzberg, Henry, Joseph Lampel, and Bruce Ahlstrand. *Strategy Safari: A Guided Tour through the Wilds of Strategic Management*. New York: The Free Press, 1998.

Mittal, Vikas, Matthew Sarkees, and Feisal Murshed. "The Right Way to Manage Unprofitable Customers." *Harvard Business Review* (April 2008).

Nakamoto, Michiyo, and David Wighton. "Citigroup Chief Stays Bullish on Buy-Outs." July 9, 2007. https://www.ft.com/content/80e2987a-2e50-11dc-821c-0000779fd2ac.

Nason, Rick. "Is Your Risk System Too Good?" *The RMA Journal.* October 2009.

Nason, Rick. *It's Not Complicated: The Art and Science of Complexity for Business Success.* Toronto: Rotman University of Toronto Press, 2017.

Nayar, Vineet. "It's Time to Invert the Management Pyramid." *Harvard Business Review* (October 2008).

Nohria, Nitin, William Joyce, and Bruce Roberson. "What Really Works." *Harvard Business Review* 81, no. 7 (August 2003): 42–52.

OECD. "Risk and Resilience." Accessed January 4, 2019. http://www.oecd.org/dac/conflict-fragility-resilience/risk-resilience/.

Office of the Comptroller of the Currency. "OCC Bulletin 2007-26: Subprime Mortgage Lending." 2007. https://www.occ.treas.gov/news-issuances/bulletins/2007/bulletin-2007-26.html.

Oliver, John J., and Emma Parrett. "Managing Future Uncertainty: Reevaluating the Role of Scenario Planning," *Business Horizons* 61 (2018): 339–52.

O'Reilly, Lara, and Laura Stevens. "Amazon, with Little Fanfare, Emerges as an Advertising Giant," *The Wall Street Journal*, November 27, 2018.

Paisley, Jo. "Building Operational Resilience: The Critical Need to Learn from Failure." Garp Risk Institute. 2019. https://www.garp.org/#!/garp-risk-institute/building_operational_resilience?utm_source=affiliates&utm_medium=email&utm_campaign=gripublication.

Parker, Geoffrey G., Marshall W. Van Alstyne, and Sangeet Paul Choudary. *Platform Revolution: How Networked Markets Are Transforming the Economy and How to Make Them Work for You.* New York: W. W. Norton, 2016.

Parker, Owen, Ryan Krause, and Cynthia E. Devers. "How Firm Reputation Shapes Managerial Discretion." *Academy of Management Review* 44:2 (2019): 254–78.

Parker Jr., Robert M. *Parker's Wine Buyers Guide,* 7th ed. New York: Simon & Schuster, 2008.

Parker, Jr., Robert M. "Making Sense of Terroir." *Wine Advocate.* Accessed January 7, 2019. https://shopcru.com/learn-about-wine/making-sense-of-terroir.

Pergler, Martin. "Enterprise Risk Management What's Different in the Corporate World and Why." *McKinsey Working Papers on Risk* 40 (2012). https://www.mckinsey.com/~/media/mckinsey/dotcom/client_service/Risk/Working%20papers/40_Whats%20Different%20in%20the%20Corporate%20World.ashx.

Pomranz, Mike. "Chef Who Gave Back His Michelin Star 'Surprised' to Find His Restaurant Back on the List." *Food & Wine.* January 22, 2019. https://www.foodandwine.com/news/michelin-stars-give-back-sebastien-bras-2019-list.

Porter, Michael E. *Competitive Strategy: Techniques for Analyzing and Analyzing Industries and Competitors.* New York: Free Press, 1980.

Porter, Michael E. *Competitive Advantage: Creating and Sustaining Superior Performance.* New York: Free Press, 1985.

Porter, Michael E. "What is Strategy?" *Harvard Business Review* (November–December 1996).

Porter, Michael E. "The Five Competitive Forces That Shape Strategy." *Harvard Business Review* (January 2008).

Priem, Richard L., Ryan Krause, Caterina Tantalo, and Ann McFadyen. "Promoting Long-Term Shareholder Value by 'Competing' for Essential Stakeholders: A New Multi-Sided Market Logic for Top Managers." *Academy of Management Perspectives* (2019).

Pulido, Alfonso, Dorian Stone, and John Strevel. "The Three Cs of Customer Satisfaction: Consistency, Consistency, Consistency." *McKinsey & Co. Insights and Publications*. 2014. https://www.mckinsey.com/industries/retail/our-insights/the-three-cs-of-customer-satisfaction-consistency-consistency-consistency.

Ramírez, Rafael, Steve Churchhouse, Alejandra Palermo, and Jonas Hoffman. "Using Scenario Planning to Reshape Strategy." *MIT Sloan Management Review*. Summer (2017).

Ramírez, Rafael, Leo Roodhart, and Willem Manders. "How Shell's Domains Link Innovation and Strategy." *Long Range Planning*. August 2011.

Rice, Condoleeza, and Amy Zegart. "Managing 21st Century Political Risk." *Harvard Business Review* (May–June 2018).

Rittenberg, Larry, and Frank Martens. "Understanding and Communicating Risk Appetite." COSO. January 2012. https://www.coso.org/Documents/ERM-Understanding-and-Communicating-Risk-Appetite.pdf.

Roberts, Joe. "Amazon Kindle: A History of the World's Best e-Reader." *Trusted Reviews*. April 13, 2016. https://www.trustedreviews.com/opinion/a-history-of-the-Amazon-kindle-2946395.

Roxbugh, Charles. "The Use and Abuse of Scenarios." McKinsey & Co. November 2009. https://www.mckinsey.com/business-functions/strategy-and-corporate-finance/our-insights/the-use-and-abuse-of-scenarios.

Rumelt, Richard. "Strategy, Structure, and Economic Performance." *Journal of Behavioral Economics* (June 1975).

Rumelt, Richard. "Diversification Strategy and Profitability." *Strategic Management Journal* 3, no. 4 (1982).

Runde, Jochen. "Clarifying Frank Knight's Discussion of the Meaning of Risk and Uncertainty." *Cambridge Journal of Economics* 22 (1998): 539–46.

Sagarin, Rafe. "Customer Service Needs to Be Either More or Less Robotic." *Harvard Business Review FAQ HBR.org*. Nov 24, 2014.

Sainato, Michael. "Accidents at Amazon: Workers Left to Suffer after Warehouse Injuries." *The Guardian*. July 30, 2018. https://www.theguardian.com/technology/2018/jul/30/accidents-at-Amazon-workers-left-to-suffer-after-warehouse-injuries.

Sainato, Michael. "Exploited Amazon Workers Need a Union. When Will They Get One?" *The Guardian*. July 8, 2018. https://www.theguardian.com/technology/2018/jul/30/accidents-at-amazon-workers-left-to-suffer-after-warehouse-injuries.

Sakai, Yasuhiro. "J. M. Keynes on Probability versus F. H. Knight on Uncertainty: Reflections on the Miracle Year of 1921." *Evolutionary and Institutional Economics Review* 13 (2016): 1–21.

Samad-Khan, Ali. "Why COSO Is Flawed." January 2005. http://www.opriskadvisory.com/docs/Why_COSO_is_flawed_(Jan_2005).pdf.

Sanchez, Ron. "Strategic Flexibility, Company Organization, and Managerial Work in Dynamic Markets: A Strategic-Options Perspective." In P. Shrivastava, A. Huff, and J. Dutton, eds., *Advances in Strategic Management*. Greenwich, CT: JAI Press, 1993, Vol. 9, pp. 251–291.

Sanchez, Ron. "Strategic Flexibility in Product Competition." *Strategic Management Journal Special Issue: Technological Transformation and the New Competitive Landscape* 16 (1995): 135–59.

Sargu, Gokce, and Rita Gunther McGrath. "Learning to Live with Complexity." *Harvard Business Review* (September 2011).

Schein, Edgar Henry. *Organizational Culture and Leadership*, 4th ed. San Francisco: Jossey-Bass, 2010.

Schoemaker, Paul J. H., and Cornelius A.J.M. van der Heijden. "Case Study: Integrating Scenarios into Strategic Planning at Royal Dutch Shell." *Strategy & Leadership* (May/June 1992): 3.

Schwantes, Marcel. "Warren Buffet Says Integrity Is the Most Important Trait to Hire For. Ask These 12 Questions to Find It." *Inc.* February 13, 2018. https://www.inc.com/marcel-schwantes/first-90-days-warren-buffetts-advice-for-hiring-based-on-3-traits.html.

Schwartz, Peter. *The Art of the Long View: Planning for the Future of an Uncertain World*. New York: Doubleday, 1991.

Schwartz, *Peter Inevitable Surprises: Thinking Ahead in a Time of Turbulence*. New York: Gotham Books, 2003.

Semadini, Matthew, and Ryan Krause. "Innovation in the Board Room." *Academy of Management Perspectives* 34:2 (2020): 240–251.

Shaw, John C. *Corporate Governance & Risk: A Systems Approach*. Hoboken, NJ: Wiley, 2003.

Sheedy, Elizabeth, and Barbara Griffin. "Empirical Analysis of Risk Culture in Financial Institutions: Interim Report." Risk Culture Project, Macquarie University. November 2014. http://www.lse.ac.uk/accounting/Assets/CARR/documents/Previous-Seminars/2014/Sheedy-Risk-Culture-Paper-Nov-14.pdf.

Sheedy, Elizabeth, and Barbara Griffin. "Risk Governance, Culture, and Behavior: A View from the Inside." *Corporate Governance: An International Review* 26 (2017): 4–22. https://doi.org/10.1111/corg.12200.

Sheedy, Elizabeth A., Barbara Griffin, and Jennifer Barbour. "A Framework and Measure for Examining Risk Climate in Financial Institutions." *Journal of Business and Psychology* 32, no. 1 (February 2017): 101–16.

Sheffield, Hazel. "The Food Waste Warriors Harvesting Success." *Financial Times*. December 31, 2019.

Sidel, Robin. "Bruised AmEx Returns to Roots." *The Wall Street Journal*. March 2, 2009.

Slywotzky, Adrian J. "What Are the Risks You Should Be Taking?" *Harvard Business Review* (October 2004).

Slywotzky, Adrian J., and John Drizik. "Countering the Biggest Risk of All." *Harvard Business Review* (September 2005).

Slywotzky, Adrian J., and Anne Field. "Turning Strategic Risk into Growth Opportunities." *Harvard Business Review* (September 2008).

Smith, Alan. "Making Sense of Divisive Trends." *Financial Times*. December 31, 2018.

Srivastav, Abhishek, and Jens Hagendorff. "Corporate Governance and Bank Risk-Taking." *Corporate Governance: An International Review* 24 (2016): 334–45.

Sutton, Ryan. "You Won't Have to Tip at Dirt Candy 2.0." *New York Eater*. November 21, 2014. https://ny.eater.com/2014/11/21/7256693/you-wont-have-to-tip-at-dirt-candy-2-0.

Taleb, Nassim Nicholas. *Fooled by Randomness: The Hidden Role of Chance in Life and in the Markets (Incerto)*, updated version. New York: Random House, 2008.

Taleb, Nassim Nicholas. *The Black Swan: The Impact of the Highly Improbable*, 2nd ed. New York: Random House, 2010.

Terazono, Emiko. "Big Business Acquires Taste for Plant-Based Meat." *Financial Times*. January 3, 2019.

Terazono, Emiko. "Burgundy Cheered as Region's Wines Outperform Gold." *Financial Times*. January 21, 2019.

Tett, Gillian. *The Silo Effect: The Peril of Expertise and the Promise of Breaking Down Barriers*. New York: Simon & Schuster, 2015.

Thomas, Daniel, and Alice Hancock. "Jeremy King Says Private Equity No Recipe for Restaurant Success." *Financial Times*. May 30, 2019.

Tolkien, J.R.R. *The Fellowship of the Rings*. London: HarperCollins, 2009.

Trachtenberg, Jeffrey A. "'They Own the System': Amazon Rewrites Book Industry by Marching into Publishing." *The Wall Street Journal*. January 16, 2019.

Trigeortis, Leon, and Jeffrey J. Reuer. "Real Options in Strategic Management." *Strategic Management Journal* 38, no. 1 (2017): 42–63.

Van Alstyne, Marshall W., Geoffrey G. Parker, and Sangeet Paul Choudary. "Pipelines, Platforms and the New Rules of Strategy." *Harvard Business Review* (April 2016).

Vancil, Richard F. *Decentralization: Managerial Ambiguity by Design*. Homewood, IL: Dow Jones-Irwin, 1979.

van der Heijden, Kees. *Scenarios: The Art of Strategic Conversation*, 2nd ed. Chichester, UK: Wiley, 2005.

van der Vegt, G. S., P. Essens, M. Wahlström, and G. George. "From the Editors—Managing Risk and Resilience. *Academy of Management Journal* 58:4 (2015): 971–80. https://doi.org/10.5465/amj.2015.4004.

Vranica, Suzanne. "Amazon's Rise in Ad Searches Dents Google's Dominance." *The Wall Street Journal*. April 4, 2019.

Wack, Pierre. "Scenarios: Uncharted Waters Ahead." *Harvard Business Review* (September–October 1985).

Wack, Pierre. "Scenarios: Shooting the Rapids." *Harvard Business Review* (November–December, 1985).

Walker, Owen. "Quants: Is It Time to Tweak the Code?" *Financial Times*. March 23, 2019.

Walton, Richard E. "From Control to Commitment in the Workplace." *Harvard Business Review* (March 1985).

Walton, Richard E. *Up and Running*. Boston: Harvard Business School Press, 1989.

Webb, Allan P. "Management Lessons from the Financial Crisis: A Conversation with Lowell Bryan and Richard Rumelt." *McKinsey Quarterly*. June 2009.

Weill, Peter. "Leading the Next Generation Business: Increased Customer Intimacy & Digital Ecosystems." LATAM CXO & Government Forum. 2015. https://www.the-digital-insurer.com/wp-content/uploads/2016/01/640-Peter_Weill.pdf.

Weill, Peter, and Stephanie Woerner. *What's Your Digital Business Model: Six Questions To Help You Build The Next-Generation Enterprise*. Boston: Harvard Business School Press, 2018.

Weitzner, David, and James Darroch. "The Limits of Strategic Rationality: Ethics, Enterprise Risk Management, and Governance." *Journal of Business Ethics* 31, no. 3 (March 2010): 361–72.

Wikipedia. "List of Female Chefs with Michelin Stars." 2018. https://en.wikipedia.org/wiki/List_of_female_chefs_with_Michelin_stars.

Wilde, Gerald J. S. "The Theory of Risk Homeostasis: Implications for Safety and Health." *Risk Analysis* 2, no. 4 (December 1982): 209–25.

Wilde, Gerald J. S. "Risk Homeostasis Theory: An Overview." *Injury Prevention* (July 1998): 89–91.

Wilkinson, Angela, and Roland Kupers. "Living in the Futures: How Scenario Planning Changed Corporate Strategy." *Harvard Business Review* (May 2013).

Wilkinson, Stephanie. "I Own the Red Hen Restaurant That Asked Sarah Sanders to Leave. Resistance Isn't Futile." *The Washington Post*. May 14, 2019. https://www.washingtonpost.com/opinions/i-own-the-red-hen-restaurant-that-asked-sarah-sanders-to-leave-resistance-isnt-futile/2019/05/14/125b4742-75a8-11e9-b7ae-390de4259661_story.html.

Williamson, Dermot. "The COSO Framework: A Critique from Systems Theory of Management." *International Journal of Risk Assessment and Management* 7, no. 8 (2007): 1089–1119.

Wolfe, Sarah. "Driving into the Ocean and 8 Other Spectacular Fails as GPS Turns 25." *PRI*. February 17, 2014. https://www.pri.org/stories/2014-02-17/driving-ocean-and-8-other-spectacular-fails-gps-turns-25.

Wucker, Michelle. *The Gray Rhino: How to Recognize and Act on the Obvious Dangers We Ignore*. New York: St. Martin's Press, 2016.

Yoffie, David B., Annabelle Gawer, and Michael A. Cusumano. "A Study of More Than 250 Platforms Reveals Why Most Fail." *Harvard Business Review* (May 2019).

Index